Portland Passages

Portland Passages

By

Edward Regory

ISBN 1-58500-357-3

About the Book

One day Alberto saw me in the hallway. He pushed, hit, and intimidated me. I cried and ran back home afterward. I told my uncle Carlito what had happened, and he was so furious that he put a razor blade in his leather jacket, grabbed my hand, and we walked briskly back to the school ... Carlito pushed open the classroom door. The teacher's voice cracked when she asked him to leave, but Carlito was determined to find Alberto. I was the only one who could point him out, and so I did....

These instances were everyday occurrences. The shootings, noise, and bizarre behavior in the projects infected us all–but our strength as a family kept us together.

I was twelve years old when we lived in the ghetto. And even though we were poor, and lived on welfare in a roach-infested project apartment, my mother believed that someday we would live in a better place. At times my father would take the meat off free lunches kids threw away to provide us with a meal; my twin brother was once stabbed to save my life. Finally, my parents scraped together enough money to send us to an unfamiliar place called Portland, Oregon, in an attempt to give us a safe, new life. But our sudden escape from the ghetto was just the beginning of my own struggle growing up in Portland.

The story describes vivid experiences of how it was for my brother and me to attend school in the Portland area, and our endeavors to better ourselves. But, because of little schooling, and past living conditions in New York, striving to do better academically was difficult for us in Portland.

I wrote about failures, triumphs, and the changes that best friends go through every day. I wrote how the loss of my mother at the early age of sixteen, and the loss of my father a few years after, were put into perspective by the love and support of a childhood friend who would later become my wife.

These sufferings are unforgettable. But the sad, happy, and

funny experiences are those which anyone will relate too.

Portland Passages is the story of my internal fight to see my parents' dream for me come true, and details the stark contrast between surviving the ghetto and facing the challenge of starting a new life in an unknown place. It shows that, like a recovering alcoholic, a person who has lived with violence must forever fight to channel all of that passion and frustration into new tools for survival. And it shows that a dream for a better life can come true. I'm an average person, but my story is everybody's story.

MY BEST FRIEND, EDMOND JEROME WAS KILLED BY A DRUNK DRIVER ONE EARLY MORNING IN MARCH 1990. I WROTE THIS BOOK FOR HIM.

To my wife, Hazel,
and to the memory of my mother, father,
and Edmond Jerome,
with love.

Acknowledgements

I would like to thank my editor, Nancy Osa, for her invaluable advice. I am more than grateful to everyone who supported me in this dream of mine to be published. They are my in-laws, Gladys and Doyle McCranie, my brothers, Joseph and Michael, and my sister, Anna Regory. I thank Betty Buffington and family for allowing me to express myself about her son and my best friend, Edmond Jerome. You will never be forgotten.

I thank Gerard Regory for giving me the brotherly advice and reasoning to continue my dream.

And, finally, for her constant support and unconditional love I thank Hazel Regory. She helped me greatly through some very difficult times. You're more than a gift of life, you're a gift from God to me. I love you.

Author's Note

Eddie Regory was born in New York City and left the projects when he was twelve years old. He now lives and works in Beaverton, Oregon, with his wife, Hazel, and their beagle, Penny.

The contents in this book have been written to the best of the author's knowledge. Character names other than those of close relations to the author have been changed. I interpret close relations to be family and friends.

Part One: The Ghetto

Chapter One—Year 1979—New York

In my neighborhood, people thought of the projects differently. I thought of them as a living hell or a sewer for criminals who lingered in unlit hallways, looking for someone to rob. If you were unlucky, you could catch a junkie shooting up heroin in the stench of his own piss, sitting on the stairwell. Sometimes it was like a "Studio 54," where a prostitute or almost anyone could be having sex anywhere. For some people, the projects were Sodom and Gomorrah; for us, the projects were home. But you couldn't look straight ahead and keep running because everywhere we looked, this shit was happening. There was nowhere to go, no place to hide, just a building full of people on welfare, including us. This was the inevitable world of living in the projects, and you either survived it or you didn't.

My twin brother, Joey, and I woke up from a commotion outside the bedroom door. I got up, opened the door slowly, and heard Mom yelling, "No, Michael, no!"
I looked down at the floor and saw drops of blood leading toward the kitchen. Barely awake, I followed the blood drops and saw my mother's little body moving from side-to-side, as she extended her arms to block the exit so my brother Michael wouldn't get out.
"No, Michael! No. You don't need to do this."
"Mom, just move. Please!"
"No, Michael! My God! Please Michael ... God please!"
"Mom, please!"
Michael's forehead was bleeding profusely over his eyes.
"Please, Michael! Sit down. I'll clean your head and it will

all be forgotten."

"No, Mom. I can't!"

"You can, baby. You can," Mom said. "Please ... sit down!"

"No, Mom! I'm gonna kill 'im!" Michael yelled one last time, then dashed toward the kitchen drawer and grabbed a butcher knife, scattering the roaches off the utensils.

He yanked the window open, leaped out, and disappeared through the next window over, into the building hallway. Mom tried to stop him, but he was too strong.

I started to cry, because I loved my brother and was afraid for his life.

Mom prayed to God for help in Spanish: *"Ay! Dios mio, Dios, por favor salva a mi hijo!"*

"Mom!" I cried, running toward her. "Mom! What happened?"

"Oh! Dios mio!" Mom prayed aloud.

"Mom? Where'd Michael go? What happened to Michael?"

"Oh, Dios! My baby! My baby!"

I grabbed Mom's apron with spots of blood on it and said, "Mom, Mom, it's okay ... it's okay ... Michael will come back ... Michael will come back."

Mom's eyes were red and her body exhausted from the worry of where Michael might be going. She struggled toward the kitchen table and sat there. I quietly stood beside her, trying to soothe the pain in her heart and stroking her hair with my small hand.

Mom rocked herself back and forth with her hands over her face as she uttered, "God will be with my Michael. God will watch him."

I later found out a junkie stabbed Michael because he wouldn't give the guy the change in his pocket. He never did find the guy that night.

When Michael got angry, there was no stopping him.

Like the day I stepped on the bad right toe he had hurt in a football game. Michael became so angry with me he yelled,

"Eddie! Ah! Ah!" as he grabbed me by the back of my hair and lifted me up.

"I'm sorry! Ow ... ow ... that hurts!"

"You stepped on my toe!"

"I didn't mean to."

"You're not supposed to be runnin' in the house!"

"Come on, Mike. Let go of my hair!"

"First I wanna see you dance," Michael yelled, lifting the back of my hair even higher.

"Okay! Okay!"

I quickly tiptoed and began to dance some kind of ballet. Michael was biting his tongue, enjoying every minute of power he had over me.

I now realized my only recourse would be Mom.

"Mom! Mom! Michael's pullin' my hair!"

"Shut up, Eddie!" Michael demanded.

"Then let go or I'll keep yellin'."

Michael let go, and I ran to Mom's room.

"Mom! Michael pulled my hair because I stepped on his toe."

"*Ay, mio,*" Mom yelled. "When you gonna learn not to run in the house? This is not a playground ... Michael? Michael?"

"Yeah, Mom."

"Michael? *Ven aca, muevate!*"

Michael reluctantly approached Mom's room.

"Yeah, Mom."

"How many times I tell you not to pull your brother's hair!"

"He stepped on my toe again."

"How 'bout if I pull your hair?"

"I'm sorry."

"Sorry nothing. Come here," Mom demanded.

She then lifted her right hand and grabbed Michael by the back of his hair.

"All right, Mom. All right ... I'm sorry!"

It was funny watching Mom's tiny body take control over Michael. The whole time, I grinned broadly, feeling vindicated.

"You get out, too!" Mom said. "I'm sick of both of you!"

Michael waited for me outside the door.

"Eddie?"

"Oh, no!" I said, then immediately turned around toward Mom's room.

Michael grabbed me and said, "Give me a hug. I'm sorry I pulled your hair, but next time be careful, okay?"

"'kay."

"Wanna go to Coney Island this week?"

I loved Coney Island. It was always Michael's way of making up to me.

"Yeah!"

"We'll go Saturday, okay."

"That would be the coolest!"

I ran to find Joey.

Freak shows were common in the neighborhood. There was always something to see or be amused by. The following day, I was playing by the living room window with my Star Trek and G.I. Joe action figures, when I suddenly heard screaming in the street.

A heavy black lady who weighed at least three hundred pounds was running around the neighborhood, dancing naked in the middle of the street. She was singing and flailing her big arms around as if she were in the privacy of her own home.

"Whoo! Yeah! Gimme some! C'mon, now ... stop! In the name of lo-ve! Whoo! What the fuck you lookin' at, nigga?" the black lady shouted at a bystander as she continued her singing. "Before you, before you bre-ake my heart ... stop! In the name of lo-ve! ... Think it o-over ... think it o-over...."

Some Puerto Rican guy sitting on the neighborhood bench shouted, "Why don't you get yo' fat ass off the street, yo. You blockin' traffic!"

His friend high-fived him and said, "Yo, man ... that was good!"

All the while, people in their cars were driving around the fat lady and aggressively honking their horns.

"Move outta the way, sicko!" one cab driver yelled.

4

"Keep singing!" people called from their windows.

"Look at the elephant!" one guy shouted from the ground.

"Throw some peanuts at her, man," another joined in. "Man, she look fatta than a French baker. Look at the rolls on her! Damn! I can't even see her pussy. Where's it at, man?"

"Ha ... ha ... ha ... ha...." the crowd laughed on.

I suddenly heard police sirens screeching through the streets. The cops rushed out of their cars in disbelief.

Our corpulent lady dancer then screamed, "Ah! Let me go! Rape ... rape ... rape! Somebody, help me! I'm a virgin! Please don't take me away! Rape!"

The cop said, "Lady, shut up! No one's gonna rape you."

"C'mon, baby, please don't take my virginity away," the fat lady pleaded.

The cop had a disgusted look on his face and began to get impatient, forcefully saying, "Lady, I'm just gonna cuff you, then take you in. Damn, I can't cuff her from behind! Her arms are too big."

"Just put her in the car," the other cop suggested.

They forced her in the car, but she kept pulling herself back out by grabbing the door jam.

The fat lady yelled, "Don't you put me in this hot box!"

"Lady, get in!" the cops demanded.

"I ain't fuckin' goin' nowhere!" the fat lady screamed. "Diana! Diana! Diana!"

"You crazy bitch!" the cop yelled, pulling his club out from his side, pushing it into her rolls of fat and trying to force her back into the police car. "She bit my finger. If you don't get in, I'm gonna shoot you!"

"Police brutality!" the fat lady shouted. "Police brutality ... police brutality ... police brutality ... police brutality!"

Because of her obesity, they had to let her out and tackle her to the ground. There must've been six cops trying to restrain her.

"They're gonna do me up the ass! Get off me, you white muthafuckas!"

People were laughing so hard you could see them rolling on

the ground in tears.

"I'll count to three," the cop said. "Then we're gonna hafta inch her in ... Go slowly. Okay, ready?"

"Ah!" the fat lady yelled. "Ain't there no justice? Get the fuck off me! You're hurtin' me! Ah! You piecea white bread muthafuckas!"

"Lady, shut up! We haven't even moved you yet," the cop said. "Here we go, guys. On three ... one, two, three! Li-ift."

"Hurry! Put her in the van!" he said, with a strained look on his face.

"Why don't you make her get up and walk?" another cop said, with a sickened look.

"She won't get up. We're gonna hafta to do it this way."

"This is bullshit!" a cop said. "I don't get paid to hurt my back. And she smells like she hasn't taken a shower for a week!"

Finally, they shoved her into the squad car.

"Whoo!" the crowd cheered over clapping their hands.

The fat lady kept yelling and banging on the windows inside the police car. "Let me out! Let me out! This is supposed to be America. How you gonna treat me like this?! Hey, bitch! You hear me, pig?! You fuckin' pig! Yo' Mamma's a ho. She got saggin' tits just like these," the fat lady shouted, lifting her cellulite tits up to the window. "You see! Look at this! Look at this! Hey!"

The cops turned away in disgust.

It was a lot for a nine-year-old to see.

To get away from this craziness, I'd sometimes sit in the living room with my family, listening to my sister, Anna, sing and my brother Gerard play the piano to my favorite song, "Let it Be," by the Beatles. Gerard's ability to play the violin, guitar, and his favorite, the piano, brought a joy to the family, lifting us away from the reality of living in the projects. These were the more serene times I remember, living in the ghetto.

My older sister, Anna, was a quiet, calm person, who kept mostly to herself and probably was closer to Mom than anyone else. She also had an occasional dislike for Michael because he would yell and argue with her over the stupidest things. That was when Gerard stepped in. He was the mediator in the family. When there was an argument or fight between any of us, Gerard would break it up and bring us back to our senses.

Michael, the oldest, was our protector. He had lionheart courage and wasn't scared of anyone. Michael had the build of an ox and was probably as strong as one. Still, there was a soft side to him that I believe only his family knew.

Albert, my dad, was a streetwise man who tried to provide a better life for us. But Dad was uneducated, which made it difficult for him to get a decent job. He didn't have an easy life from the start: At fourteen, he was supporting his mother (who was often beaten by his father), trying to make ends meet. He told me stories about how his mother, sister, and two brothers slept together in a one-room tenement apartment because they couldn't afford heat and their bodies would keep them warm.

My twin brother, Joey, was the skinniest person in the house and probably those most fragile. But he was a lovable, innocent, yet curious person and, at times, mischievous.

Santa, my mom, was our light. She was the glue that held the family together, and she showed us the importance of love, faith, and hope. She believed we would get out of the ghetto someday and live like normal people. Mom also made sure our stomachs were full, even if it meant her not eating. She was Dad's right arm. But Mom was a temperamental woman, not to be messed with. Her authoritative, strong will and Catholic background gave her the respect she so deserved. I believe if it weren't for her, we would not have been a family.

Me, well, I was always trying to be like Michael, often trying to emulate his style. Trying to become the strong, respected bodybuilder he was in the neighborhood. And whenever I didn't succeed in something, I never gave up.

Chapter Two

One day when I was about eleven, Dad set me aside and asked, "Eddie, did you know your father fought in the Korean war?"

"What's that?"

"Just a place where men fight to live," he continued. "But before I went, I supported my mother, two brothers, and sister. We slept in a one-room tenement. Do you know what a tenement is?"

I was wondering why Dad was telling me all this, but he did this sometimes. I think he needed someone who would look up to him and listen, and not judge him for his past.

"No," I answered.

"It's no place to be proud of, but it was shelter," Dad said. "It's worse than this place we live in now. This hole! I remember roaming the streets tryin' to scam somethin' to eat, and when I couldn't find anything, I stole it! I'm not sayin' what I did was right, but that's what I did. Don't ever grow up like your dad ... I'm nothin' to be proud of. Grab me my cigarettes from the drawer."

I pulled the drawer out and gave him the pack of Kools. He proceeded to light one up and continued.

"Your mother's the best thing to come into my life. She knows the importance of family. But I can't give her the one thing she wants the most."

There was a moment of silence and I asked, "What, Dad?"

"Out. Out of this hellhole."

"Hellhole?" I asked, with a confused look on my face.

Dad bent over and looked me straight in the eye, blowing out one last breath of smoke from his lips and said, "Son, go play with your brother."

I left with one last look from him. It wasn't long before I forgot what Dad told me.

Every day, Joey and I would face the drugs and prostitution in the neighborhood. Because of this, we didn't want to go to school. We were fearful of getting into a fight with some other kid. When I was in class, I thought about Joey, wondering if the other kids were teasing him or threatening him with knives they brought from home.

There was one mean, ugly-looking kid named Alberto. He looked like Godzilla with his rough face, short, Brillo-like hair, and dark skin. When Alberto saw me walking to class, he rushed toward me and pushed me backward by my face. Afterward, I was too embarrassed to go to class, so I ran to my uncle Carlito's house on Essex Street.

"Carlito! Carlito!" I cried out, banging on the front door.

"What is it, Eddie? Whatta you doin' outta school?"

"Alberto pushed me in the face!"

"Alberto? Who's Alberto? Whatta you mean, he pushed you in the face? Where is this kid?"

"At school."

"C'mon. Let's go!"

Carlito threw his leather jacket on, took a razor blade out of the bathroom cabinet, grabbed my hand, and briskly walked me back to school.

"Where's Alberto's class?" Carlito asked.

"This way," I replied, guiding Carlito down the hallway toward Alberto's classroom.

When we got there, Carlito kicked open the door and yelled, "Where the fuck is Alberto?!" Slowly, Carlito removed the sharp razor blade from his jacket and looked around the classroom.

The teacher, with a crack in her voice, politely said, "Sir, you're going to have to leave."

Carlito ignored her and focused his attention on the older kids.

I couldn't believe it! I could see Alberto's face swelling and the rest of his body paralyzed with fear at the back of the classroom. I was the only one who would point him out.

Carlito pushed aside a chair and walked over to him as the other kids watched the massive frame of my uncle slowly move past them.

Carlito bent over, gazed straight into Alberto's fearful eyes, and angrily said, "If you ever fuck with my nephew again, I'll kill you!" He held the blade close to Alberto's rough face. "You fuckin' understand? I don't goddamn care how old you are! You fuck with my nephew, you die!"

The teacher didn't say a word while this all happened. Alberto, with his mouth partially opened and eyes suddenly wide, nodded his head. Carlito walked back to me.

"Let's go."

I grabbed his hand.

"Where's your classroom?" Carlito asked.

"That way."

"Where's that?"

"A couple doors down."

"I'll take you there."

Carlito walked me to the front door, squatted down to my height, and said, "Listen, if this Alberto kid messes with you again, you let me know?"

I nodded my head.

"Now go to class," Carlito said, patting me on the back.

For that moment, I forgot about Michael and idolized my uncle.

After school, Joey and I rushed home to play. Joey looked out the window.

"Eddie," Joey called, "Look! They got the fire hydrant on. Let's see if Mom will let us go out!"

"You know she won't. It's too dangerous."

"She might."

"Let me see," I said, watching the other kids outside take their empty tin cans with the top and bottom lids off. They tightly held a can over the spout on the fire hydrant to see the water rush out at least twenty-five feet, soaking everyone within distance.

"Joey said, "Look! Hillea's out there.

Hillea was the neighborhood sweetheart. She had a nice body, too.

11

"She's got big boobs," I said, watching them gracefully bob up and down.

"Yeah she does," Joey agreed.

We knew Mom wouldn't let us go out, so, often, to pass time, we brought our heads close together and sang into the silver doorknob on the bedroom door, watching the reflection of our heads take different shapes.

"Duke-Duke-Duke- Duke of Earl-Earl Earl- Duke of Earl-Earl-Earl- Duke of Earl-Earl Earl ... " we sang over and over.

I would add my own flavor into the song.

"La-a-a-a ... la, la, la, la, la-a-a-a ... la, la, la, la, la-a-a-a ... la, la, la, la, la-a-a-a ... "

Then Joey interjected with this high-pitched nasal sound.

"Wa-a-a-a-a-a ... wa, wa, wa, wa, wa-a-a-a-a-a ... wa, wa, wa, wa, wa-a-a-a-a-a ... wa, wa, wa, wa, wa-a-a-a-a-a."

"Stop it!" Mom yelled.

We giggled. And when we heard Mom's feet stamping toward the bedroom, Joey and I ran for cover under the blankets.

Mom forced opened the door.

"I don't want to hear that song again. Not for the rest of the day ... not forever! You hear me?"

"Sorry, Mom," I said.

"Sing something, something else. Anything but Duke."

"We don't know anything else."

"Then go to bed," Mom's last words were, as she slammed the door shut.

"Joey?"

"Yeah?"

"Go get G.I. Joe."

I couldn't understand why the neighborhood kids were so cruel to us, and the grown-up people were just as foolish. Who knows what goes through some people's minds? As confusing as it was, we just dealt with it.

Another day at school during recess, Rocheet was on the playground. Rocheet was a black, skinny kid with crooked teeth and a growing Afro. He loved to pick a fight with me, so fighting became a routine for us.

"Eddie?"

"What Rocheet?"

"I feel like fighting."

"Rocheet, leave me alone before I whip your ass again."

"You got lucky last time," Rocheet said. "Now I'm gonna get lucky this time. C'mon!" he shouted, motioning me to come closer.

"Rocheet, can't we just be friends for today?"

"No."

"Rocheet if you don't leave, I'm gonna pound you."

"Bring it! Spic."

I glared at him with fury in my eyes, then grabbed him around his skinny neck, using the weight of my body to force him toward the ground.

"Ah!" Rocheet yelled.

"Had enough?" I shouted, with my right arm tightly wrapped around his fragile neck.

"Let go! Let go!" Rocheet pleaded. "Okay! I had enough! I had enough!"

As soon as I let go, Rocheet declared, "C'mon! Let's fight!"

"You gotta be kiddin'."

"C'mon!" Rocheet shouted, motioning me to come closer. "C'mon white boy!"

"Arrghhh!" I yelled, lunging at him with no remorse, nor any reservation over how skinny and fragile his body was.

"Ugh," Rocheet gasped.

"C'mon! C'mon!" I shouted, hitting him anywhere I could find a clear shot.

"Stop! Stop!" Rocheet begged. "I won't fight anymore. I won't fight you anymore."

"You promise you'll leave me alone?"

"I will!"

"I swear to God, Rocheet, if you mess with me one more time, I'm gonna wipe you all over the street!"

I let him go. Rocheet brushed his right hand over his nose then charged at me like a bull.

"Ah! You bit my arm!" I yelled in pain.

"I'm gonna kick your ass, Eddie."

"Rocheet, don't you ever give up?"

"Nope."

We tackled each other on the ground. Some teachers saw the fight and ran over.

"Stop it! Stop it!" one teacher demanded, forcing her body between us.

"Rocheet started it!"

"Eddie, I don't care who started what. I'm sick of you two fighting! Both of you come with me."

The teacher took us into the principal's office. Bruised up, scraped, and tired from fighting, we sat there, waiting for the principal to say something.

"What is it with you guys?" our principal said. "Almost every day, Rocheet, you feel this need to fight Eddie. And Eddie, almost every day, instead of reporting to one of the teachers, you indulge Rocheet in a fight. What am I supposed to do? I could suspend both of you, but that would do no good. I could expel you, but that wouldn't be good. Or, well, I could just quit. You're both suspended for the day."

I stared at Rocheet up and down, noticing the holes in his shoes and ragged secondhand clothes he wore. I began to feel sorry for him, but wasn't about to take the blame for what he had started.

"He started it!" I exclaimed, glaring at Rocheet, then pointing my finger at him. "He always starts it!"

"Did not!"

"Yeah you did!"

"Settle down!" the principal interjected. "I don't care who started it. You're both going home to cool off. I'll call your parents and make them aware of it. Tomorrow will be a new day, and maybe you guys can get along. Now I want you to shake hands and promise you won't fight again."

Rocheet seemed hesitant, but proceeded to walk toward me with his head partially hanging down. He brought his head up and sort of smirked, then brought his hand out for me to shake.

"Sorry."

I was shocked by his apology.

"Sorry, too," I replied.

"Now go home and come back tomorrow," the principal said. "From here on out, I don't want any more trouble."

Dad knew that Rocheet and I always fought. Dad once asked him, "Why do you like to fight my son, Rocheet?"

Rocheet gladly answered, "Because I like it."

I believed that somewhere in Rocheet's heart there was a good person and a possible friend, although he never gave me the chance to find out. Until this day, I wonder if he's still around and what he's done with himself. But thinking that makes me realize: life in the ghetto is like living in a land of no opportunity and no place to go.

Chapter Three

When someone picked on Joey, Joey would tell me, and I ended up scaring or fighting the guy. If someone bigger picked on me, my oldest brother, Michael, took care of them.

Papo was another bully who would harass me after school. I often tried to avoid him, but he was always hanging around the neighborhood with his buddies.

"Whatta you in a rush for?" Papo asked one time, blocking my way toward the stairs that led up to my house.

"Leave me alone, Papo."

"Hey, fuck you, kid! You know who I am? I'm the baddest Puerto Rican in the East Side, *esse* ... I do what I want and no motherfucker says otherwise. You ever seen one of these?" Papo asked, pulling a stiletto out from the back pocket of his polyester pants, then brushing it close to my face. "This is my guardian. I slice anybody up who gets in my way. And you know what? I don't even care if they're a cop. If it's a cop, I do it to him."

I could see Papo was high on dope. I felt cold sweat drizzle down my tearful face.

Terrified of what might happen, I tore myself away from Papo, ran up the five flights of stairs to the apartment, and banged on the front door.

"Mike!" I yelled from the hallway, waiting for him to open the door, "Mike, it's me, Eddie! Open the door!"

"What's wrong?" Michael asked, "What are you yellin' for?"

"Papo ... he put ... he put a knife to me."

"What?"

"Papo ... Papo tried to stab me," I cried, wiping the tears from my eyes.

Michael became furious. He grabbed a baseball bat from the bedroom closet and briskly walked downstairs to find Papo as I followed behind. When Michael saw him, he grabbed Papo by his nylon shirt and pushed him against the wall.

In an authoritative, angry voice Michael promised, "If you ever, ever mess with my little brother again, I'll kill you, then break both your legs. Do you understand that English?"

"Man, I didn't do shit! I was just showin' him the blade. That's all."

"Shut up!" Michael shouted, holding the bat tightly against Papo's jaw. "Let me tell you something ... this is my blood, my brother. You mess with him, you mess with me—understand?"

"Yeah, man," Papo answered, his right eye twitching in fear.

"If it happens again, I'll inflict pain, then shove your Puerto Rican ass in the East River."

"All right, man. It's cool ... won't happen again."

Michael then grabbed his hair and began to pull it hard toward the ground, forcing Papo to his knees.

"Ma', get the fuck off my hair!" Papo declared.

"What did you say?" Michael's eyes went wide, and I could see his temper begin to flare through his skin, and he said, "Say you're sorry!"

When this happened, I felt like I could kick Papo's ass myself. But I thought Michael had a handle on it. At first Papo hesitated, but Michael pulled even harder.

"Ah! Ah! Okay, man. Okay! I'm sorry!"

The whole time, no one would dare interfere. Michael let go. Then he cleaned Papo's hair grease from himself by brushing his hands off on his pants.

"Eddie, c'mon."

I followed Michael outside and heard Papo yell, *"Maricon!"*

We crossed the street to the Spanish store and shared a *Malta* drink.

"Mike?"

"What?"

"Thanks."

He kissed me on my forehead, chuckled and said, "You just gotta put a little fear in these bozos."

I used to love the disco bouncing off the hallways of our apartment building, echoing to the sound of the Bee Gees. And if I stepped outside, I saw people acting cool, dancing to the beat of Donna Summer. If I had a pair of polyester ajays, a silk, long-sleeved shirt, and the Puma shoes to match, I was sure to fit in.

But with five kids and one income, Dad couldn't afford for us to fit in. So he got us only what we needed, including our crew-cut hairstyles.

But our short haircuts gave the neighborhood bullies like Angel, Frankie, and Edwin another reason to tease us. Angel and Frankie didn't bother me much, they were like wannabes. If they could hang with the other guys in the 'hood, they thought they were cool. Edwin was the one I was afraid of. He was fourteen years old and looked tough. He had a flattop haircut, a medium-size build, and knuckles the size of nickels. This Puerto Rican really intimidated me, and my brother Michael knew it.

I hated Edwin because I couldn't stand knowing I was afraid of him. So one afternoon I was outside playing with a rubber Spalding ball the size of a baseball by throwing it up against the project building, trying to see if I could reach the fourteenth floor. Edwin was nearby, spray–painting slogans with a can of orange paint on a brick wall behind the iron bars that stood beneath the first floor.

I walked toward the bars. With each step my legs felt heavier and heavier, and my breathing got shorter and shorter. But I was determined to overcome my biggest fear and bully … Edwin. I suddenly had a burst of courage, and with my last breath I yelled, "Edwin's got a Juicy Fruit head."

As I turned away from him, I saw Michael walking home from his workout at Nick's gym. I then had another burst of courage, and made a complete turnaround in Edwin's direction and repeatedly taunted, "Edwin's got a Juicy Fruit head, Juicy Fruit head."

This time, he walked toward me, put his face flushed up against the bars, and angrily said, "Shut the fuck up, white boy!"

I thought the bars between us would buy me enough time for my brother Michael to get there and stop the fight, if there was one. Edwin walked around the bars, marched over, and focused his enraged eyes on me. By then I felt I had the strength of ten men and dug my small-knuckled little fist into Edwin's bulletproof face. His face felt like a rock.

"What the fu'!" Edwin said in disbelief.

I don't think I even budged him. Then he punched my face.

"Ah!" I cried out, covering my face with my hands.

I went into a temporary, standing knockout. Still standing, I awakened, looked at Edwin, saw my brother Michael, and almost cried. Yet pride wouldn't let me.

Without thought I blurted, "You fuckin' asshole! I ain't scareda you...," desperately holding back the tears from the pain in my face.

"What the fuck did you say?" Edwin shouted, clenching his hand into a fist and bringing his arm back for another punch to my face.

"You heard me. Fuck-face!"

"Whoa. Whoa," Michael intervened, "Edwin, you're bigger than my little brother."

"Your little brother was calling me names, then hit me in my face."

"Is this true, Eddie?"

I kept silent.

"Well, is it?"

"Well, well I only called him a Juicy Fruit head."

"Why did you say that?"

"'Cause."

"'Cause why, Eddie?"

I lifted my chest up and firmly pressed against Michael's body, which separated Edwin and me, and shouted, "'Cause I'm tired of him messin' with me. I ain't scared of you, Edwin. I'll take you on anywhere—anytime!"

Michael said, "Follow me. Come with me. Both of you."

Michael brought us through a side door of the building; we could smell the urine on the stairwell as he led us up to the first floor, where no one was around.

He paused and with calmness in his voice said, "You can

both finish the fight here."

I looked at Michael, then Edwin (who didn't look as if he had a scare in him), and I felt tears pour down my sore face. Michael rested his hand on my shoulder and said, "Okay, okay. You don't have to fight, but you're gonna have to make friends."

"Why I gotta make friends first?" I asked, sniffling and wiping the tears from my eyes.

"You don't wanna make friends."

"I didn't start it."

Meanwhile, Edwin acted like he didn't have a care in the world.

"Come on, Eddie," Michael said. "Either you make friends, or I let you guys finish it off here."

That's when I reluctantly brought my hand out, knowing that if I didn't, I might have to face Edwin in another standoff.

"Sorry I called you a Juicy Fruit head."

"Yeah," Edwin replied, in this tough-guy voice.

"Now, Eddie, go upstairs while I talk to Edwin."

"Why?"

"Just do it."

I began to climb the stairs, feeling embarrassed for crying.

"Edwin?" Michael said.

"Yeah."

"I'm only gonna say this once, okay? I know Eddie can be stupid, but you're twice his size, so I'm gonna have to trust you not to hurt him next time."

"Well, whatta I do next time he fucks with me?"

"You tell me, and I'll take care of it, but I don't think he will. You understand me?"

"I don't know."

Michael bent over and gave Edwin a serious look, and said, "Edwin, I can't touch you. I know that. But if my little brother comes home hurt on account of you doin' the hurtin', I'll make it a point to get someone your age who will hurt you. Now do you understand what I'm talkin' about?"

"Yeah."

Michael picked up his bag and said, "Good."

Joey and I did have a few friends we liked, like Louie and Nanny. Louie lived beneath us, on the fourth floor at the back side of our building. He was a skinny kid who had black, curly hair and laughed like a hyena. He was a lot of fun, too.

One boring day, Joey and I decided to see what Louie was up to.

"Louie? Louie?" Joey yelled out the window.

Louie leaned out his bedroom window.

"Joey!" Louie exclaimed. "I got a new toy."

"Let's see it!" we said.

"I'll be back."

Louie rushed back with a fire engine truck.

"Look! I got it for my birthday."

"Cool!" I said. "Can you come up and play with us?"

"I can't. My parents aren't home."

"Throw the truck up!" Joey suggested.

"Okay!" Louie said. "You guys catch it, okay?"

"Okay," we replied.

"Here," Louie yelled, then tossed the fire engine truck up as hard as he could.

Joey and I felt the toy truck touched the tips of our fingers, but then it fell into the bushes below.

"Heh ... heh ... heh ... heh ... heh ... heh!" Louie heckled loudly.

"We gotta go get it," I said.

"Hey, watch this," Louie said, hanging out his window and peeing on the fire engine truck, acting as if he was putting out a fire. "Woooo - woo - woo - woo - woo - woo ... woooo - woo - woo - woo - woo - woo."

"Louie!" someone yelled from below. "Get back inside 'fore I tell your mother."

"Oh, shit!" Joey and I said, moving away from the window as quickly as we could.

Louie always knew how to stay out of trouble. He pulled his own weight by talking his way out of a fight or running.

Nanny was a pudgy kid, and Edwin's little brother. Nanny

lived on the second floor and would often invite himself to our houses for a free meal. When we were bored, Joey, Louie, Nanny, and I would go spy on the flirtatious Spanish lady on the fourth floor. Sometimes we felt she knew we were spying on her, but I think she enjoyed us watching her naked through the keyhole of her front door.

"Hey, Louie?"

"What?"

"Look!" I said, "her door is open a little."

"Let's go check it out," Nanny suggested.

We surreptitiously inched our way toward her front door.

I peeked through the keyhole and quietly said, "Damn! Look at those tits."

"Let me see!" Joey said. "I wanna see!"

She was slouched on a torn-up chair, watching television with no bra on. Louie started to chuckle and whispered, "Open the door, Eddie."

I was almost too scared to even look through the keyhole.

"You open it!" I replied, stepping away from the door.

"I'll open it," Joey volunteered, giggling the whole time.

"Okay, do it!" Nanny demanded.

Joey hit the door open. We backed up, and the lady, with a shocked look on her face, covered her breasts and chased after us through the hallway, like a vicious dog with rabies. We laughed so hard we couldn't breathe.

We ran up a stairwell, and I opened the steel door to the fifth floor. She followed us up the stairs until Joey jumped on her back and started to squeeze her breasts. I couldn't believe what Joey was doing as she yelled, "*Puerco … estupido*! … *no me toques*! *No me toques*!" She spat and tried to get him off.

I managed to touch one of her breasts.

Nanny shouted, "Eddie! Run!"

The naked Spanish lady struggled up the stairwell after me with Joey on her back.

"Joey!" I shouted from the top of the stairwell. "Get off her!"

"I can't," Joey stressed. "She's pulling my hair."

Joey let go and ran down the stairs. The lady chased after him. We followed behind as she frantically yelled, "*Puerco! Puerco! Puerco!*"

Joey got away, and Nanny, Louie, and I ran back up the stairs toward the fifth floor. When we got there, we rolled on the dirty cement ground and couldn't stop laughing.

"Man, did you see her face?" Louie asked, still laughing.

"Yeah. I can't believe what Joey did," Nanny said, holding his stomach from all the laughing.

I looked outside the hallway window to see if I could find Joey.

Then we heard a door bang shut.

"Joey! Where'd you go?" Nanny asked. "How'd you get away?"

"Ha … ha … ha … ha … ha," Joey laughed. "Did you see me?"

"Yeah. I can't believe it," Louie said. "You're lucky she didn't get you."

"Joe, you think she'll tell Mom and Dad?" I asked, in a distressed tone.

We went quiet for a moment, then Nanny said, "Nah. She won't say nothin'."

"Man, if your Dad finds out, he's gonna hit you hard," Louie said, in a simpering manner.

"Shut up, Louie!" I shouted. "Your dad's gonna hit you, too."

"He's not gonna beat me like your dad does," Louie shouted back.

"You better take it back!" I said, stepping toward him with an angry face.

"Come on, guys, she won't say anything," Nanny said.

"What if she does?" Joey said.

"She won't," Nanny said. "She had some big ol' tits."

We laughed.

"I know ... I know. And I touched one of them," I proclaimed proudly.

"How did it feel?" Nanny asked.

"Like a big Twinkie," I replied.

"It felt like ... like—sort of mushy," Joey added.

"You think that's like having sex?" Louie asked, in a serious tone.

"Probably pregnant now," Joey said. "Isn't she Eddie."

"She's not pregnant!" I exclaimed.

"I'm glad I didn't touch her," Nanny said. "What if she is?"

"That's stupid," Louie said. "My mom says you can only get pregnant if you stick your dingy in them."

"Dingy?" Nanny replied, with a confused look.

I said, "I know I didn't stick my dingy in her."

"Yeah, me too," Joey added.

"Let's go play catch," Nanny suggested.

"Okay," we replied, no longer worried about the Spanish lady.

Dad respected women, so if he found out, he would've hit us with the leather belt he kept in the bedroom closet. But the Spanish lady never did say anything to him or Mom.

Chapter Four

In time Dad kicked a few habits, like smoking cigarettes. But when he quit, he began eating all the time, which eventually put him at a high seven hundred pounds, disabling him from work. It got to the point where he had to rely on Gerard and Michael for everything, even cleaning his rectum and in areas he couldn't reach. Finally, his weight would put him in the Veterans Hospital.

"Dad!" I yelled, happy to see him during a visit. "What's that in your hand?"

"It's a Bible, son," Dad said. "Michael? How's Santa doin'?"

"She's fine, Dad. She loves you, you know."

"Yeah, but she never comes to visit," Dad said sadly.

"Dad, you know, Mom's upset about some things. You just gotta give her time."

"Time ... some time," Dad said. "Eddie, you been sayin' your prayers?"

"Prayers," I said. "I don't know how."

Dad said, "Push me to that window."

"Okay," I answered, excited about grabbing the handles to the back of his wheelchair.

Dad had this peaceful look on his face as we stared out at the grass from the hospital window.

"You know, son, there was a time when your mom was very, very sick and almost died."

"She was?"

"Oh, yeah," Dad said. "None of us knew what was wrong with her, and we thought she was going to die."

"Dad," Michael interrupted. "You think you should be telling him that story now?"

"He's gotta know someday, right?"

Michael sighed.

"Anyway," Dad continued, "you weren't born at the time, and your brother Gerard was three years old."

"Uh-huh?"

"Your brother Michael and I were watching television one night, and Gerard walked into the bedroom where Mom rested. Gerard saw a bright light shine through the window. Do you know what an angel is?"

"No," I replied.

"It's somebody who watches over your every step in life. Someone who cares for who you are. We couldn't put Santa in a hospital because we couldn't afford it. Well, something great happened."

"What?"

"An angel appeared and knelt in front of your mom and began to pray."

"For what?"

"Probably for your mother to get well again, but that same angel saw your brother Gerard and taught him how to pray also."

"He did?"

Dad nodded and said, "The angel asked Gerard if he would like to learn how to pray and taught him the 'Our Father.' After that, Gerard left the room and came back two or three times more. Then the angel was gone."

"What happened next?" I asked anxiously.

"Well, the next day your Mom was well again. Her sickness passed."

"It did?"

I looked over at Michael as if looking for some confirmation to Dad's story. But even Michael had the same truthful look in his eyes.

"Would you like to learn how to pray?" Dad asked.

"Yeah, Dad. Yeah."

We bowed our heads and Dad taught me the "Our Father."

The following weekend Mom let us play baseball with the other kids in the neighborhood. We looked like the whitest kids out there. It was Joey's turn at bat. He nervously walked toward the batter's plate.

"C'mon, Joey! Home run it! Over the fence, Joe!" I encouraged him from the sidelines.

Some of the kids began singing, "Play that fuckin' mu-sic white boy ... play that fuckin' mu-sic white boy ... play that fuckin' mu-sic…."

I glanced over to the kids who were singing then to Joey and yelled, "Forget 'em, Joe. C'mon! Swing it outta the park!"

Pitch one was thrown. Then Joey swung as hard as he could and missed the ball by just a hair.

"Ha ... ha ... ha ... ha ... ha," a kid named Hector yelled out. "You suck! That ball went smack in the middle ... in the middle."

I stood erect with my chest out, pointed at Hector, and yelled, "You're a liar! You know that ball wasn't even close to the middle."

"Shut up! *Pollo*!" Hector shouted with an offensive tone.

"Whateva," I replied.

The pitcher pulled his pants down and bare-assed Joey.

Joey shouted, "Look at that hairy butt. Looks ugly!"

"Just for that, I'm gonna strike you out."

Pitch two was thrown, and Joey slammed it hard between the pitcher and third baseman. The pitcher dived for it but scraped his elbow on the concrete.

"Yeah, Joe! Run! Run! Run! Run!"

Suddenly the kids who were laughing began to yell, "Whoo! Go Joey! Go!"

Joey ran to first base.

"Stay there, Joe! Stay there!"

The next batter was Abraham. He was the best ball player out there and also the oldest. Hector didn't say a word when it was Abraham's turn because if he did, he'd get his ass kicked.

There was silence, then the ball was pitched. We watched in awe as Abraham swatted it out of the park, hitting the front steps of PS-188.

"Joey!" I called out. "Walk your bases."

Joey jogged over the bases into home plate.

29

"Heh ... heh ... heh ... heh ... heh," Abraham chuckled, as he proudly jogged around first, second, and third base.

Mom stuck her head out the fifth-floor window and yelled, "Ed-die ... Jo-ey ... Ed-die ... Jo-ey."

It was embarrassing whenever Mom yelled for us to come in because you could hear her yell echo between the project buildings.

"Ed-die ... Jo-ey ... " one kid mimicked. "You betta go home, girly boys!

Joey and I picked up our baseball gloves and jogged out of the park.

"I wish Hector would die!" Joey said resentfully.

"Ed-die ... Jo-ey ... Ed-die ... Jo-ey!" Mom continued yelling.

"Okay," we answered.

Before we got into the building to run upstairs, Mom yelled down, "Why didn't you answer when I called the first time?"

"We were playin' ball," Joey answered.

"We didn't hear you," I added.

"Hurry up! Time to eat."

We ran up, pinching our noses as we passed a smelly drunk on the steps.

"He stunk!" Joey blurted.

"Hurry! Or I'm gonna throw up!" I added, referring to the atrocious urine smell which led toward the fifth floor.

The next week, Michael and I went to the welfare office, and the line was so backed up, I thought, *How could so many people be out of work?* It was so hot in the building that an old lady waiting on the same line fainted, and somewhere a man shouted, "See whatcha guys did to the old lady? She fainted 'cause y'all take so long."

Michael bent down and held the lady's arm, "Lady, lady, you okay?"

"I'm hot," the lady answered. "I need me my check."

"Hey!" Michael shouted, to one of the welfare officers. "Can't you see the lady fainted here? It's too hot in this building and ya make us wait all day long! Why don't you just give her her check so she can go home."

One of the managers came out.

"Lady? Are you okay?"

"Hey, bozo? Of course she's not okay. You think she'd be layin' on the ground for her health?"

The manager looked up at Michael with resentment and said, "Hey buddy, I'm tryin', okay?"

Shortly afterward, the ambulance came. The lady got her check, and they took her to the hospital.

One black man blurted out from the crowd, "Goddamn! If all I had to do was faint to get my check, I woulda dunnit a long time ago!"

The crowd reacted with a sudden burst of laughter.

Dad hated welfare, but knew how to manipulate the system to his advantage. He would sometimes misquote *Fiddler on the Roof* to me and say, "Son, there ain't no dishonor in being poor, but there ain't no honor in it, either."

Chapter Five

Dad lost hundreds of pounds. When he got out of the hospital, he started a little *piraguas* stand (a snow-cone cart we built from pinewood) we pushed through the neighborhood. In the summer, *piraguas* stands were how people got by when there wasn't work.

My dad's own *piraguas* stand. I was proud. I watched him scrape scraps of ice off that big, cold block. He also volunteered to give out the free lunches funded by the park to the kids. And when the kids threw away their sandwiches, Dad would take the meat out of them and provide us a meal.

Our neighbor Salvador and I would help Dad push the cart to every park in walking distance. Salvador was funny, and a man of many talents. He could read a book and remember it paragraph for paragraph. But Salvador never took advantage of his talents. Instead, he hung around the neighborhood like everyone else.

Once we were selling snow cones on the corner of an intersection, and Dad was yelling at the cars, "Hey buddy! Hey! Snow cones … frosty snow cones. Buy one! Bring some home to ya kids."

Because Dad and Salvador were so consumed with selling another snow cone, I walked to the nearby park. I sat on a metal swing, and a guy who looked about eighteen or twenty years old crimped his eyebrows, came up to me and demanded, "Get off the swing." Sticking his chest out he clench his hands into fists.

I didn't know why he wanted me off. I wasn't bothering him. So with a cocky tone I replied, "No."

He punched me in the face.

"Ah!" I fell off the swing and blurted, "You asshole!" and ran back to Dad's cart. Out of breath and my face in pain, I said, "Dad, Dad. This guy hit me."

"What?"

"Some guy hit me," I said, covering the hurt left side of my face.

Dad was surprised because he didn't realize I was gone.

"Sal, go find this guy for me," Dad said, in an authoritative voice. "I can't chase anyone down."

The guy who hit me started to walk in our direction anyway (I don't think he knew I was with my dad.)

"That's him!" I blurted, pointing him out.

"Hey! C'mere!" Salvador yelled at my attacker. "Hey! C'mere!"

"What?" the guy answered with an attitude.

Salvador pointed at me and asked, "Did you hit him?"

"Fuck you wanna know!" the guy answered with a scowling face, slowly backing away from Salvador.

Salvador walked briskly toward the guy, who warned Salvador, "Man, you betta step off 'less you wanna get slammed!"

Salvador still walked closer, and Dad followed.

"I said step off!" the guy shouted. "Fuck you!" And he brought his right arm way back past his chest and hit Salvador dead on the right eye.

I couldn't believe it. This guy was on a punching spree.

"You punk kid!" Salvador said in disbelief.

The guy was quicker and swiftly moved out of Salvador's range.

Dad was trying to catch up to both of them saying, "Just hold the guy for me, Sal … just grab ahold of him for me."

Once Dad got ahold of anyone, they were history.

The guy yelled, "You fuckin' losers!" He flipped us the middle finger and ran across the intersection, disappearing into the crowd.

"I can't believe that guy," Salvador said. "He hit me right in the eye."

"Goddamn kid!" Dad said. "Sal, you okay?"

"Yeah, Al."

"I swear if I see that kid in the streets, I'm gonna run 'im down."

"Don't worry about it, Al."

"Let me grab some ice," Dad said, scraping ice off the block, then putting some into a hand towel he grabbed off the cart. "Here, put this over your eye."

"Thanks, Al."

Dad then turned to me and said, "Where'd you go, Eddie?"

"I just went to the park up there, and that guy came from nowhere, then hit me."

"How many times I tell you not to take off without me knowin'? Dad said. "When we get home, you're gonna be punished."

"It's not his fault, Al," Salvador said, in an apologetic tone. "Kid should be able to go to the park without some prick hitting him."

"He shouldn't have taken off like that, Sal."

"Hey Al, if it ain't botherin' me, it shouldn't bother you. I mean, I'm the one who got hit, here."

Dad looked at me, then Salvador and said, "He was a fast little demon wasn't he?"

Salvador chuckled and replied, "Too fast."

"Sorry, Dad."

"It's okay," Dad said. "Come on, let's go home."

We pushed the cart through the intersection and made some extra money selling more snow cones on the way home.

There was always trouble in the neighborhood. Weeks later, I saw a guy named Polo hanging out with Papo. Polo was a short kid with curly, reddish hair, and one of the most feared kids in the neighborhood. He would beat on anyone just for the sheer pleasure of having power over them.

Carlton and I stayed away from those two, but they were always looking for trouble.

One day we were walking in the park in front of my building when we saw them heading in our direction. Polo was on crutches. We didn't want to show them we were scared, so we decided to walk toward them. Polo passed Carlton and gave him a look of hate. Polo stopped, rested on his crutches, and blurted,

"What the fuck you lookin' at, nigger boy?"

Carlton was scared. I could see it in his face and knew it wasn't going to get better. Papo stood there laughing, then showed us the handle of a gun he had hidden under his leather coat.

Carlton submissively answered, "Nothin', Polo, nothin'."

Polo aggressively hobbled closer and angrily shouted, "Fuck you ain't ... you big, black, motherfucker!"

I didn't know what to do and thought, *I wished my brother Michael was here.* I wanted to hit Polo so bad I could feel his blood in my hand. Polo suddenly lifted his left crutch over his head and hit Carlton over the face with it.

Carlton dropped his keys and begged, "Stop it, Polo! Stop!"

"I ain't stoppin' shit, nigger!" Polo shouted. "Don't tell me to stop, black boy!"

"Hit him," Papo encouraged Polo, "Hit the nigger in the face again! Look at him go down ... ha, ha, ha, ha, ha, ha ... whoo!"

"Please, stop, Polo! Stop! I'm sorry!"

I don't know why I stood there in hatred without helping. I realized I was afraid, too. Polo stopped, picked up Carlton's keys, and threw them at a nearby bench, laughing as he and Papo left us. I then held Carlton in my arms, humiliated and disgusted with myself, and asked, "Are you okay, Carlton?"

"Yeah, Eddie, I'm okay," Carlton replied, wiping the tears from his eyes.

I picked up Carlton's keys and held them tightly in my hand, and said, "We'll get 'em Carlton. We'll get 'em."

A few days passed.

"Mom? Can I got outside and play?"

"No. I don't want you or your brother goin' out. It's dangerous."

"Please, Mom! I'm just gonna play catch with Nanny."

Mom could see the hope in my eyes.

"Okay. Only for an hour."

"Thanks, Mom. I'll be back in an hour."

But I didn't go out to play catch. Instead, I sat on the neighborhood bench, hoping and waiting to see Polo walk by. I felt I owed it to Carlton to avenge his beating by Polo, and to take the guilt off my heart for not helping him that day.

I sat there with my hands in my coat pocket. The minutes seemed like hours, as I was in deep thought about what I was going to do if I saw Polo. This time I didn't care if Polo had Papo with him.

Suddenly, I saw him, walking with Papo. They were heading my direction, and I thought, *Is he going to say something or just walk past me?* I was scared, but I sat there on the top, back edge of the bench, clenching my fists, waiting for any surprise.

This time Polo wasn't on crutches, as I hoped he would be. I rested my feet firmly on the seat of the bench, and my face flushed with anger. I looked Polo straight in the eyes as the pair strutted past me.

Polo stared back, and for a moment I thought I was ready to encounter or react to anything. Instead I froze, my eyes glued to the ground like a sad puppy dog.

"Get off my fuckin' bench," Polo demanded, while Papo stood there laughing at me.

"Hey," Papo smirked. "This guy was with that nigger we fucked up."

That's when I realized I was committed to my plan. I suddenly went blank, not thinking or feeling scared anymore, and brought my head up.

I looked at them and confidently replied, "No. Fuck you, Polo!"

Polo was shocked I stood up to him. He then slowly walked toward me as Papo stood behind and watched. I psyched myself out thinking, *This punk piece of shit isn't anything without his friend Papo.*

Remembering how he hit Carlton, my body tensed. I slowly stepped off the bench and advanced toward Polo. I knew I was going to have to hit Polo first. So I punched him with all the anger and hate I had for him, right in the face.

Polo stepped back, touched his face, and shouted, "You motherfucker! What the fuck! You hit me!"

Polo lunged at me like a raging bull. We fought our way behind the bench onto the muddy grass. People rushed from the park to see us fight like two roosters in a cockfight.

"Hey man, look at 'em fight! Goddamn!" one guy said.

"Go Polo, go!" some of Polo's followers cheered on.

"Kick some ass!" the crowd shouted.

"I got money on the chubby kid," a guy in the crowd said, referring to me.

I kept thinking how I was on my own, hoping somebody would stop the fight. We rolled in dog shit. I wrapped my right arm around Polo.

"You motherfucker!" I shouted. "I'm gonna kill you for hittin' Carlton. You're dead! You hear me! I'm gonna kill you! Arrghh!"

"Ugh," Polo yelled. "Get off me! You're dead, Eddie! Dead!"

Finally, I was getting the better part of Polo, and we both knew it. We temporarily separated, and I quickly scanned over the crowd and saw a glimpse of Joey standing there, yelling, "C'mon, bro, c'mon, Eddie."

Afterward, I focused my attention back to Polo and saw him reached into his pocket.

I whispered, "Oh, God."

Polo pulled out a pocketknife with his right hand.

I remembered what Dad said to me once: "If anyone should pull a blade out on you son, your best defense would be to take off your coat and use that as a guard."

When he said that, I didn't think it was possible. Now I brought the coat in front of me and obstructed Polo's path like a matador does to a bull.

But Polo was moving his knife arm aggressively back and forth, hoping to stab me somewhere. I lost my balance, and my knees buckled to the ground. I was terrified, and still no one did anything to help.

Desperately, I yelled, "Joey! Joey! Help!"

He came running onto the grass and stepped in front of Polo's vicious anger. I got away.

"Ah!" I heard an indescribable scream.

"Joey!" I shouted. "Joey! Joey!"

I saw blood streaming from his leg. I was about to help him when suddenly I felt this heavy weight on my back.

"Ugh!"

Papo had jumped on it, and it was hard for me to breathe.

"You fuckin' coward, Papo!" one guy shouted from an apartment window. "I'm gonna come down there and tear your balls out!"

Someone else yelled, "You sonsabitches, I'm gonna come down and kill ya!"

He came down with a stickball bat.

"Cops are comin'. Don't do it, man," a guy said to the man with the stickball bat.

The sound of sirens was all around me. Suddenly police officers came running toward us.

"Knock it off!" a cop ordered, breaking up the fight and motioning Polo to go to the bench. "You, stand over there."

"Man, I saw it all!" somebody said.

"Is my brother okay?"

"Eddie?" Joey cried.

"Joe," I said running to his side. "Joe, you okay?"

"I'm bleedin'."

"Joe. Hey! My brother's bleedin'!"

The cop rushed over.

"Let's see," the cop said to his partner. "Radio an ambulance? Then cuff the kid with the red hair."

His partner went over to Polo and said, "Give me the weapon."

Polo handed it over.

He continued, "Turn around and give me your hands."

A few minutes later, the ambulance came, and they put Joey on a stretcher as I went along.

Later, when Mom and Dad found out about the fight, they scraped together every cent they could save to send us far away from the projects. That's what Mom and Dad wanted for Joey and me. The hope of a new life. Gerard and Anna had already left home, moving far away from the ghetto. Mom and Dad sent us away to join our brother and sister in another world: Portland, Oregon.

Part Two: Portland, Oregon

Chapter Six—A New Beginning

My brother Gerard was nineteen years old when a friend told him to see what Portland was like. Gerard liked Oregon. He told Mom and Dad that this would be a better place for Joey and me. My sister Anna followed. She was sixteen when she decided to stay in Portland with Gerard. Slowly, my family was leaving the neighborhood. Even though the money was hard to come by, Mom and Dad were determined to fulfill their dream for the rest of us.

One cold morning in 1979, my parents woke Joey and me up early. My eyes squinted open drowsily when Mom said, "*Ven mi bebe, q' vamos de viaje.*"

"A trip? Where Mom?" I asked curiously.

"Where there's no pain. *Tu vas* a Portland, Oregon."

"What do you mean?" I asked groggily.

Joey and I didn't know what Portland was, nor had we ever been on a trip before.

"C'mon Joey!" I asserted, trying to get him up. "Mom said we're goin' where there's no pain."

Mom had two suitcases ready for us, but I saw tears in her eyes and wondered, *Why is she crying if we're only going on a trip?* I helped Joey put his pants and shoes on as Mom and Dad went into the kitchen to talk with Michael.

Joey began to rub the sleep from his eyes, looked at me, and said, "Eddie, you're tying the shoe wrong."

"Don't worry … doing it right."

It was time to go, and Dad walked us to the exit door, where Michael waited.

"Eddie, Joey, give me a hug," Michael said hugging us tightly. "I love you guys."

Confused, Joey asked, "You comin', Mike?"

Michael's voice was a little choked up as if he was about to cry. "No, I'm not, but you're gonna go see your brother and sister."

Dad opened the thick, steel door that led us out the hallway. We were about to use the elevator, but the elevator door was off its hinges again. So we walked down the semi-dark, smelly five flights of stairs, passing a junkie on the way down. Mom covered her face with her scarf like she always did before she went outside.

She held our hands and softly expressed, *"Mis bebes yo los quiero."*

We didn't ask what she meant, because we felt it.

Because it was so early, no hookers, pimps, or any of our friends were outside. Just graffiti and the wind carrying the pollution through the streets. We got into the junker station wagon and drove off. We weren't too interested in a last look at the ghetto, so Joey and I played in the back seat. When we got to the airport, Joey put his hands on the car window and yelled with excitement, "Wow, wow! Eddie, look!"

"I see—Mom, Dad are we goin' in one of those today?" I asked, staring at an airplane elevating high into the air, and began to maneuver my way toward the front of the car.

"Yes, you kids are," Dad answered, calmly laying his hand on my hair.

"What about you, Dad, Mom?"

"No, just you and Joseph," Dad replied.

Once inside the airport, I didn't think about the neighborhood or my friends, just about this place Mom and Dad called Portland, Oregon. And by the looks of it, I felt Joey was thinking the same. We waited in the lobby until the plane was ready to be boarded. Joey and I sat there in astonishment, still watching these huge, winged, chunks of metal, going up and coming down. I could hear Joey say, "Man, how do they do that?"

While Joey was lost in amazement, Dad was comforting Mom. So I got up from my seat, held Mom's hand and asked,

"Are you okay, Mom?"

"*Si, mi bebe, estoy bien*," she answered, laying her hand gently behind my neck.

Our plane was ready to board, and Mom embraced us with a long, last hug and softly said, "*Mi bebes va a empezar una nueva vida, gracias mi Dios.*"

Mom cried tears of joy as Joey and I waved bye down the corridor. "I love you…" were her last words.

We sat in our seats and waited for the airplane to take off. I buckled in and put my right hand on the glass window, hoping to see one last glimpse of Mom and Dad. The plane started to taxi away from the entrance. It moved faster and faster on this long, stretched-out road in front of us. We were scared, but excited too. I took my hand off the window, inched it over to Joey's hand, and held it.

"Are there any roaches where we're goin'?" Joey asked anxiously.

I knew Joey was scared of roaches. I couldn't resist but to smile and answered, "No, flying fat water bugs!"

"Na-ah."

"Mm-hmm," I said, in a convincing tone, "There is too."

"How do you know?" Joey asked.

"'Cause Dad said 'flying roaches are everywhere,'" I replied confidently.

The plane took off, and for that moment, I could feel this tingling feeling in my stomach. I looked over to Joey with my eyes wide and asked, "Can you feel it?"

"Feel what?"

"The tingle?"

"Yeah! I feel it."

My face flush against the glass, I saw other ghettos I never knew existed as the plane passed near the Statute of Liberty.

I suddenly felt a deep, hurt inside of me and thought, *What about Carlton? I'll miss you Carlton; I'll miss you.*

It was strange leaving our home. Except we weren't sad, we were happy: something Mom and Dad called "better" was waiting for us.

When we stepped off the airplane and into Portland, the first thing I thought was, *This is like walking into Paradise.*

I felt like an alien on a new planet. The best part was, nothing reminded me of our neighborhood, except for the blue, junkered Ford that Gerard and Anna met us at the airport in. I couldn't believe all the green trees, unpolluted areas, and people with blond hair.

"I thought you only saw people like this in magazines!" I said, curiously, looking at everything I passed as we exited the airport. "Wow! This is beautiful, Gerard."

He and Anna looked at each other and chuckled. Still in awe, we hurried into the car, and I anxiously rolled down the window.

"Everything is smaller," I said. "Is all of Portland like this, Gerard?"

"Pretty much, except for a few buildings downtown."

We drove over bridges, and passed quiet, green, grassy neighborhoods. It all seemed like a dream. After a twenty-minute or so drive, they took us to an area called Northwest Portland. It looked like a little town, and everything was so clean.

Gerard parked the car by a little store. It didn't look like the Spanish store Mom went to back in the neighborhood.

They showed us across the street to an old building called The Katherine apartments. We walked in and a few feet ahead us was a wide stairwell that twisted slightly toward the second floor. We proceeded up the stairs and my nose inhaled fresh air instead of the smell of piss or the odor of a junkie sitting in the stairwell shooting up heroin.

As Gerard led us down the hall to our new home, I noticed the other apartment doors weren't made of two-inch thick steel, like the doors in the projects. Eager to see what our new place looked like, Gerard unlocked the front door and I saw hardwood floors. It was nothing like the old torn linoleum we were used to. Joey and I hurried to the living room window where there was a balcony. We pulled up the window and noticed other balconies that extended to each apartment below.

"Wow!" Joey blurted. "Anna, look! This is cool!"

"Yeah. This is cool!" I added, touching the balcony. "Gerard can we go outside on it?"

"Yeah, go ahead."

Joey went first and I followed. It was great. We looked around and saw the little buildings and houses around us.

The day passed and that evening, I looked out the living-room window again. There was a quiet, peaceful feeling I had never felt in New York. I looked up into the cold, dark sky and stared at the glimmering stars.

Soon after, I lay on the floor and covered myself with blankets. Staring around the dark room, I had memories of what we had left and thought of this new life we were going to start: we didn't have to worry about getting stabbed, or Mom looking out the fifth-floor window seeing if Joey and me were okay. I fell asleep, anxious for the next day to arrive.

The next night, about eight in the evening, Anna, Joey and I walked up a hill to a place called Washington Park. Back in the projects, we wouldn't even think about walking out our front door at that time. As we approached the entrance of the park, I gaped at the city lights downtown.

"Eddie, are there any animals in this park?" Joey asked curiously.

"Yeah, big, huge bears!" I teased, making like a huge bear myself.

"Really!"

"I don't know."

"Then why'd you say it?"

"'Cause."

We sat on some nearby swings and I asked, "Are we on a mountain, Anna?"

She chuckled and replied, "We're on the highest mountain in Portland, and we're free here."

Chapter Seven

It wasn't long before the day came for Joey and me to sign up at Chapman Junior High School. As Anna walked us to our new school, I noticed the street signs read Lovejoy, Northrup, and 25th and Pettygrove Street. We then saw something incredible: a huge field of green grass, with kids playing soccer on it. There were beautiful homes on both sides of the park, and the houses didn't look dirty or broken into.

Joey asked, "Anna, what park is this?"

"Wallace," she answered, leading us toward the front doors of the school.

When we entered, the school was like a huge mansion, with no bars or vandalism anywhere. In bewilderment, Joey's mouth went wide and exclaimed, "Whoa!"

People said "hello" and "good morning" to us.

By now I thought for sure I was in a dream.

At first we didn't trust anyone, but being from where we came from, that was considered street-smart. We didn't become popular overnight, either.

After a while we adjusted, and Joey met his first friend, Jaeger. I liked Jaeger because he was funny, outgoing, and considered, like one of us, "scum." Because the school was divided into to groups, rich or poor, the rich kids had labels for everyone.

So Joey and Jaeger decided to start their own club of friends. They wore green jackets with silver letters that read, "THE LORDS." But I think they really started the club after we saw the movie *The Warriors* at The Esquire Theater.

The principal began to tell lies about my brother's club like: "The Lords are beating up kids for their lunch money and stealing bikes from around the playground."

Fact is Joey, Jaeger and whoever else was in the club never did these things. I wanted badly to be involved in the club, but they wouldn't let me.

Since I couldn't be a part of the club, I would visit Jaeger and listen to records at his house on Northwest 23rd and Kearney, just one block away from the Esquire Theater.

Since Joey and I lived nearby, we'd go see a movie when Gerard let us. One of our favorites was Grease. When the movie came out, Joey, Jaeger and some of their friends, wore nylon shirts and greasy gel through their hair. They seemed compatible, and that was the reason why they were perfect friends.

At Chapman School, we even met twin, pudgy girls named Hazel and Tamara, who lived on 27th and Upshur, in the Upshur apartment complex just a few blocks north of Chapman. At first I thought they were Mexican, but then they told me they were Peruvian.

No girl was interested in a sixth or seventh grader, but I still tried to impress them. One day, another girl came up to my locker. I concealed the titles of my books so she wouldn't know what special classes I was taking. She said, "Eddie if you want to be cool, buy a pair of Nikes."

I looked down at my feet and noticed I was wearing the same cheap shoes I'd had before we left New York. After that embarrassing moment, my goal was to get a pair of Nikes.

Gerard and Anna couldn't afford to buy us clothing, so when the school found out, they set up a social worker for us. She was a nice lady who took me shopping at JC Penneys (Joey went another time.)

I got some jeans and shirts, then she asked, "Do you want a pair of shoes?"

I saw this as my prime opportunity to get the Nikes I'd been wanting. We went to the shoe department, and I pointed them out. "Thirty-five dollars!" she blurted in a shocked tone.

"Yeah, thirty-five dollars," I replied casually.

"Are you sure you want these shoes? There are better ones in the store," she suggested. "How about those over there."

All I could think was how bad I wanted those shoes.

So I randomly pointed out another pair of shoes and said,

"See, these are cheap because the rubber won't last long. And … and those over—I used to have those. They're no good."

The social worker smiled and asked, "When did you become an expert on shoes?"

"Uh … I just know!"

She picked up the shoe I wanted off the rack, saw my face filled with hope, and said, "Okay. We'll buy them."

"Cool!" I said. "Thanks! Thanks a lot!"

When I went to school in my new Nikes, the same girl came up to me and said, "Eddie, you got a pair of Nikes?"

"You like them?"

"Yeah, I do. They look nice."

For sure I thought I was on the road to stardom, and maybe the girl had an interest in me, but nothing became of it.

I didn't have a lot of friends, so to occupy my time, I exercised. Running through the streets of Portland with a white towel wrapped around my neck was how I had my fun.

Once I jogged to Jaeger's house in the snow, and I was tired after running several miles. Joey and Jaeger's friend Gino were there, listening to the soundtrack Grease. I didn't like Gino because he thought he was intimidating. But little did he know he was just ugly. His face looked like it had craters on it, and he had scrappy, long, dirty, blond hair, which looked like he never washed it.

I think Gino knew I wasn't scared of him, but wanted to find out for sure.

He said resentfully, "Whatta you lookin' at?"

I shrugged my shoulders and replied, "Nothing important."

I sensed Gino didn't like my response, and because I was afraid of Jaeger's dad knowing a fight was about to occur upstairs, I proceeded to walk away, when Gino blurted, "What's your problem? Scared?"

I turned my head sharply and replied in a cocky tone, "What's your problem?"

Next thing you know, we were fighting.

"Ah! You punk-bitch!" Gino shouted.

"I'm gonna tear you a new asshole!" I shouted back.

49

Jaeger shouted, "Stop! Guys, stop!"

Joey yelled, "C'mon, Eddie. Kick his ass!"

Jaeger's dad heard the commotion, rushed upstairs, forced himself between us, and yelled, "What the hell? Take it outside! Take it outside!"

Gino ran outside and yelled, "C'mon, Eddie! C'mon!"

I ran out there slipping on the snow.

"C'mon crater face!" I yelled, "gonna fuck you up!"

I body-slammed Gino on the ground, and seeing his position, I grabbed his head and banged it against a car bumper.

"Umph!" Gino gasped.

Jaeger's dad wrapped his arms around my shoulders and exclaimed, "Jesus Christ! This kid is strong!"

"Let go!" I yelled, "I'm gonna fuck you up, Gino!"

"Eddie, relax!" Jaeger said. "Come on … it's over, man."

Gino was out of breath, wheezing because of his smoking.

"Eddie, you cool? You okay?" Jaeger asked, resting his hands on my shoulders.

"Yeah, but he shouldn't have fucked with me, Jaeger," I said, "I don't take shit from nobody."

Jaeger chuckled and said, "I know you don't … I know."

"Gino, go home," Jaeger's dad said. "You too, Eddie. I don't want to see you guys here for a while."

Gino reluctantly walked away and shouted, "You ain't seen the end of me."

Jaeger said, "Hey, man, I'll see ya tomorrow."

"You comin', Joe?"

"Yeah," Joey said, as we walked away from Jaeger's house. "Man, you kicked his ass. He won't mess with you again."

I slowly turned my head to Joey and said, "He better not."

The teachers at Chapman realized how behind we were in our education, so they kept us in these special classes for longer than I wanted to be. I really longed to be with the other smart kids. So I studied as hard as I could, even though it always felt like I wasn't getting anywhere.

I managed to excel in math and get into a more difficult

science class, but I still felt behind. And when I thought I had reached a learning plateau, I mainly focused on exercising. Doing this was a getaway from temporary failure. I often felt if I couldn't be mentally smart, then I would be physically strong.

One place we hung out at was Couch Park. It was fun going there because of the high structure we played tag on. And after a hard game of tag, we went swimming in the school pool at the park.

The neat thing about the school was, Old Man Dean kept the place running smoothly. He was a soft-spoken, fairly tall, heavy-set man who wore thick glasses and had little hair on his head. He was always polite and encouraging to us all.

Dean believed we could accomplish anything if we wanted it bad enough. He even had his own achievement board of the kids who reached certain goals: the most sit-ups, chin-ups, push-ups, laps in the pool, or dumbbell curls. Anything he could think of to build up our self-esteem.

Nothing was better than the person who did the most sit-ups. Jaeger was the all-time champion. When I looked at the board and saw one thousand sit-ups for Jaeger Decaro I exclaimed, "Wow! Did he really do this, Dean?"

Dean proudly replied, "He sure did. I sat here and counted every one."

"You think I could do the same?"

"C'mon. I'll hold your feet and count. You can stop anytime you want, and this will give you the practice you need to build up to a thousand."

"All right!"

Later, I asked Jaeger how he felt about doing a thousand sit-ups and he theatrically replied, "Yeah, I did it. But my butt was raw, after."

We both started laughing.

Meanwhile, everyone in the family was trying to save money to bring Dad to Portland.

Chapter Eight

The hot sun was blazing on my body while I jogged in my new Etonic running shoes toward Couch Park, grabbing the white, cotton towel wrapped around my neck to wipe the beads of sweat pouring down my face. When I arrived at the park, I rushed to the water fountain adjacent to the bathroom and tried to drink more than I could consume.

It felt good splashing it over my face with the satisfaction of knowing I'd just run several hard miles. I stood under the shelter close to the bathrooms, when I noticed this guy from a distance sitting on a rail not far from the entrance of the school. I don't really know what drove me to get closer to him, except I wanted to meet him.

I casually walked up some stairs, approached the guy, picked up a nearby basketball and said, "What's up?"

"What's up?" he answered hesitantly and under his breath.

"My name's Eddie," I said, bouncing the basketball.

"Your name's Eddie? My name's Eddie, too," he replied somewhat surprised.

We chuckled.

"Wanna play a game of hoop, Eddie?" I asked.

"Just call me Ed," he insisted politely.

"Okay, c'mon Ed," I said, dribbling the ball toward the free-throw line.

"Hey," I yelled at two guys playing a game of Horse. "You wanna play two-on-two?"

They looked at each other and nodded their heads.

Ed asked, "Should I call you Ed?"

"Just call me Eddie," I replied shooting a lay-up.

"Okay, Eddie, nice to meet you."

"Yeah! Me too, Ed."

"Yo, winners outs, right?" I asked the two guys.

"Yeah, that's cool," they replied, looking at each other and nodding their heads.

"Ed, you shoot the die, see who gets the ball."

"Okay," Ed replied, dribbling the ball to the second line above the free-throw line.

Ed made the shot and it was our ball.

I dashed out for a pass and yelled, "Ed! Right here, man. I'm open!"

Ed passed the ball, but the guy behind me intercepted it, cleared it at the second line, and shot a two-pointer.

"It's all right, man," I said reassuring Ed. "We'll get 'em."

"Winners outs, right?" the guy asked.

"Yeah," Ed answered.

"Let's 'd' (defense) these guys," I said, giving Ed a low five with my hand.

"Ball in," Ed said, handing the guy back the basketball to resume the game.

The guy passed it out to his friend, and he shot the ball but missed the rim. Ed rebounded it and passed it back to me, then I shot the ball from the free-throw line, swish through the net.

"Yeah!" Ed exclaimed. "One."

It was 2 to 1, their lead.

"Ball in," I said, passing the ball to Ed.

Ed dribbled the ball, working his way outside the free-throw line. He passed it to me, and I maneuvered my way between the two guys. I faked the shot and passed it to Ed, and he shot it.

"Good shot," I praised Ed. "That was butta!"

"Two to 2, tied," Ed declared, as he proceeded toward the free-throw line for another check.

Ed passed it in to me, and the guy stole it.

"Shit!" I muttered with my arms extended out, defending him as close as I could.

The guy quickly dribbled the ball around me, jumped in the air, and shot a lay-up leading the ball with his left hand. It appeared as if that was his best shot. We played hard like that for two games. They won one.

After the game, we headed back down the steps toward the shelter to eat free peanut butter and jelly sandwiches funded by the park.

"Man, we could've crushed those guys," I said. "Can you

believe that scrappy dude shootin' the ball from under his leg? What the hell was that shot?"

"I don't know, man," Ed replied, shaking his head from side-to-side. "It was ugly, though."

"Yeah it was," I said, "dude wasn't even lookin' at the hoop."

"No way," Ed said, still eating his sandwich.

"You're pretty good," I said. "Where'd you learn how to play?"

"I'm not very good," Ed replied modestly.

"Man, you were kickin' it out there."

Ed smiled and said, "You're pretty quick."

"Think so?"

"Yeah, you're quicker than me."

"But you got the outside shot," I said, "wish I had that."

"That comes with practice," Ed said. "You come here a lot?"

"Sometimes."

Ed said, "I've never seen you here before. You go to school here?"

"Nah. I go to Chapman," I replied.

"I go to Lincoln," Ed said. "How do you like Chapman?"

"It's cool. Lotta rich kids, though."

"Same at Lincoln," Ed asked. "Wanna come over my house?"

"Sure!"

After eating, we walked a few blocks west of the park. Ed lived on the first floor in the Villa Florence apartment building on Northwest 22nd and Glisan Street.

"Come on in and meet my mom," Ed insisted in a friendly manner.

I followed him into the apartment and saw a lady about five feet four inches tall, with brownish hair and a welcoming smile.

"Hi, Mom! This is my new friend, and his name is Eddie too."

She welcomed me in a soft-spoken voice, "Well, hello, my

name is Edith. We have two Eddie's in the house, now."

"Nice meeting you, Edith," I said, following Ed to his room.

His room was so organized, I wondered if he cleaned it himself. He had a picture of Clint Eastwood hanging above his bed.

"That's a cool picture," I said, walking closer to it. "What movie is this from?"

"*The Good, the Bad and the Ugly*," Ed said proudly.

"You clean your own room?" I asked curiously.

"Nah, man, my mom does it."

"That's cool," I said, "my mom does my room, too."

We stayed in his room and talked about everything: girls, sports, school, and what we were going to do the next day. I soon realized Ed had the same interests and goals as I did, like exercising and going to movies. But we especially loved jogging.

Ed was fourteen years old, and I was twelve. Yet age was no barrier to an evolving friendship I felt would last forever. Weeks flew by hanging out with Ed, and I wished I could be in the same grade as him so we could be together more. I was thankful to have someone by my side whom I could now call a friend. I hadn't felt this way since I left Carlton in New York.

It was my seventh year at Chapman. Mount Saint Helen's erupted, and Dad had come to live with us in a small, two-bedroom basement apartment on Johnson Street in the Northwest. We lived there until it was time to bring Mom down. Back in New York, Michael had met a new girl named Ellie and planned on staying in the projects until it was time for them to come to Portland.

Part Three: Year 1981

Chapter Nine

Sometimes when jogging in the Northwest, I would visit Hazel. When I got there, she would offer me a piece of cheese because she knew how much I liked it.

I couldn't think of Hazel any other way but as a friend. Besides, she knew who I liked at Chapman. I even once told Hazel what a "fox" the girl was. I didn't know if she liked that, but felt at the time I could confide my thoughts to her.

The girl I like was named Heidi, and she was the most popular girl at Chapman. She had sandy blond hair, light brown skin, and pretty brown eyes. At the time she was seeing a guy named, David, who was also a soshe. Many times I felt Heidi knew I liked her, but never thought I had a chance.

It was a windy day when I sat on the bench in the park watching the same soccer game as Heidi was. I didn't like soccer, but stayed because she was there. Suddenly her body began to move toward me. My heart started to pound, and my stomach felt like it froze. It was like watching her in slow motion as she inched closer to me. Then words started to come out from her mouth, but because I was so absorbed by her beauty and the lips she spoke the words from, I didn't even hear what she had said to me. My ears miraculously cleared themselves, and I heard her say, "Eddie, if you could take me out, how would you do it?"

I didn't know how to respond to her question, and never in my wildest dreams thought she would ask. Not sure of what she wanted me to say, I replied, "We could … uh … go to the park."

She looked to her friend Mary, smiled, then left giggling. I felt like the park idiot. For the rest of the day and night, I hated myself for blowing my big chance to be with the most beautiful girl in the school.

The next day her friend Mary approached me and said, "Eddie, Heidi would like you to come over to her house."

For a split second I was in a state of shock and almost didn't have a tongue.

I replied confidently, "Sure. Sure, no problem."

I listened carefully as she began to tell me Heidi's address.

"So, can you remember that?" Mary asked in a snobbish tone.

"Yeah, cool … no problem."

"You know what time to be there?" Mary asked.

"Yeah, I got a handle on it. Thanks."

The following weekend I jogged to Heidi's house with butterflies in my stomach. I rushed down a gravel driveway, which led to her house, then knocked firmly on the door.

"Eddie? Hi!"

"Hi, Heidi."

"Come in. My mom's out at an event."

"Oh ... okay."

We sat at an oak table in the kitchen. In the center of the table there was a wooden bowl filled with fruit.

"Would you like an apple and Coke?" Heidi asked.

"Yeah. That's cool. Thanks."

"Here, the apple's from Fred Meyer," she said, with a smile.

"Looks good," I said, setting the apple on the table. "Wanna share the Coke?"

"Sure."

For a few seconds, we sat there and looked at each other.

"So, how do you like Chapman?" I asked.

"It's okay. I can't wait for high school."

"Yeah, me too. Being a freshman's gonna be weird."

"Why?"

"I don't know. Just 'cause it's kind of a big step, I guess."

"Do you like records?" Heidi asked.

"Yeah. I don't have any, though."

"Do you like the movie *Fame?*"

"Heard it was good," I replied. "Why?"

"I've got the album here. I'll put it on."

"Okay."

In my heart, the sharing of the Coke and conversation we had was the beginning of my first relationship. But in my mind there was the question of, *What about David?*

Soon after our first date, I decided next time I saw Heidi, I would pop the question I'd desperately been wanting to ask. I jogged through the back streets of Northwest Portland, anxious to get to her house. Nervous and unsure of how I was going to approach her with the question, I rang her doorbell with anticipation.

"Eddie?" Heidi asked, surprised to see me, "what are you doing here?"

Suddenly, without thought, I looked deep into her eyes and blurted, "Heidi, would you be my girlfriend?"

She was stunned.

"Yes," she answered, nodding her head happily.

I felt like we had just eloped and that I was capable of doing anything.

I jogged over to her house almost all the time, but not without first stopping to say hello to Hazel.

Once I went to Heidi's house and went through my visit ritual by first opening the refrigerator and grabbing a piece of Tillamook cheddar cheese. She didn't understand why I had this fetish for cheese, but there was always a supply when I got there (Hazel did the same for me.)

Hazel knew we were dating, so I felt comfortable bringing Heidi over there.

I knocked on the door and Hazel answered.

"Hazel, this is Heidi."

"Hi."

"Can we come in?" I asked.

"Yeah," Hazel said quietly.

Soon after, I took out this can of Copenhagen snuff that a kid gave me.

When I showed it to Heidi she curiously asked, "What's

that?"

"A can of chew."

"Chew?"

"Yeah, chew."

Hazel stood in the kitchen and watched us playing girlfriend and boyfriend in the living room. I was slipping the can of chew back into my back pocket when Heidi blurted, "Let me try that!"

"Try this?"

"Yeah, try that."

"Okay, but don't get mad at me if you get sick," I said, taking the can out of my back pocket, carefully lifting the lid off.

Heidi stepped back, pinched her nose and blurted, "Oh, my God! That stuff stinks!"

"Whatta you mean it stinks?"

I held the can close to Hazel's nose and asked, "Do you think this stinks?"

She smelled it and with her big, brown eyes looked at me and quietly replied, "No, it doesn't stink."

"See, Hazel doesn't think it smells. Try it!" I insisted in a cool manner.

She hesitated then proceeded toward me and said, "Well, okay, just a little though."

"So you wanna try it?" I asked.

"Yeah, I'll try it."

Heidi amateurishly dug her fingers into the can and said, "It feels mushy," and proceeded to put a small amount under her bottom lip. A look of disgust crossed her face.

"What's up? Is it okay?"

Heidi's eyes went watery. She grabbed her chin and mumbled, "No."

I chuckled, then grabbed the can and said, "Let me show you."

I dug my right two fingers into it, making it seem like I had years of experience and put a large amount under my bottom lip. I desperately tried not to show my weakness to the dreadful taste in my mouth.

"Oh, man. I think I'm gonna get sick."

60

Heidi said, "Me too," and spit the chew on the gray carpet.

I laid on the carpet, nauseated and said, "Oh ... oh ... I feel like throwin' up."

"I gotta go," Heidi said. "I need to throw up."

We began to walk away from Hazel's house and Heidi vomited.

"Heidi," I asked, "you okay?"

"No. Just get me home."

We took a shortcut through Macleay Park toward her house.

I was serious about Heidi and wanted to share every moment I could with her. I was excited about graduating from the eighth grade, but even happier that Mom was soon coming to Portland. Before we graduated, Debi, a girl in our school, decided to have a party at her mom's house (her mom was out of town at the time.) So I invited Ed, Jaeger, Joey—anyone who wanted to party and have a good time.

The day of the party, Ed and I walked up Westover Street to where Debi lived around these million-dollar homes. I loved going there because it was unreal! It was like walking into a mansion, and her backyard was like a forest.

When we got to the party, one of Debi's good friends, Sarah, answered the door.

"Eddie!" Sarah blurted. "Debi, Eddie's here. Who's your friend?"

"Yo, this is my brother," I said. "Ed, this is Sarah."

"Hi, Ed!" Sarah asked, "Is he really your brother?"

"Yeah, he's my brother. Don't we look alike?"

Right then, Debi came up from the basement and said, "Party's downstairs, guys."

We followed them downstairs, and I saw a foosball table. I loved foosball and had almost become champion at Friendly House Community Center playing the game.

"Man, where'd they get all the alcohol?" Ed asked.

"I don't know, man, and I don't care. But I'm gonna go crush someone in some foosball, c'mon!"

As we were playing foosball, we saw Sarah walk down the

stairs, holding a bottle of Manischewitz in her left hand and a can of Budweiser in her right.

"Sarah," I asked in a sarcastic tone, "you think that's enough booze?"

Between sipping the wine and taking gulps of the beer, she slurred, "I'm just gettin' ... gettin' started."

Soon, people were getting tipsy, slurring their words, and walking sloppy. Ed and I laughed as we watched everyone make fools of themselves.

The party was now out of control, and one guy broke the glass to the liquor cabinet to get the tequila. Some of the party moved upstairs. I didn't know where Joey or Jaeger were, but I suspected they were flirting with the girls. Suddenly, Debi came running down the basement stairs yelling, "Eddie, Eddie, come upstairs, quick!"

"Yo, Debi, what's up?"

She ran toward me and whispered something. I backed up and exclaimed, "What?"

"What's up?" Ed asked, restlessly waiting for an answer.

"Man, you're not gonna believe this."

"What? What?"

"C'mon, bro, follow me!"

We ran upstairs and noticed some girls surrounding the bathroom door. I saw Heidi covering her nose and repeating, "Oh, my God! ...Oh, my God!"

"Heidi, I didn't know you were here," I said, surprised to see her.

"Eddie, we tried to help her, but we couldn't get her out of there."

Ed, standing behind me, looked at Heidi and said, "Looks like you saw a ghost."

"Worse," Heidi replied, walking away from the bathroom door.

I forced my way through the body of girls blocking the door, when Debi grabbed me and said, "Just be ready."

"It can't be that bad."

I slowly cracked opened the door. "Holy shit!" I blurted,

62

shocked, "what do you expect me to do?"

"We don't know," some girls replied.

"What the hell is goin' on, man?" Ed wanted to know.

"Ed, I'm gonna need your help."

"With what?"

I opened the door and showed him.

"With this!"

"Holy shit!" Ed cried, backing away from the door.

"That's what I'm sayin', man," I told him, quickly closing the door.

Sarah had drank that bottle of Manischewitz and topped it off with another can of beer. She was sitting on the toilet, holding her stomach as she groaned in pain, and from her waist down, her clothes were off. There was shit on the floor, the walls, and on her underwear, which dangled off her right ankle.

We didn't know what to do.

Debi suggested, "She needs air. We'll clean her up, and you guys can take her outside in the backyard."

Relieved I didn't have to clean her myself, I looked at Ed and said, "Man, I'm glad I don't drink that shit."

"Yeah, me too," Ed replied, with a relieved tone in his voice.

We then heard a knock on the front door.

"Who's that?" Debi asked, looking at all of us.

My first thought was, *Maybe a friend of Debi's showed up late.* Debi walked briskly to the door to see who it was, looked through the peephole, and exclaimed, "Oh my God!"

She ran back to us, frantic, and said, "Sarah's mom is here!"

"What?" Heidi said. "No way!"

"Sarah's mom is here. She's at the front door," Debi said. "What am I going to do?"

The doorbell rang again, and everyone panicked. Instantly, people tried to find a place to hide.

"What are we going to do?" one girl asked.

"Take her outside, now!" Debi demanded, pacing around trying to think of a quick fix to her dilemma.

"Okay, we'll take her out, but you gotta buy us some time," I told Debi.

Before they could finish cleaning her, Ed and I picked Sarah up and rushed for the backyard. Debi left to go answer the door.

"Oh … uh … Mrs. Welton, hi." Debi filled us in on this later.

"Have you seen Sarah?"

"No, I haven't," Debi replied, keeping the door slightly cracked.

"What's going on in there, Debi?"

"Nothing," Debi answered shiftily.

"Well, where's your mother?" Mrs. Welton asked, trying to look over Debi's head to see into the house.

"At the store. She'll be back," Debi answered quickly.

Mrs. Welton didn't believe Debi, so she inched herself in and noticed beer bottles and cans everywhere.

"Oh my God! Debi, what's going on here?"

Minutes later, Ed and I heard this yell for Sarah.

"Sarah … Sarah … Sarah!"

A girl from the party came running outside and shouted, "Sarah's mom is coming!"

"Shit!" I said. "Ed, help me bring her down the hill."

At the bottom of the hill, stood a cyclone fence, which stopped us from going any further. Sarah was still groaning in pain. So in desperation, I looked over to Ed and said, "Let's throw her over the fence!"

"What? Are you crazy, Eddie! You're nuts! She'll be torn apart."

"Well, whatta we gonna do?"

"Throw leaves over her," Ed suggested, picking the leaves up off the ground and quickly spreading them on Sarah's drunken, sick body. "C'mon! Help me?"

"Man, just leave her here?"

"Well, you were gonna throw her over the fence!" Ed said. "Don't you think this is a better idea?"

"Okay, okay," I agreed, then began to help.

After coating Sarah's drunken body with wet, dirty leaves, we ran from the scene. Mrs. Welton eventually made her way out the backyard, still yelling Sarah's name. She then noticed some feet at the bottom of the hill and ran to see who it was. She frantically brushed the leaves off, and freaked out!

"Mrs. Welton, it's not what you think," Debi said. "She just had a little too much to drink."

"Drink!" Mrs. Welton said. "Oh, Sarah ... wake up baby ... wake up. Debi!"

"Yes?"

"Help me take her to the car."

They rushed her inside the car, and Mrs. Welton's last words were, "Your mother will hear of this, Debi."

She rushed Sarah to the Good Samaritan Hospital on 21st and Lovejoy.

When Debi's mother found out about the party, Debi was grounded for a very long time. We felt sorry for her, but there wasn't much we could do, and for weeks Debi's party became the talk of the school.

Chapter Ten

A couple of months later, the phone rang.

"Hello?"

"Eddie?"

"Hi, Heidi. What's up?"

"Could you come over? It's important I talk with you."

"Yeah. I'll be there in a jif."

"Okay, bye."

"Bye," I said, and hopped on a cheap bike I'd put together from parts I found around bike shops.

When I got there, I jumped off my bike, dropped it on her front porch steps, and hurried to the front door.

She opened it and said, "I want to talk to you, Eddie."

"About what?" I asked, breathing hard after riding my bike several miles.

"About something important," she replied calmly.

We sat down on the front porch and she asked, "Eddie, I don't know how to say this except for just saying it."

"What?"

"Have you ever done it?"

"Done what?"

"You know, have sex."

In bewilderment, my mouth went partially opened and responded, "Wha'? No, why?"

"Do you want to try it?"

I was getting this really weird feeling inside of me. I kept quiet for a few seconds and then replied, "I don't know."

"Do you have any rubbers?" Heidi asked.

I could not believe her forwardness.

"No, no I don't … what are rubbers?"

"You know what it is, don't you? It's protection … just in case," Heidi said confidently.

"Well, yeah … yeah, I sort of know, but I really don't know how to handle this." I hesitantly asked, "How do I get them?"

"Go to Fred Meyer. They got all that stuff."

I was fifteen years old, and I didn't know if I could even buy them.

"How?"

"Just get on your bike and get them," Heidi said firmly.

"Man, I don't know. I've never done anything like this before."

"Do you want to just forget it?" she asked, standing up, about to go back into the house.

"No, no! I'll try," I said, lifting my bike off her steps. "I'll be back!"

"Okay, bye. I love you!" she said, giving me a look of confidence as I rode off on my bike up her gravel driveway.

When I got to Fred Meyer, I walked toward the pharmaceutical department, with no knowledge of what a box of condoms looked like.

So I asked a nearby clerk, "Hey, uh ... do you know where the rubbers are?"

"You mean condoms?"

"Um, yeah that's it."

He pointed his finger to an aisle and said loudly, "Over there are where we keep all of the prophylactics."

I looked around to see if anyone heard him.

As I walked slowly passed the aisle, I became overwhelmed with all the different kinds they had. I tried to be discreet because I didn't want anyone to know what I was doing. I then saw a familiar name and whispered triumphantly, "Trojan!"

I saw three, twelve and thirty-six in a box, not knowing which one to buy. I began to talk to myself, "Okay ... okay ... think about this, Eddie. No, I don't want those, not enough. What the hell's a Sheik?" I said, glancing at another brand of condoms. " ... Here it is! This is what I need."

Since it was the first time, I thought, I had to do this right. So I grabbed the biggest box of Trojans they had and a pack of Wrigley's Spearmint gum.

I briskly walked toward the nearest open register.

68

"Holy shit!" I mumbled.

The only person checking was a woman, and all I could do was move forward. When it was my turn, I hesitantly placed the contents on the counter and thought, *Oh man, she's not going to sell them to me.*

Just when I hoped for nothing to go wrong, the lady looked at the gum and condoms, and said with a smile, "Nice combination."

I paid for them and left as fast as possible. I rode back to Heidi's and she led me to her room in the attic, where she then turned off the lights. I could see these self-adhesive stars and moons glowing on her ceiling. I noticed she was embarrassed and hesitant to take her clothes off. So I tried to make her feel comfortable even though I wasn't myself.

She laid down on her back and I laid on top of her. I touched her gently and asked, "Are you okay?"

She replied quietly, "Yeah, I guess."

I didn't know where to start and asked, "Um, could you ... could you show me?"

"Yeah," she said, guiding me to where her vagina was.

I started to feel myself penetrate her.

"Go slow ... slow ... it hurts a little."

"Okay ... sorry," I said, comforting her any way I could. "Is there anything you want me to do?"

"No. Just, just keep going," Heidi replied.

Nothing seemed to be happening for us. Then I thought, *How could adults like this sex thing so much?*

When we were done, we went downstairs, put a record on and sat quietly for a while.

Heidi looked over to me and asked, "What did you think of it?"

"I don't know. How 'bout you?"

"It was okay. It hurt a little."

"I'm sorry."

"Do you want to try it again?" she asked.

"Sure. Yeah, let's try it ... I guess."

We went back upstairs and proceeded to go through the

same physical motions. This time it was different. I started to feel something inside. A feeling I thought at first was going to hurt me.

We kissed each other hard, and I said, "Something's happening, oh, God! Oh man … oh … oh … oh!"

This huge burst of something came rushing out. I didn't know what was happening, but whatever it was, it couldn't be stopped.

We now knew why adults liked sex so much.

Even though our relationship continued, our desire to love each other began to dissipate. I felt Heidi and myself lose interest in each other, so we ended the relationship. To keep my mind off of her, I found other things to do, like make up for lost time with Ed.

Chapter Eleven

The school held our 1981 eighth grade graduation in the gymnasium and I wore my rayon shirt, Britannia jeans, and Nike shoes. My shirt was soaked with sweat as I danced the night away. Some clapped their hands to the beat of the music, and I was bringing the heat out of my shoes. After several songs, I stopped dancing to get a cup of juice and noticed Heidi talking to David. I pretended it didn't bother me.

The strobe lights lit the floor and everyone was dancing to the song by the Police, "Don't Stand So Close to Me." Soon after, I stepped outside to get some air and saw Hazel and Tamara.

"Eddie!" Hazel voiced from a distance.

"Yo, what's up?" I replied, happy to see her.

"How do you like the party?" she asked.

"It's cool! How 'bout you?"

"It's nice."

It was unusual for her to be so outgoing, considering she was normally shy toward me. I guess she was feeling gutsy.

I brushed my hand through my hair and said, "I'm gonna go back inside, okay. See ya!"

I heard her say "bye" as I walked back into the school. For the rest of the night, I danced and showed off every step I could.

Joey and Jaeger were leaving the dance to go party elsewhere.

"Hey, Joey, where you guys goin'?"

"Me an' Jaeger gonna go trip."

"Whatta you mean?"

"C'mon Jaeger," Joey said, ignoring me then motioning Jaeger to follow.

At about nine thirty the dance was over, and I decided to hang out at Wallace Park for a while. I walked toward the basketball court and saw my friend Timmy talking with some guys. Timmy was a skinny Cuban kid, who lived across the street from the park and played football with me and the guys most weekends. We had become good friends at Chapman.

I cupped my hands around my mouth and yelled, "Timmy, Timmy!"

"Eddie, what's up, man?"

"Nothin', whatta you doin' here?"

"Just kickin' it with Tito."

Tito was always around the park drinking beer and telling stories about how hard his life was and all the fights he had won in the past. At times it was even comical. Tito had dark hair that reached down to his shoulders, a rough bearded face, a voice that sounded a lot like Wolf Man Jack's voice, and more muscles than I've ever seen. He looked pretty tough. That was why no one ever questioned him about his stories.

Tito gestured a greeting with his 32-ounce bottle of Old English 800 beer and said with his raspy voice, "Hey, brutha! What's up?"

"Hey, Tito," I said sarcastically, "I see you're fuelin' up."

"Congratulations, little guy," Tito chuckled, referring to my graduation. "What the fuck you gonna do with your life now?"

"I'm gonna move on to bigger and better things, man, you know, talk to women and be a bad ass," I replied, tucking my hands into my pants pockets.

"Ha, ha, ha … yeah, you can't depend on anyone else to be a bad ass for you," Tito said, taking another gulp of his beer.

"Hey Timmy you gonna play football next week?" I asked.

"I don't know, how 'bout you?"

"I'll play if you play—Man, I graduated … isn't that great!"

"Man, you're crazy. Everybody graduates," Timmy said, acting as if I was stupid for saying it.

"Not in my old neighborhood, man. You're lucky if you could make it through the sixth grade without gettin' stabbed. Hey, my mom's comin' down too!"

"Hey that's great, man, so now you're gonna be a goddamn mamma's boy," Tito said, laughing and taking another gulp of his beer.

"How can you handle that shit?" I asked, with disdain.

"This is a man's mutha-fuckin' beer—eight ball!" Tito declared. "Wanna drink, graduate?"

"Nah, man, I'm savin' myself. Thanks anyway."

"For what? This shit will grow hair in your ass!" Tito said laughing.

"Thanks, Tito," I said, briefly waving my hand, "I think the hair on my ass is fine."

"Okay, *Rocky*," Tito said, referring to the movie.

"Hey, Tim, I gotta cruise, but I'll call you tomorrow, okay?"

"Okay? Check out my new shoes."

"Those are cool!" I said, leaning over to touch his new Converse sneakers.

"These things were thirty-five bucks," Tim said. "They're the best!"

"They look cool!" I said, "I gotta go. See ya tomorrow."

"Okay."

As I was walking away Tim shouted, "Eddie!"

"Yeah?"

"Congrats, man."

"Thanks, Tim."

Tito blurted, "I'm about to get teary here ... heh ... heh ... heh ... heh ... heh...."

Chapter Twelve

Before Mom came to Portland, Dad was going to make her proud. So we moved out of our Northwest Johnson Street apartment and into a two-story pink house in North Portland. It had three bedrooms, dinning room, guestroom, 1-1/2 bathrooms, a basement, and a backyard that I hated mowing. This was a dream we never thought could come true. And even though we didn't own it, it was home.

The day Mom came into the airport, we were so happy to see her. Her scarf was draped over her neck and a smile painted on her face I'll never forget.

"Mom!" I yelled with excitement as she extended her arms to hug us all.

I saw Dad wipe the tears of joy from his eyes.

As we showed Mom how much we'd missed her, I heard Dad say, "I have a surprise for you."

Joey was on the left side of her and I was on the right. She caressed our necks and asked, "Are you okay, *mis bebes*?"

"Yeah, Mom," we replied.

Mom was so amazed at the sight of Portland. I saw contentment in her face, as if she had this sudden peaceful feeling inside her.

"Portland's so clean!" Mom said. "I love you all so much … so much!"

When we got to the blue, junker Ford car, Mom remarked with her broken English, "I see we haven't change our taste in cars."

Everyone laughed.

The airport was about fifteen minutes away from our new home. Mom must've felt like she was in a wonderful dream, which had become a reality.

Dad was parking the car when Gerard said, "What do you think, Mom?"

"What a beautiful home."

Gerard helped Mom out of the car as the rest of us stepped out. I held Mom's right hand and walked her in.

I looked up to her and said, "I love you, Mom!" as we entered our new home on North Albina Street.

"This is cool!" Joey said, "I'm gonna explore. Come on, Eddie!"

I left with Joey rushing through the house and anxious to see the rest of it.

The next day I decided to explore the attic and to walk on the two-by-four beams that laid across the ceiling.

I brought a pen flashlight with me, but the light stopped working. So I shook the pen a couple of times and when I did this, I lost my balance and my left foot slipped off the beam and onto the dusty, flat surface of the ceiling. Seconds later, a good portion of the ceiling came crashing down into Anna's bedroom, and my leg along with it.

Anna screamed and frantically ran out of the room yelling, "A burglar's in the attic … a burglar's in the attic!"

No one knew what was going on, and my leg was still stuck between the beams and sheetrock.

I struggled to lift myself to safety, and the rest of the family ran upstairs to see what had happened. Dad rushed into Anna's room with a stick, Mom hid behind Dad, and Joey stood there as he gaped at the debris and big hole in the ceiling. Everyone waited and watched, including my frantic sister.

I slowly peeped through the hole and, right then, Anna saw her burglar.

The summer passed, and freshmen year came at last. My first day at Lincoln High School, and everything seemed much bigger than Chapman. I saw Ed in the hallway heading toward the office to sign up for his senior year classes.

"Ed!" I yelled. "What's up, bro? Man, isn't this a trip? All these freshmen."

"Yeah, man. Hey, you going—"

Interrupting, I pointed at a girl and said, "Ed, check out that

76

girl."

"What girl?"

"The one over there!" I exclaimed, pointing my finger again at a girl wearing a pink dress on a figure you only saw in the movies. "Can't you see her?"

"Oh, yeah. She's fine!" Ed said, acting like it was no big deal.

"That's it. 'She's fine' is all you can say?"

"Yeah, she's fine," Ed reiterated. "What do want me to say?"

"A little more than 'she's fine' would be nice."

I placed my hand on Ed's shoulder, turned him around, and said, "Well, you obviously don't care about God's creations walkin' by, so will my askin' you to go running tonight be okay?"

"Yeah, sure, maybe we can go to Mount Scott."

"What's Mount Scott?"

"It's a place you can box at."

"Box?" I exclaimed. "Why would I want to put boxes away at Mount Scott?"

Ed laughed and showed me a "one-two" punch like a professional boxer does when he shadowboxes in front of a mirror.

"No man, not that kind of box, boxing like in fighting!"

"No way, man," I said. "You mean just like the movie we saw, *Rocky*?"

"Yeah. You wanna go check it out?"

"Yeah!" I said, standing there ready to go.

"We'll go tonight," Ed said. "This guy Aaron is showing me the ropes right now."

"Cool," I asked, "Hey, you wanna go see *Rocky* at the Esquire?"

"Yeah, let's do that," Ed replied.

Ed got into boxing for medals, but I started doing it to feel inspired and stay in shape. Ed had flair when he fought in the ring. At times we'd listen to the *Rocky* soundtrack during our

77

workout because it inspired us to train harder. The first time I saw one of Ed's fights was at Mount Scott Community Center. It lasted three rounds. Ed always put his heart into his fights, even when he knew he was losing the match.

Ed also had a charm the girls would die for. Handsome, witty, smooth as silk, and filled with lots of pizzazz. And because of these special traits, Ed's first girlfriend was Carrie.

Ed often talked about Carrie's blue eyes and began to spend more time with her. During their relationship, I felt left out of Ed's life. And since we only had some of the school year left, I wanted to make the most of it.

So one day I convinced Ed to skip class.

I asked, "Ed, do you love Carrie?"

Surprised at my immediate question and at first not knowing how to respond, Ed replied, "Yeah, I do Eddie. She's great, isn't she?"

I didn't want to hurt his feelings by asking him to spend more time with me, so I sadly replied, "Yeah, man, she's fine. You guys are a great couple."

That was the first time I lied to Ed and thought, *At least I felt better for not saying the truth.*

Girls didn't stop Ed from being athletic though. He also participated in cross-country. And if he didn't win a race, it didn't matter. As long as he knew he tried. Jamie, another track runner who attended Lincoln, was Ed's toughest competitor, and one of those gifted runners who could probably win a race with little training. When I saw them train together, I often noticed how hard Ed worked to keep up with Jamie.

Because of Jamie's talent as a runner, Ed felt the track coach, Mr. Brown, liked Jamie more.

Ed also had this natural talent in being funny. If I felt down, Ed was the guy to have around. His mom even thought of him as her most "precious jewel."

To make his mom laugh, Ed often made funny sounds and acted out these funny gestures. While doing this, he would manipulate his face into funny shapes. His spontaneous, creative, and sometimes musical acts brought an unforgettable euphoric feeling from his family and friends. Ed also had characters he randomly made up.

One of his favorites was Bill. Bill had a high-pitched voice, funny face, and always walked weird. At first it was sort of strange getting used to Ed's eccentric behavior, but he grew on me quickly, and after a while, I tried to emulate him. We were like a pair. In fact, an act without the both of us didn't seem right.

Chapter Thirteen

Since Ed was in the class of 1982, I couldn't accept him graduating because I didn't want to be without him for my remaining years at Lincoln. So I went over to his house all the time, trying to spend as much time with him as I could.

My way of knocking on Ed's front door was to yell his name outside of his apartment window. In the projects that's how most people communicated.

"Hey Ed! Hey! Hey Ed!" I yelled, waiting for him to look out.

He stuck his head out the window and yelled back, "When you gonna knock on my front door?"

I laughed and replied, "As soon as I learn how."

We went to his room and Ed showed me his new pet ferret. We played with it for hours.

"So, where'd you get the ferret?"

"My mom got it for me. Isn't it cool!"

"Yeah, man. It is. Let's take him outside and see what he does on the grass."

"He's free, man, and does whatever he wants. He's like a bird on the ground."

Some of the things Ed said astonished me. He talked as if he were a wise, old man. A trait I always admired about him.

Ed always looked for a new challenge, too. I remember when he became a counselor at outdoor school and told me all of the wonderful experiences he had, being with those kids.

When he got back, he said, "Man, Eddie, I wished you were there with me—able to see all those kids' faces happy and learning with affection and love. It was great!"

I said, "You know, no one in the projects would believe me about outdoor school."

"Why not."

"'Cause ... just wasn't normal over there," I replied.

"What was normal?"

"I don't know. Maybe fightin'."

"Fighting?" Ed asked, "Why would fighting be normal in the projects?"

"'Cause that's all I ever did. It was like all the time."

"Damn. That would suck."

"Not really, I mean, I kinda got used to it."

I picked up a necklace made of rope with a round, wooden pendant at the end of it. They gave it to Ed at outdoor school. It read with the nickname, "Scooter."

I said, "My counselor at outdoor school was named Duck."

"That's a cool name," Ed said. "The kids also had other names for me, but I liked Scooter the best."

"I think it's a good name for you," I said. "You ever think about havin' kids?"

"Yeah, someday I'd like to build my own house and have a good wife with a couple of kids," Ed said, changing the subject. "You should try becoming a counselor. It's very rewarding."

"Always wanted to. Maybe someday."

The same year, Ed went on a sailing trip with Carrie and some of his senior friends. I waited eagerly for him to come back. He was gone only a week, but it felt like a lifetime.

When he finally got back from his trip, I decided to go pay him a surprise visit. I walked behind the building, cupped my hands over my mouth and yelled, "Yo, Ed! ... Yo, Ed!"

He looked out and when I saw him, I felt good and excited inside because he was home.

"Hey Ed, what's up? Hey, c'mon down and bring your ferret."

"What's up, Eddie? I gotta tell ya 'bout my trip," Ed said, almost shutting the window. "I'll be down in a heartbeat."

"Hurry up!"

He rushed toward the front entrance and we walked to Couch Park and watched the ferret go crazy on the grass.

"This is cool!" I said playing with the ferret.

"Yeah, he's neat, isn't he?" Ed said, picking up the ferret and letting it crawl on his clothes.

"He looks like he wants to lick you," I said, getting closer to the ferret's face.

"Maybe he does," Ed said, putting the ferret's nose flush to his own nose. "His nose is cold."

I chuckled and began to pet the ferret.

"Think he's sick?"

"Nah," Ed replied.

"Whatta you think?"

"He's just checkin' us out," Ed said. "Just wondering who these giant people are."

It was getting dark so we went back to Ed's house.

Later that evening, we went back to Couch Park and played tag with Joey and Jaeger. We played hard and did some crazy stunts on that wooden structure. But I have to say Jaeger was the most daring when it came to jumping off certain heights from the structure.

He could jump from the top of what we called "the bird house" all the way down toward the barkdust. The structure also had a bridge with twists and turns, making the game much more competitive.

My favorite place to hide was under the structure, beneath all of the massive two-by-fours. Ed and me crawled underneath, ignoring any barkdust we might've gotten on our bodies and hair.

I heard Jaeger yelling, "I can smell you, Eddie ... you can't hide from the *tag king*. Boy, I'm gonna get you."

Ed inched beside me and whispered, "This reminds me of a scene in *Mission Impossible*. Eddie, I'm gonna dash out, Jaeger will see me, and I'll run for the safe place and you can meet me there."

"Okay, man. Good luck!" I said, showing Ed a thumbs up.

It was sometimes too dark to see where any of us were running, but that didn't stop us from playing. Ed was probably the fastest person on the structure, but I maneuvered the quickest. Suddenly, Ed dashed out from underneath the two-by-fours. Jaeger saw him and chased him down like a Lion chasing his prey.

"I'm gonna get you, Ed! You're mine!"

Ed's diversion gave me time to get out from underneath and run for the safe place.

"I'm safe!" I yelled. "C'mon Ed ... run!"

"Whoo!" Jaeger cried out. "Whoo!"

"Don't touch the barkdust, Ed. Don't touch it or you'll be it."

Ed ran through the structure trying to avoid Jaeger anyway he could. My sixty-second rest was up, so I began to run through when Jaeger tagged me.

"Damn!" I said, now trying to get Joey.

"Whoo!" Joey yelled. "You can't get me."

"I'm gonna get you, Joe," I said, breathing heavily from all the dodging and running I was doing.

We played through the night and into the morning.

I enjoyed the first few months at Lincoln. We loved our house on Albina Street and everything seemed to be going great. I had a best friend and a family I wouldn't trade for the world. Michael finally came to Portland and got his own place on the Southeast Side with his new wife, Ellie. I felt God looked over us.

So in celebration of our new start in Oregon, we feasted at a Chinese restaurant downtown called Tuc Lung's. It had been a long time since the family had eaten in a restaurant. Everyone was so happy.

Gerard stood up and said, "I wanna make a toast."

"Go 'head Gerard," Michael said. "Make a good one."

We stayed silent as he poured some wine into his glass and said, "Mom, Dad, you gave us the gift of life and showed us happiness is attainable even in the worst of times. From all of us, your children, thank you for showing us the meaning of love so we could be here as a family today. We love you."

We all clapped.

I saw some hot Chinese mustard on the table and said, "Gerard, you dare me to eat this mustard?"

Michael's attention focused on me and said, "Go 'head, dummy, do it!"

"You dare me? Do ya?"

"I dare ya, Eddie," Gerard said, "go 'head, I double dare ya. I'll even give you five bucks if you do it."

That was enough incentive for me to quickly pick up the bowl and swallow all the hot mustard I could. Soon after, I had this disgusted look on my face.

Gerard snickered and said, "Well, you've earned it!"

"Told you I'd do it," I said, picking up a glass of ice water then gulping it.

I got my five dollars, but my mouth burned terribly. After a lot of laughing and joking, Mom was tired and said, "We should go now. I'm very tired."

"Okay, honey," Dad said. "Gerard we should leave now."

"Okay guys. Let's doggie some of this up."

Later that evening Dad wanted to talk with me.

"Son, there's no such thing as luck. Everything you want out of life, you'll have to earn."

I didn't know why he said that. I guess he felt that believing in luck was more disappointing than working hard for what you believed in. He grabbed his Bible and read a scripture on how God sacrificed his son for our sins.

Dad then said, "Eddie, all your life you will work for happiness. I know, because I had failed to achieve it at your age. Until I found God. All the materials and successes this life has to offer are short. The only long-term, tangible thing you will be able to hold on to is God. He will give you everlasting life and happiness."

"I know, Dad. I know," I said hugging him.

"Now go to bed," Dad said, taking his handkerchief out from his left pocket and blowing his nose.

"Hey, Dad?"

"Yeah."

"I had a good time tonight."

"So did I. So did I, son."

Chapter Fourteen

I hurried downstairs one day to jump rope in the basement. I noticed Mom was coughing and feeling nauseated.

"Mom, are you okay?" I asked, concerned.

"Yes, baby. I'm fine," Mom replied, still sweeping the dust out the front door.

"Want some water?"

"No, baby." Mom asked, "Are you hungry?"

"No. I'm gonna go work out right now," I replied, walking toward the basement door.

The next day Dad took Mom to see a doctor. They arrived at Oregon Health Sciences University, where the doctor looked at Mom.

"Well, Mr. Regory, it would be good if she had some rest," the doctor said, assuring Dad she was okay. "She seems to be fine."

Dad brought Mom back home and Mom retired to bed early with an irritated throat. To me, it might've been a simple cold or the dust from the floor she had swept away the day before. That was the assumption from all of us because Mom was healthy and rarely got sick.

But Mom was getting worse by the day. So Dad took her to the hospital again. Later when he came home, it wasn't with Mom.

"All of you come into the living room," Dad said solemnly.

"Yeah, Dad?" Gerard asked, "What's wrong?"

"Your mother needs to stay in the hospital for a night."

We didn't know how to react to what Dad said, and for a moment we sat there quietly.

Gerard said, "Why?"

"I'm not sure ... we'll have to see tomorrow. That's all I've got to say for now."

Dad got up and left. Later that evening, we all went to bed

confused and scared, missing the one most important person in our lives. But overnight turned into another day and another, until the results were finally back. Once more Dad sat us all down in the living room. He began to cry and I thought, *My dad crying? Why? He never cries.*

We heard him gasp for words, trying to tell us what had happened to Mom. I was scared, and we didn't know what to do.

Finally Dad said, "Your mother has cancer of the lungs ... 'cancer,' the doctor said. I don't ... I don't know how or why ... just know the doctor said she had cancer and it spread too fast to catch."

Dad draped his shaking hands over his head and cried out an indescribable pain. He looked, as we all felt, helpless. Quiet and confused, we didn't know what to think. We sat there in the living room, waiting for Dad to say something more, but he never did. Joey and I didn't know what this cancer was but understood it wasn't good.

Dad got up and proceeded to his room as Gerard followed. Joey and I wanted to hear what they were talking about, but they would not let us into the room. The rest of the family stayed in the living room. I walked sadly up the stairs and sat there.

Joey asked, "Eddie, what's cancer?"

"Don't know."

"Dad was crying," Joey said, "Dad never cries."

"I know," I said, staring at the steps with my hands cupped under my chin.

"I wanna see Mom."

"Me too," I said. "Wonder if Dad's gonna tell us what it is?"

"Think Mom will come home?"

"Yeah, she'll come home. She's our mom."

"What if she doesn't?"

"Don't say that!" I said. "She will. She will."

We kept quiet and stared at the bottom of the staircase, thinking of what was going to happen next.

Days after Dad broke the news to us, he took Joey and me to see Mom at the hospital. We sat in the waiting room and when the doctor came out, he had a look on his face like "hope" never existed.

He walked toward my dad and in a sympathetic tone said, "Mr. Regory, your wife is very sick. At this point, her condition is terminal."

Dad sat down as if he had been drained of all his energy. He looked up at the doctor with his fatigued eyes and anguished face and asked with one last breath of hope, "Is there anything you can do? Anything?"

The doctor, remorseful and hesitant to reply, answered, "I'm sorry, Mr. Regory."

It seemed as if every breath Dad took was difficult and every question hard to ask.

Dad still believed something could be done for Mom and asked, "Doctor, what if I gave her one of my lungs?"

The doctor sighed and softly expressed, "I'm sorry. I'm sorry."

Dad brought his head down as we reached out to comfort his pain. The doctor left the waiting room and we sat there silently.

As I approached the door of the Intensive Care Unit where Mom was, my heart pounded with fear. I was in deep thought about a lot of things like, *What is Mom gonna look like? Is she gonna be awake? Is she gonna be the same mother I had before this cancer came?*

It seemed as if everything was in slow motion. Gerard took us in and guided Joey and me to where Mom was. The curtain to her room was slightly open, and I slowly walked in as Joey followed behind. I didn't want to see what I saw. Every inconceivable thought of what Mom might have looked like came true.

She laid helpless in bed with tubes in her nose and in her mouth, and an oxygen tank helping her breathe, with these round, white patches stuck to her chest. I wanted desperately to pull them off, then denial hit me. I felt as if everything happening was a nightmare and that I would soon wake up. I thought, *This isn't Mom. It can't be. None of this is really happening.*

Feeling drained out of my own life, I knelt by her bedside and saw her eyes were barely open. I held her right hand and said, "Mom, I love you, Mom."

I would not cry because I didn't want Mom to worry about me. My heart felt anger, and I was confused, wondering, *Why?* But there was no answer to my internal cry. Joey didn't even stay long enough to look at Mom because he was so emotional.

Dad was at the hospital every day. He came in early and left late, if he left at all. He prayed day and night hoping for a miracle to happen. One day I went with Dad to visit Mom, and we sat in the waiting room. Dad was holding the Bible in his right hand and a handkerchief in the other, and looked like he had finished crying. I noticed a yellow and green notepad Dad had on the seat of his chair.

I asked, "Dad, what's that?"

He said softly, "Nothing, son. It's nothing."

When Gerard came in, they talked quietly amongst themselves. I guess Dad felt it was better if we understood Mom as being alive than of knowing she was going to die.

The doctor came out as we looked at him with hope in our eyes and said with care in his voice, "Mr. Regory, I feel it would be okay for her to go home."

"Okay, thank you, doctor," Dad replied softly, getting up off his seat then stroking his hair back with his hands.

Dad prepared for this and made enough room for her hospital bed and oxygen tank at home. When we got Mom home, we sat around the bed daily, taking turns comforting her. Every day, day and night, Dad wrote and read Mom poems while she slept.

I knew each day that passed was a day closer to her death. I even wished we could go back in time and live in the old neighborhood because that's when Mom was healthy. All the dangers we faced then would be small problems now. It was the only time in my life I ever wanted to go back to the ghetto.

Later I discovered the yellow and green notepad was a short diary of Dad's pain before Mom died. When I read it, only then did I know what he was going through. And the empty, dark deadness my dad felt and with tears of ink wrote this:

December 19, 1981

"These first six days were hell. But though I pray and have faith, God made it <u>bearable</u>. She is still with us all. You live all your life, but you don't know how important someone is until something happens to that one. I love my wife! I remember when she came to Oregon, full of life and hope. We all came with hope of a new start. She loved it here. She felt comfortable knowing Edward and Joseph were safe going to school. I thank God for that. I don't understand this cancer. It comes so fast and destroys the person you love, and no one seems to know what to tell you or what to do.

"When she got off the plane, she was full of life, hope and so beautiful. When I saw her, I fell in love with her again. She is my right hand! She is my hope! She is my life! She is <u>soft, hoping, loving</u> and <u>gentle</u>. We were happy together. I found that just touching her made me feel good."

December 20, 1981

"God gave us another day. That's what we asked for ... one day at a time. She looks so nice! There's color in her face today. They made her more comfortable by changing her bed. Mike came but not Ellie. It was difficult for her I guess. The doctor and nurse have been so kind to her. She is still very weak. Where is Ellie?

"Bonita (Gerard's Friend) came into the Intensive Care Unit and let her kids sit by her. The doctor checked her blood to see if she's getting oxygen."

LUNCH...

"She is eating well. It is good to see her this way. She

couldn't drink the distilled water because it choked her. The doctor told me the x-ray he took three days ago showed the same results. But I have **HOPE!** As long as she lives ... one day at a time. Anna just came in, and how happy she is to see her. I hope Joe and Eddie are okay. Gerard just came in. He told me Joseph is worried what will happen if Mom dies. Gerard told Joseph, 'God will keep us together.'"

December 21, 1981
"There is no change. Our hope now rest with God. Gerard came with me this morning. I see now she is beginning to understand she has cancer and is going to die. She's lost lots of weight; she is now 99 lbs. I love my wife when we first met, but I find my love is greater now than at first. She is resting now. The nurse gave her medicine (codeine). It is hard for her to breathe."

December 22, 1981
"She was sitting up when I came in this morning. A brother and sister (Jehovah's witnesses) came in to see her. Santa said, 'no! I do not know yet.'"

December 23, 1981
"Anna came in today. She's happy when Anna is here. I sometimes wonder that, when someone you love dies, you ask yourself, did I do everything possible? Did I make the right decisions? Our marriage was long but not always happy. Not because of her, but because of me."

December 25, 1981
"Eddie and Joe came to see her. It made her feel better. She gained a little weight today. I thank God for this day. She seems to be getting better. She said that 'Even with oxygen, her chest feels tight.'

"The oxygen has been lowered to number three. She feels she has not been the kind of mother she would've liked to have been. But that's not true! She was a better mother than I was a *father.*

"I find people are so nice here! Not like most hospitals I've been in. They take their job more than just a job. They love her, and they kiss her when they come in."

December 26, 1981

"She looks tired today. I don't know what's happening to her. One day she gains weight, the next day she looks no better.

"Eddie and Joe came in with me to see her. They don't understand what's happening. Like Santa said, 'They're young.'

"Today will be a big day for her. All her children will be here. We talked about writing grandma in New York.

"I guess it's time I pray for a miracle! I asked God to take me instead of her. The nurses are nice here. Life is hard from birth to death, and yet we fight to live no matter how hard life is.

"Santa told me Nilla (Tim's mother) saw her today. She seems to like her. I look at her and want to lay beside her and die with her. But life is not like the movies. It's real.

"I tried to think of our lives together. I can't remember! I don't know why. She says, 'How hard it is to breathe.'

"It must be the cancer taking its toll. She's getting weaker and weaker! I don't understand why they can't give her some medicine to breathe, but there is none. Her lungs are getting worse. Oh God, don't let her be in pain, please!

"I feel like I'm in a daze. In the morning I don't want to wake up. I feel afraid of each day. Soon we will take her home to sleep with her family around her."

December 27, 1981

"She is eating a little better; she is in pain. The doctor wants to talk to me again. He's letting her come home. There's nothing more they can do.

"I read her a poem that Bonita gave me, and she liked it. Her stitches she got from the operation bother her a lot. She just wants to go to sleep."

December 28, 1981

"They talked of her coming home—our only hope is God! Maybe it's best she's coming home. She wants to be with her family."

December 29, 1981
"They asked her if she will let the Gynecologist look at her. She said, 'No!' She looks much better. Gerard and Bonita are coming over. She did not eat much. Dr. Wolf is looking at her."

January 2, 1982
"She is asleep (died)."

That second day of January, Gerard walked in and found her not breathing. He then came out with a distressed look on his face, closing the door behind him, and said, "She's dead."

I looked over to Joey and he started sobbing so hard I wondered if people could hear him outside. Anna embraced Joey's pain in her arms, then Joey yelled, "Why couldn't we save her? Is it because we're poor? ... Why? Why?"

I couldn't cry, and I didn't know why. Maybe it was because I felt she was asleep and we would see her alive and happy again someday.

"Gerard," I asked, "can I go see Mom?"

Gerard looked over to Anna, then me, and said, "Yeah. Go ahead."

When I entered the room, I sat by her bedside and held her fragile, little, pale hand in mine. I looked at Mom's still body and slightly blue face and said, "I'll make you proud of me, Mom. I promise."

Joey came in and sat beside me with tears in his eyes and asked, "Can I hold her, too?

"Yeah," I said, gently setting Mom's left hand into Joey's.

"Her hand is so soft," Joey said, with drops of tears descending onto his white shirt. "Did you say anything to her?"

"Yeah," I said firmly, holding back my tears. "I made her a promise."

"What was it?"

94

"To make her proud of me."

Joey knelt closer to her still body, sniffling his nose and saliva wetting his lips and said, "I'm gonna make you proud of me, too, Mom. I promise."

We left the room together, and I hugged Joey.

The next day, friends found out about Mom's death. Denny's family (a friend we played football with at Wallace Park) came by.

"Hi, Eddie."

"Oh, um, hi Mrs. Resnick."

"We're real sorry about your loss. We wanted to drop this by and give this to you and your family."

"Okay," I said, taking the ham and bread they gave me.

"Eddie," Mrs. Resnick said, "If there's anything you need, let us know, okay?"

"Okay."

"Bye, Ed," Denny said in sad tone.

People we didn't know and neighbors we'd never met also brought food. Dad couldn't believe the kindness that came our way.

Then Heidi called me ...

"Eddie?"

I was surprised but happy.

"Hi, Heidi."

"I heard," she said, "I'm real sorry. Are you going to be okay?"

"Yeah, I think so, but I don't know about Joey."

"Did they take her to the mortuary?"

I didn't know what mortuary meant, so I was hoping to give her the right answer.

"Yeah, they did."

"Well if you need anything, just call," Heidi said in a caring way.

"Thanks, Heidi."

Afterwards, I called Ed.

"Hey, Ed."

"Eddie, what's up?"

"My mom died."

There was a moment of silence.

"I'm sorry, Eddie. Do you want me to come over?"

"It's okay. I wanna be alone for a while."

"Okay, man. But if you need me for anything, let me know, okay?"

"Okay. Thanks Ed."

The next few days, Dad cleaned out Mom's closet. It's funny—when people are alive, all the materials around them exist, but when they die, everything they work for means nothing.

Dad grieved every day, but slowly began to change his life around. We heard him early in the mornings exercising to the Richard Simmons show, trying to lose the weight Mom always wanted him to lose.

Chapter Fifteen

One morning, walking down Albina Street to take the number 4 bus to Ed's house, I suddenly saw this black puppy walking toward me. I bent over and petted it and noticed her stomach was bloated.

I picked her up and said, "You wanna come home with me, doggy? Sure you do."

I brought her back to the house and showed her to Dad.

I yelled with excitement, "Dad, look! A puppy dog."

He petted the dog and said, "She looks sick."

"Can we keep her?"

"Yes, son. We can. I'm tired of death. I don't want to see it anymore."

So I took the dog to a veterinarian and got her fixed up. Soon after, we named her "Yoko," and she became a part of the family.

We moved out of our dream house and into a smaller place on the same block. The new place was divided into two rentals, upstairs and downstairs. We lived downstairs. It was three bedrooms, one small bathroom. Not as nice as the pink house, but after Mom's death, Dad wasn't going to live there anymore.

Three months later, Michael's wife, Ellie had a baby girl. They named her Racheal. Anna soon moved out and got her own place.

Ed and his mom moved out of the Villa Florence apartment building on 22nd and Glisan to a place on the Southeast Side of town. It was a small, two-bedroom apartment. I went to see Ed and their new place. When I got there, Edith said with her polite, soft voice, "He went running, honey. He should be back soon. Would you like to wait for him?"

"Yeah, Mom. Thanks," I said, walking into their apartment.

"Would you like some cookies, sweetie?"

"Oh, no Edith. Thanks."

"Are you sure? I just bought them today."

"Um, thanks anyway, Edith."

"Well, you make yourself at home."

"Thanks."

I went into Ed's room, lay down on his bed, and waited. I heard a knock on the front door and thought it was Ed, but it was his sister, Connie. "Hi, Mom," I heard Connie say.

Connie was a nice person, but she often seemed troubled. I could hear indistinct sounds off the walls of the small apartment.

I then heard Connie yell, "It's all your fault for the way I am! It's all your fault I can't walk anymore! I hate you! I hate you!"

Edith screamed, "Eddie! ... Eddie!"

At first I didn't know what to do, then quickly got up, opened the door, and ran toward the kitchen, where I saw Connie trying to hit Edith's face. I barged between them and blocked Connie's hands and said, "Connie, stop! This is your mother."

"It's all her fault for the way I am!" Connie cried out. "I hate you! I hate you!"

"Connie, what are you talkin' about?" I asked. "Why are you doing this?"

"Because it's her fault for the way I am," Connie said. "I'll never be able to walk normal again."

I turned to Edith, surprised and somewhat apologetic for Connie's actions, and asked, "Are you okay, Edith?"

"Yes, I'm fine," she replied, wiping the tears from her eyes.

Tears continued to pour down Connie's face as she limped away to the recliner in the living room to smoke a cigarette. I went back to the bedroom and waited. When Ed arrived, I stayed in the room while Edith told him what had happened. I'm not sure what he said to Connie, but knowing Ed, he had a way of making a bad situation good. He began to joke with Connie and make her laugh.

Shortly after, he came into the room and said, "Hey, Eddie! What's up, buddy?"

"What's up?" I replied, happy to see him.

Ed didn't tell me what had happened out there, nor did I ask.

"Wanna go to the arcade?" I asked.

"Yeah. Let me get some money from my mom," Ed replied, leaving the room.

"Okay. Hey!" I asked before he left, "How far'd you run?"

"Three miles."

"Cool ... are you gonna take a shower?"

"Yeah. I'll be back," Ed replied, closing the door.

Later, we took the bus to Wallace Park instead of going to the video arcade. We sat in the back of the bus.

"Hey, Ed."

"Yeah."

"Mind if I ask you a question?"

"What's up?"

"Whatever did happen to Connie?"

Ed stayed silent for a minute, then said, "She tried to commit suicide off the Fremont Bridge."

"Damn," I said, surprised. "How'd she ever survive?"

"Sometimes I think about that."

"And?"

"I feel God was with her."

"Oh," I responded, dropping the subject.

Shortly after, we got off on 23rd and Pettygrove in Portland and walked one block west to Tim's house. Ed knocked on the door, and when Tim answered, Ed exclaimed, "Hey, Cuban!"

I chuckled and added, "What's up, Castro?"

Tim laughed and replied, "Hey, if it isn't the two Eds."

I said, "Lend us your ball and come on out?"

"Okay," Tim said, "let me get my cleats."

"Hurry up!" Ed said, running toward the park.

Tim ran out with his football in his hand and shouted, "Ed, catch!"

Ed turned around and ran for the pass.

"Right here, Ed!" I yelled, running deep into the muddy field.

We played football for about an hour, and afterward walked

up to the Greek store on 21st and Lovejoy to buy two ham sandwiches.

A few months later, Ed and his mom moved again, into a new place on Southeast 37th and Powell. The great thing about Ed's new place was, there was a video arcade called "Good Times" down the street. A few yards west of the video arcade was a restaurant called DeNicola's, our favorite pizza place. Sometimes Edith treated us there. We spent every last quarter we had playing our favorite games, Donkey Kong or Donkey Kong Junior. And when we had no quarters left, the manager at the Bales Thriftway store on Glisan would let us stack bottles for money.

Chapter Sixteen

Once, Joey and I were walking across the school field while the varsity football team was training.

This big guy they called Dirk yelled, "You better get your freshmen asses off the field."

I looked over to Joey, startled, and asked, "What'd he say?"

Joey thought it was funny, so we ignored his remark. Because of that, Dirk became angry. In a huff, he marched over to us. And seeing his blue, squinted eyes and helmet over his sweaty, rough face, I thought, *Yep, I've seen this look before.*

Dirk gazed down at us and shouted, "Get off the fuckin' field!"

I thought, *Man, I've dealt with tougher guys than this.*

I looked him in the eyes and shouted back, "Who the fuck are you talkin' to, man. I'll kick your fuckin' ass all over this field. I'm from New York! Mutha-fucker!"

Coach Riley ran up and got between us and asked, "What's going on here?"

I answered, "This guy told us to get off the fuckin' field."

"Is this true?" Coach Riley asked, eyeballing Dirk and waiting for an answer.

"No," Dirk replied, showing a slight attitude.

I pointed my finger at Dirk and shouted, "You fuckin' liar!"

"Hey, relax!" the coach interjected, "we don't want that language here."

I restrained myself from saying anymore.

Coach Riley proceeded to ask, "Now, Dirk, did you say that to them?"

Dirk wouldn't say a word.

"Well, I don't care who said what. I want both of you to shake hands and forget this even happened."

Dirk looked at Coach Riley, then me, and hesitantly said, "Sorry."

"I'm sorry, too," I said shaking his hand.

Everyone on the team was surprised I stood up to the biggest guy in the school. And when word got around about what I did, the other seniors at school respected me more.

I guess the experience with Dirk inspired Joey and me to join the freshmen football team. But it was nothing like the "Pop Warner" football we played in eighth grade.

Besides me being the hardest-hitting right guard on the team, Joey was an aggressive wide receiver. Joey's love for the game increased every time he played. When we played together, nothing could stop us.

Sometimes when I finished a football practice, I'd go train with Ed at Mount Scott. Edith saw us getting so much into our boxing that she used her Montgomery Ward credit card to buy us athletic shorts and shirts. We wore them with pride. Yet when Ed came to school wearing sunglasses, it was usually because he'd gotten a black eye from a boxing match the day before.

Ed decided that after graduation he would register for the selected services. I knew registering didn't mean you were going to war, but knowing the possibility of Ed getting hurt in a war scared me to death.

Dad said to me once, "Son, if you wanna fight, fight for God. Man can take away life, but God can resurrect him. Don't fight for mankind or a piece of cloth. Fight for a higher power, a power no government can ever kill. War is no fun. I know. I fought in the war at seventeen years old, and I never understood why we send young men to a war for an old man's glory.

"When I joined, it was because my Catholic teacher said I wouldn't amount to anything, and I was illiterate and should join the army. That was why I joined. Don't make the same mistakes your father made. Instead, learn from them."

He told me that story more times than I can remember, and every time I listened. Dad may have never finished school, but he was brilliant in other ways. His street smarts, wise words and love were the words I carried in my heart everywhere I went.

I was at my house when Ed decided to talk with me about

his plans.

"Hey, Eddie."

"What's up, bro?"

"I'm gonna join the Airborne Rangers."

"What? What's that? Whatta you mean?"

"The military. I'm gonna go Airborne, just like my dad was."

At first I couldn't believe it and didn't understand why he wanted to leave.

I began to feel angry and said, "Ed, I thought you were just gonna register? You don't need to join the military to accomplish a duty."

"Yeah, I know, but they pay for your college when you get out."

"College? Ed, you can get a regular job for that. What if you die? What am I gonna do?"

"I'm not gonna die," Ed said. "Besides, I'm not going to war. I'm just doin' my time and gettin' out and afterwards, goin' to college. At least we'll have money when I visit and won't have to stack bottles anymore."

"I don't care about that. I just want you to stay."

"Eddie, I know what you're feeling, man, but there's nothing else I can do here. I don't wanna flip burgers all my life."

"You won't. We'll both get jobs somewhere. A cool job we'll both like, like the arcade or something."

Ed said, "You won't need to work in any arcade 'cause I'll have money. Just think, we'll buy one of those Donkey Kong Junior games and play all the time."

"How we gonna do that? You won't even be here," I said sadly.

"I'll be here. I'll always be right here," Ed said, lightly touching his right hand to my heart.

"Yeah ... guess so."

Ed put his arm around me and said, "You wanna go runnin'?"

I chuckled and replied, "Yeah, man, yeah."

"C'mon, Puerto Rican."

This was almost the same empty feeling I had when I left Carlton in New York.

A few months later, Ed signed into the Airborne Rangers for four years. He wrote letters and told me how things were going out there at Fort Lewis, but I still felt empty inside knowing he wasn't around. Meanwhile, I kept going to school and averaged a "C," and sometimes if I was lucky, a "B."

I decided to join the freshman wrestling team, and the head coach Mr. Chong thought I was good enough for varsity. Which I later realized wasn't good for me, because some of the guys I competed against were twice my size. I once wrestled this guy who thought he could easily beat me because I was a freshman and inexperienced.

The bell rang and we rushed at each other. We wrestled hard, yet cautiously. The bell rang for a break, then again for a second round. Suddenly, the other wrestler did an unexpected move on me. I found myself flat on my back. Sweat poured over my eyes, obstructing my vision. I worked out of his tight pin and almost pinned him down twice.

He squeezed out of my hold and proceeded to go the distance. After two rounds of what felt like combat, I was ready to take a long rest.

The third bell rang, and what little energy I had left, I poured into the last round. It ended with him winning because of the most points. I was so exhausted I felt like vomiting.

There were competitions going on all day.

Mr. Chong said, "Okay, Eddie, you've got one more guy to wrestle."

"One more?"

"Yes. You have to use your quickness on him 'cause he's big, real big. Remember what you've learned. Get low, move fast. Tire him out. Okay?"

"Okay."

I suddenly saw who I was going to wrestle next.

He was at least six feet tall, had long, dark hair, a hairy body, and they called him "Gorilla." He looked like one, too.

The bell to the first round rang. The gorilla guy lifted me up and practically threw me flat on my back. "Ugh!" I gasped as he pinned my shoulders down to the mat.

My body felt like someone squeezed all the air out of it. The referee dropped to his stomach to see if my shoulders were evenly flush with the mat. He counted as he slammed his right hand on the mat, "One, two, three!"

It was all over, with the gorilla guy winning.

After the match, I didn't want to wrestle anymore. In fact, I decided to take up a less strenuous profession—girls.

Chapter Seventeen

Nineteen eighty-five was a great year for me. Not because I was a senior, but because I met a girl named Cynthia. She was beautiful. She had blond hair, and a smile that could brighten anyone's day. I never thought she'd be interested in me. A group of us walked to the McDonald's on Burnside after a football game, and Cynthia came along with a friend. They sat across from us.

I looked over to Cynthia and asked, "So, how'd you like the game?"

"It was fun. How about you?"

"I don't know ... think we should of won it."

"Yeah," Cynthia replied, then chuckled. "Seems like we never win."

"But it was a cool game, though," I said.

"Yeah, real cool," a friend of mine, Jayjay included. "We only lost by twenty-one points."

I turned to him and said, "Yeah, but, we had heart out there."

"Oh, yeah, a lot of heart, Eddie," he replied, looking at me like I was crazy.

"It ain't the game, it's the guts!" I exclaimed, with a tight-fisted pat to my chest.

Then Jayjay joined in, "Yeah! Guts! Guts! Guts!"

Cynthia and her friend, Stacey, smiled.

While Jayjay was talking to Stacey, I leaned over a little and whispered, "Hey Cindy, whatta you got goin' on this weekend?"

"I don't know. Why?"

"Well, I um, thought maybe you might wanna hook up?"

"And do what?"

"Well, you could come over to my place ... or, really, my sister's place."

We had "innocent passion" in our eyes. I felt like I was in a "love daze" or something.

"Sure."

"Cool, we'll hook up this weekend."

I was excited the rest of the week about Cynthia coming over. She showed up at my sister's studio apartment at the Lownsdale apartment complex on 15th and Taylor, just north of Lincoln High School. Cynthia's mom dropped her off in a new, white Audi. She wore a black outfit that clung to her slim figure.

"Hi. I'm glad you came. Come on in, come in."

"Thanks," Cynthia said. "This is a nice place. Really close to the school, too."

"Yeah. That's one thing I like about it. If I stay the night, all I gotta do is walk a couple blocks and I'm there. Would you like something to drink? Let's see, I've got juice and soda."

"I'll take a soda."

"It's Coke. Is that cool?" I asked.

"That's fine."

I popped the tab and said, "Here ya go."

"Thanks."

We sat down on the bed.

"Where are you from?" Cynthia asked curiously.

"New York."

"How did you like it?"

"It was cool," I answered in an evasive manner.

"Where did you live?"

"Manhattan," I replied, hoping she wouldn't ask me where.

"Where in Manhattan?"

"On the East Side."

There was a moment of silence, and I inched my body closer to hers and kissed her.

"Wow," Cynthia said softly. "That was … was nice."

"Is it okay with you?" I asked, gentleman-like, hoping she would let me continue.

"Yes. I liked it a lot," Cynthia replied, with a smile and advanced toward me with a kiss back.

"Um … what time's your mom coming?"

"Why?"

"Well, I really like being here with you."

"So do I."

We kissed again.

"You, uh, kiss really well, Eddie."

My head blew up about the size of a mountain. I began to carefully slide my left hand around her waist and sensed she was now tensed.

"If you don't want me to do this, I won't."

"No, it's ... it's not that at all. I've just got this feeling inside my stomach."

"Is it a good feeling?"

She nodded her head.

"I'm glad you like it," I said, leaning toward her once more and kissing her soft lips.

Time wasn't a concern until the buzzer to the apartment rang.

"Could that be your mom?"

"Is it ten o'clock already?"

"Yeah, it is," I said. "I'll walk you to your car."

"Okay."

As we approached the exit door, I could see her mom's white Audi out front. I wanted so badly to kiss Cynthia good-bye, and sensed she wanted to do the same.

"Well, I guess I'll see you at school."

"Count on it," Cynthia said with a smile.

After our first date at my sister's place, we were inseparable. We ate lunch at school together, attended parties, and did my favorite, watched movies at her house.

Another time Cynthia scheduled a date at her house near Pittock Mansion. I'd heard how nice Pittock Mansion was, but I'd never been by there. I grabbed my Sony Walkman, two dollars off the kitchen table, and my *Rocky* tape and jogged up West Burnside to Cynthia's house.

It took forever to run up those hills. When I got closer to her house, I was in disbelief in some of the houses I saw around me.

As I passed them I thought, *If Mom were alive she would love to have that house or that house.*

I didn't know which hill or driveway was Cynthia's. Suddenly, I saw her standing by a mailbox at the end of a driveway.

"Cynthia!" I said with excitement. "Hey, what's up? I couldn't find your house."

"Hi. It's okay. That's why I waited down here."

"You live up here?"

"Uh-huh. Follow me," Cynthia said, grabbing my hand as we hiked up a long driveway. We turned the corner at the end of the driveway, and I noticed a red sports car with a Porsche emblem on it. To my left was a basketball pole embedded into the concrete. The outside of the house looked small, but when we walked in, it was awesome!

In amazement I blurted, "Wow, whatta cool place."

"You like it?"

"Do I like it? This is sweet!"

"Come on. I'll show you around," Cynthia said, taking my hand into hers.

I never thought in my wildest dreams people lived like this. They even had their own bathrooms. There was even a part of the house laid out in white, plush carpet. Every souvenir, appliance and television was of high quality.

It was like the *Lifestyles of the Rich and Famous*.

Yet that wasn't all. She brought me outside to her patio, and it was nothing like the porch, that overlooked our grass on Albina Street. Cynthia's patio was made of red brick and was at least a quarter of a city block long, with a panoramic view of downtown Portland. I was mesmerized and wordless.

"Are you okay?" she asked.

"Yeah ... uh ... I'm okay," I answered, still in awe of everything around me.

"Well, this is my house."

"It's a very ... very nice place," I said. "Are your parents rich?"

"Well, they're not rich, but they do pretty good."

"How does it feel to have all this?"

"It feels ... it feels good. You get used to it."

"Can you get whatever you want?"

"Not whatever I want, but I get nice things," Cynthia replied, as if it wasn't a big deal.

"It must be really nice to live here," I said, walking around the patio, looking at the scenery and dreaming of what it would be like if I lived here.

We later went into the movie room.

"What kind of movies do you have?" I asked.

"We have a few down here," Cynthia said, opening a cabinet and showing me rows of videotapes neatly stacked. "Pick your choice?"

"Cool. I love movies. It's like my favorite thing to do," I said. "How's this one?"

"Officer and a Gentleman? That's a really good one. You wanna watch it?"

"Yeah, let's check it out."

She put the tape in and we sat close to each other for the duration of the movie.

I could never live up to her standards, I thought. I tried not to be jealous and happy for her instead, but it was impossible.

Whenever Cynthia wanted to come over and meet my family and see my house, I often came up with excuses for her not to, because I was embarrassed of where we lived and how poor we were.

Kegs were common at Macleay Park. If you said "beer" to the freshmen at Lincoln, they ran with their wallets open. One time, Bubba, a friend I met at Lincoln and who had also attended Chapman, helped me carry a keg up the trail as far up as we could. He also watched the tap so no one would steal it.

Bubba was a character. He reminded me a little of Carlton because of his size and strength. He weighed about two hundred pounds, had dark, thick hair, thick eyebrows, and more hair on his body than the gorilla guy I once wrestled. He was funny, and the kind of person who could keep a party alive and crazy.

Sometimes my friend Tim would help me collect the money at the bottom of the trail right before the first bridge, which overpassed a running creek. Even when the keg was dry, we would still charge three bucks per person. Of course, they didn't know the keg was dry until they got to it.

Bubba could drink anyone under the table if they dared to challenge him. I remember the time he drank forty-eight sixteen-ounce cups of beer at Cynthia's birthday party at Tim's house. He got so drunk, he laid his body out on the driveway in front of Tim's house and vomited from the side of his mouth. The puddle of vomit crawled down the driveway toward the sidewalk.

Tim's mother walked outside to see what was going on, and when she saw Bubba, she ran back in the house and hysterically yelled with her broken English, "Ay! Timmy, Timmy, Timmy! Bubba vomit all over floor—outside!"

Timmy calmed Nilla down and quickly went outside to see if Bubba was okay.

"Bubba, get up, man. People think you're dead out here."

Bubba let out a long belch and replied, "Okay, man, you gotta a dip a Copenhagen?"

Tim chuckled and said, "Yeah, man. But first you have to come inside."

Bubba struggled awkwardly back in the house and had his hand on his stomach and asked, "You have any food?"

Tim grinned, motioning to the kitchen and answered, "Yeah, in the 'fridge."

"Bubba, you hungry?" Nilla asked, lifting a piece of birthday cake off the table, putting it in front of his face.

Bubba was nauseated and replied, "Nah, Nilla, nah. I don't want cake."

Nilla kept forcing the cake on him, saying, "Bubba … you eat. It's good for you—you feel better!"

"Nah, Nilla, I can't Nilla. I don't want cake right now."

"Bubba you eat, eat," Nilla repeated putting the cake closer to his face.

Bubba grabbed the cake and threw it against the dishwasher

machine, splattering it all over the kitchen sink and refrigerator and on the linoleum floor. Tim's mom ran frantically around the house yelling, "Ay! Timmy ... Timmy!"

But then a bizarre thing happened. Nilla started laughing. During this craziness, I walked outside and saw Cynthia standing beside the park drinking fountain. She seemed sad.

Concerned, I advanced toward her and asked, "Are you okay, Cynthia?"

She stared sadly at the ground and replied, "I'm okay."

"Are you havin' a good time?" I asked, holding her hand in mine.

"Yeah, I am. How 'bout you?"

"This is normal for me. I mean, I go out with the boys and have a good time, ya know. Does it bother you that I'm here or I brought you here?"

"No, not at all."

I hugged her and asked, "Is it my friends you're upset with?"

"No, it's not anyone. It's just, well, I wonder if I'm good enough for you."

I was shocked. I looked into her eyes and softly touched her face and said, "Cynthia, from here on out, you're my girl."

She looked at me with passion in her eyes and said, "I love you!"

"I like you, too," I replied, gently holding her chin with my right hand.

"You don't love me?"

It was difficult for me to say the "love" word, but I knew if I didn't, she might think I didn't like her either.

"No ... no it's, it's not that. I do love you."

"You do?"

"Yeah, I do," I replied.

Cynthia hugged me and began to cry.

"Hey, hey, it's okay, come on. This is supposed to be your day."

She wiped her face with her hands and quietly said, "I'm sorry."

"Cynthia, you don't have to cry. I'm here for you."

"I know. You're just the first guy I've ever loved."

"And hopefully the last, right?" I asked, smiling at her.

"Yeah," Cynthia answered, hugging me again.

"Let's go inside," I said, holding her hand in mine back to the house.

Chapter Eighteen

Lincoln had honor classes I often wanted to be a part of, but couldn't because my grades just weren't good enough. Which made me think, why was I so different? Were these kids smarter because of the money their parents had, or was I mentally deficient? I couldn't come up with an answer, so I accepted it as temporary failure. I also stuck with what I did best, sports.

One night I came home and told Dad, "Dad, I'm sick of the dumb classes I'm in."

He said, "Eddie, there's no such thing as a dumb class, and you can do anything you want if you put your mind to it. You just gotta believe in what you want and you'll get it. And keep going to school. I wished I stayed in school. Instead, I joined the army."

"But what am I supposed to keep tryin' to do? I can't do math, English, or nothin'. What am I gonna be good at."

"What do you like the most?" Dad asked. "What makes you happy?"

"Movies."

"Well then, be in movies."

"How?"

"Work. Work harder than anyone you know and I promise you, you will be good at acting or writing or whatever it is you want in life. All it takes is the will and dedication."

"Yeah. Thanks Dad," I said, hugging him, then walking toward my room.

"And Eddie?"

"Yeah, Dad."

"Never, ever give up."

"But sometimes I want to."

"We all do," Dad said, " but we can't, Eddie. We can't."

Dad's health began to deteriorate. He gained more weight

than he had tried to lose, and blood clots on his calves spread to his ankles. Even though an in-house nurse who came treated them daily, that didn't seem to make a difference. Luckily he was still able to walk, but not without effort. Dad's obesity became the center point for harassment too. Once he had just gotten back from the Sentry Market by Jefferson High School in North Portland.

"Hey, Dad, what's up?"

"Nothing, I'm just gonna go lay down."

"You okay?"

"I'm okay."

Shortly after I walked in.

"Dad, I know something's up."

"Eddie, nothing's up. Now let me get some rest."

"Dad, I'm gonna keep buggin' you until you tell me."

"Oh, man. You don't quit, do ya?"

"Well, you come home all quiet and everything. What am I supposed to think."

"Okay, fine. Some kids at the store were botherin' me."

"Who?" I asked angrily. "Who bothered you?"

"It doesn't matter who. It just happened."

"Well, what happened."

"They just said I was fat."

I was furious at this. I couldn't imagine anyone wanting to hurt my family, especially Dad. So I asked, "Where are they? Tell me!"

Dad peacefully said, "No, son. That's not how God taught us to be. Besides, I talked to them."

"What did you say?"

"I said, hey, c'mon, isn't there enough pain and problems in this world than to hate a fat, old man. Then they turned around and left."

"Why did they want to beat you up?"

"Like I said, because I was fat," Dad replied, disgraced with himself. "That's just they way the world is."

"That's a dumb reason."

"Isn't fighting for any reason dumb, Eddie?"

"Not if someone tries to hurt you."

"They hurt Jesus. What makes you or me any better?"

"It's just not right."

"Then you did learn something from this."

"What?"

"To treat others the way you would want to be treated."

When Dad said those words to me, I promised myself I would never maliciously make fun of fat people, or anyone for that matter.

Every weekend there was a party somewhere. This time there was a party at Woody's house. Woody was a white, skinny, rich kid who lived on the hill in a nice neighborhood, several blocks from Council Crest Park. He quickly became our friend when he would invite us to his house to party.

He also had an alcohol cabinet with every kind of liquor imaginable. He had the keg in his backyard, and as usual, Bubba took charge and proudly tapped the keg.

Cynthia didn't have a curfew that night, so I took advantage of the time we had together.

"Hey, Cindy, you wanna go somewhere?"

"Okay. Where?"

"Come on," I said, grabbing her hand in mine.

"Where are we going, Eddie."

"You'll see. I wanna show you something," I said, opening a door to one of the bedrooms. "Isn't this cool."

"Wow. It's nice," Cynthia said.

The room was beautiful and had a queen-size bed that looked like royalty slept on it. Everything was perfect. There was a cool breeze, which whispered through the window. Cynthia and I kissed each other, and the heated romance of our bodies forced us to softly lay our clothing onto the plush carpet. The white curtains, which floated from the breeze, gave me reason to get even closer to her. She crossed her arms over her breasts.

"Cynthia?"

"Yeah," she replied softly.

"You've got nothing to be embarrassed about."

I held her hand in mine, and we proceeded to get under the covers. I took a condom out of my wallet and slowly caressed her soul into my hands, and we made love.

"How do you feel?" I asked a while later, delicately moving my hands through her hair.

"Okay," she replied.

She had this glow emerging from her face.

"I can't believe we did it." Cynthia held me tightly and asked, "Do you think it will always be like this?"

"Do you want it to be?"

"I do," Cynthia said. "Think they're wondering where we are?"

"Probably. You wanna go back?"

"Might be a good idea."

"Okay."

We got up and proceeded to make the bed.

"Oh, no," Cynthia said.

"What?"

"There's blood on the sheets."

"Don't worry. I'll get a wet towel."

"Could you?"

"Hold on," I said, rushing to the bathroom outside the bedroom door, and back in with a towel moistened with hot water and soap. "Here. Try this."

Cynthia rubbed vigorously to get the bloodstain out. I then helped her make the bed. We went back to the party.

After that experience at Woody's house, Cynthia would often lie to her mom about staying the night at her friends, so we could go to cheap motels on Interstate Avenue and be together.

Weeks later, some friends of Cynthia's and the rest of the guys decided to drink some beers and California Coolers. Shortly after my third beer, I was drunk. We then drove to Sauvie Island.

When we got there, Timmy parked the car in front of a high, steel-mesh, cyclone fence. There was a huge field of grass and foliage on the other side. I awkwardly stepped out of the car and began to climb the cold fence.

Bubba said, "Eddie, get down, you idiot."

"Get down before you get hurt," Tim added.

I began to sing, "Taking Care of Business -Every day - Taking Care of Business -Every way ... takin' — hey, Tim? "

"You drunk! Come down, Ed," Bubba demanded.

"Come on up here. It's cool, man," I said.

Cynthia shook her head and watched me make a fool of myself saying, "Eddie, get down from there, please."

I looked at her, then Bubba, and back over to Cynthia and blurted, "You know what you need?"

"No, I don't know what I need. Are you going to tell me?"

"A good fuck!"

Bubba couldn't believe what I'd said and quietly muttered, "I'm gonna stay out of this one."

"I can't believe you. How could you say that? I can't believe it!" Cynthia said, with a shocked tone in her voice. She ran away to some steps that led toward the river.

"You better beg for forgiveness now, Eddie!" Stewart said, laughing at me as I stumbled down the fence after her.

Stewart was another friend of ours who lived on the hill with his parents not far from Macleay Park. He wasn't the average, "stuck-up" rich kid who looked down on anyone either. He was more of a rebel. It always seemed as if nothing ever bothered him. And because of the big head and long neck he had, we gave him two nicknames, "Charlie Brown" or "Bottle Neck."

"Fuck off, Bottleneck!" I shouted, flipping him the middle finger.

When I finally caught up with Cynthia, I tried to maintain my composure so I wouldn't smirk, but the alcohol was in charge of my emotions.

"What do you want, Eddie?" Cynthia asked, trying to avoid me by briskly walking ahead of me.

"Cynthia, look, I'm sorry! I'm sorry! It's just the alcohol. I don't know what more you want me to say."

"Just leave me alone," Cynthia demanded, running away

from me.

I grabbed her arm and turned her around.

"What else can I say, I mean … I'm sorry!"

"You're sorry?"

"Yeah, I'm sorry," I repeated, thinking I'd finally got her to listen.

She had this calmness about her, inching her face to mine and with a smile said, "I'm sorry, too, 'cause, well, you're not gonna get any sex from me for a long time."

"Whoa, that's cold," I said. I kissed her while I still had the chance.

"You think that's going to make things better? Kissing me, thinking you can say whatever you want? How could you embarrass me in front of everyone like that?"

"Well—"

"Well you can't, Eddie. Don't ever talk to me again that way!"

"Okay, I won't. I'm tellin' you, it's just the beer talkin'."

"Just the beer?"

"Yeah, c'mere," I said, slowly working my way even closer to her.

"You always have some way of making light of things, don't you?" Cynthia said, smiling.

Chapter Nineteen

Ed had successfully finished boot camp, traveled across a couple of countries, and came to visit. During his stay, we boarded the number 9 bus to downtown, then the number 15 to Wallace Park. We hung out under the shelter near the basketball court and made up for lost time.

Ed noticed a girl playing basketball with a group of sweaty guys, and watching her every move asked, "Who's that girl?"

"That's Missy, why?"

He had the look of *love* gleaming from his eyes and replied, "She's fine! That's why."

I said, "She goes to that MLC School in Couch Park."

I couldn't blame him for being interested, because Missy was beautiful. She had a chest any guy would die for and often gave me an excuse to challenge her in a game of basketball. She was somewhat reserved yet mysteriously dangerous. She came from a middle-class family, but she never seemed snobbish or too stuck-up to want to converse with anyone at the park.

Missy walked over to us, wiping the drops of sweat off her forehead. "Hi."

"Hey, Missy, this is a friend of mine, Ed. Ed, this is Missy."

"Hi, Missy," Ed said, "you play pretty good.

"Thanks."

Missy smiled, then looked over to me and said, "Whatta you guys doing here?"

"Oh, we're just kickin' it. Not much."

"Wanna go to a party?" she asked.

"Sure," Ed asked, "where's it gonna be?"

"My house."

"Cool! We'll be there," I said, nodding my head.

The guys were calling Missy for another game.

"I gotta go, but maybe I'll see you tonight."

"Count on it," Ed said, glancing at me.

We showed up at the party and mingled around. It wasn't long after before Ed and Missy became a couple. The one thing about the party that I can selfishly admit is, during Ed's visit, he now wanted to spend more time with her than me.

But we managed to go play video games at the arcade and eat pizza at DeNicola's. It felt like old times. Yet I noticed something different about Ed. He was cussing more, which he had never done before. He also seemed a lot tougher than he was before he left for the military.

We could be somewhere, and Ed would suddenly start singing military songs.

I once asked him, "Ed, what are you singing?"

"A song I learned in the military."

"What's a commie-killin' soldier?"

"The type of people who want dictatorship over countries," Ed said. "You know Eddie, you don't know how free you are until you're living in another country."

"Whatta you mean?"

"This is the freest country in the world. When you've been where I've been, you'd be thankful for where you live now."

"Think so?"

"Yeah, I do."

Ed invited Cynthia and some of our friends to his house to celebrate his visit. I brought the chips, and Edith bought the beer for us. Tim had just showed up, empty-handed as usual. The guys partied in the living room, and I slipped my way into Ed's room with Cynthia.

"Eddie, what are you doing?"

"Don't worry, baby. I got it under control."

"You think it's a good idea to do this here?"

"Yeah, it's fine," I said, "Ed's real cool about these things."

I slipped a condom on and began to make love with her.

"Oh! Cindy, you feel so good."

The bed backboard kept slamming against the wall.

Ed knocked on the door and whispered, "Hey, Eddie, keep it down, man."

"Sorry, bro."

Ed closed the door.

Cynthia giggled, "I can't believe what we're doing."

"I can."

Soon after our lovemaking, we tried to secretly step out of the bedroom to avoid embarrassment, but instead had a standing ovation. I nodded my head, gesturing for them to settle down, and said, "Okay, guys, that's enough."

By now, Ed and I were crocked from the beer. We hung out and laughed and talked for hours.

"Hey, Tim," Ed said, "you should join the Rangers. Uncle Sam will take care of ya."

"Will he get me a good job when I get out?" Tim asked.

"That and college money."

"He can't join no army," I said. "Look at him? He's skinnier than a toothpick."

"I've got muscles," Tim said making a bodybuilding pose for us.

"Tim, I could wrap my hand around that arm of yours."

We all laughed.

To me, Tim didn't seem like military material, but I sensed he wanted to be respected more since he was picked on the most. Late that night, everyone went home, and I slept over.

Two weeks passed, and it was time for Ed to go back. Edith and I drove him to the airport. Before he boarded the plane, I said, "Hey, Ed?"

"Yeah."

"I'll pray for you."

"I'll pray for you," he replied, giving me a thumbs up.

Edith put her arm around me and with her sweet, tender voice said, "My Ed might have left, but my other son is here with me now."

With those words she would be the mother I lost. That evening I went to Lincoln High School and jogged six miles in flat shoes around the track. I did it for Ed.

I often comforted Missy when Ed was gone, and because we

were such good friends, we would call each other and talk for hours. Once Missy was baby-sitting for a friend up the street, and she called me.

"Eddie?"

"Oh, hi, Missy."

"Whatta you doing right now?"

"Nothin'. Just hangin' out. Why?"

"I'm bored."

"Well, want me to come over?"

"If you want."

"Sure. I'll be there in a bit."

"Okay."

I got on my ten-speed bike and rode to where she was.

"Hi, Eddie! I'm glad you came."

I looked around and asked, "Whose house is this?" curiously looking and touching anything within arms' distance.

"It belongs to a friend of mine." Missy asked, "Would you like some juice?"

"Yeah, I'll take some. This is a cool house."

I stood behind the kitchen bar while she sat on a stool across from me. We temporarily eyed each other as if we had some sort of connection. I turned our attention to something else.

"So, the people who own this house, what do they do?"

"I think the dad's an engineer, and I'm not sure what his wife does."

"What's an engineer do?" I asked.

"I think it has something to do with computers."

"Oh, that's cool."

We talked late into the night, then sat on the beige leather sofa and listened to Jazz music.

I looked at Missy's pretty, blue eyes and asked, "Do you love Ed, Missy?"

She replied in a sad tone, "Yeah, I do. But he's always gone. I need him more than just a few weeks out of the year."

I knew by her saying those words that something was going to happen between us.

"Missy, you think it's good for me to be here?"

"Do you feel uncomfortable?"

"Well, um ... not ... I mean ... not totally uncomfortable. I like being here with you, it's just that I'm wondering if it's—"

"I know what you mean, but do you like being here?"

"Yeah. I ... I do."

"I like it, too."

Missy reached over and kissed me. Instead of pulling away, I reacted with a kiss. She grabbed my hand and guided me to a nearby bedroom.

"Come in," she said, holding my hand in hers. "It's okay."

I sighed and said, "I feel ... I feel really awkward."

"I feel a little different, too."

We inched closer toward each other. I lifted her shirt up over her head and caressed her breasts. She began to fondle my groin and unbuckle my belt. The clothes gracefully slipped off, piece by piece, until we were naked. Still wondering if I should do this, desire drew me passionately closer to her and our breathing got harder. We laid on the bed and she helped me find her vagina.

There was no way I could avoid knowing that the heavy burden of guilt and betrayal to my best friend would weigh itself upon my chest for the rest of my life.

I felt like I had just committed adultery. We didn't say a word to each other. I then put my clothes back on, got on my bike, and left.

I began spending more time with Cynthia and never told her what had happened between Missy and me. I also got a new job at the Oregon Health Sciences University Hospital for the rest of my senior year. At first it was hard for me to work there, because of Mom's treatment on the north side of the hospital, but I tried not to think about it. I learned a lot about food and nutrition, even if I didn't always take my job seriously. That was obvious when it was time to clean the trays and dishes that were brought down from the patients' rooms. I often instigated a water fight and almost lost my job several times for it. But at $3.35 an hour, I didn't care.

That same year, Missy had decided to go to college. She wrote Ed a letter once, and at the end it read, *"Ed, At first it was you who was away, now it's me."*

When Ed read the letter, he called me from his barracks and cried over the phone, "Eddie, why did she leave me? What did I ever do to make her run away from me?"

"Ed, you didn't do anything to hurt her. She just felt she wasn't good enough for you, and that you were gone too much."

"No, Eddie, I know why she left me, because she's a slut! She just wanted to meet other guys. She used me!"

"Ed, you can't feel this way, bro. We both know there're plenty more girls out there. Besides, every time you come down, girls are lookin' to go out with us."

There was a silence over the receiver, then Ed replied, "You're right. Look, man, I have to go, but I'm gonna try to come down and see you soon, okay."

"Okay. Cheer up, man. You'll be okay."

I knew my encounter with Missy had something to do with their break-up. As soon as he hung up, I had this eating feeling inside of me. I wanted to let Missy know how bad she hurt Ed and that she wasn't worthy of him, but at the time I felt neither was I.

Chapter Twenty

I was getting tired of school, and for some reason, Mom's death became more real to me now than when it happened. So I began missing school.

Dad was curious about my attendance at school and asked, "Eddie, don't you have any school today?"

"No, Dad. Teachers are havin' a meeting."

"A meeting? They're always havin' meetings."

"I know. I can't imagine why."

"Eddie, do you want to talk?"

"No, Dad."

"Son, school's important. You hafta go."

"I know, Dad. I am going. Don't worry, okay?"

Dad knew I was lying, but at the time, I felt the truth would hurt him more. Being a senior was something I was proud of, but homework wasn't easy for me.

There weren't many fights at Lincoln. Except for the time Joey and I were walking to class and some students heard disturbance around the corner of the hallway. When I looked behind me, Joey wasn't there anymore.

I turned the corner to see what was happening and saw Joey fighting two Iranian guys. I couldn't believe it. One minute Joey was there, the next, he was fighting.

Joey was yelling, "C'mon, c'mon! You wanna fuck with me! I'm from New York!"

I stood there watching him with his fists clenched go into this "blank state" of anger. What surprised me the most was, he took both of them on. I began to boost his confidence (like he had always done for me) and shouted, "C'mon bro! Kick their asses, Joey. Fuck 'em up!"

Joey picked up a nearby garbage can and bent it with his hands, as if he was possessed by some demon.

"Holy shit!" one student said. "Did you see that."

There was so much yelling from everywhere that it sounded like a million people were there. The teachers came running out of their classrooms.

"Stop it! Stop it!" one teacher demanded, forcing her arms between Joey and the Iranian guys.

"Knock it off!" a male teacher angrily shouted, grabbing Joey by his shirt. "I said knock it off."

They were separated.

He continued, "Both of you follow me. We're going to the principal's office."

Joey and the Iranian guys were later suspended for the day.

Some of the teachers at Lincoln genuinely cared about our education, unlike the teachers back in New York. One teacher I'll never forget was Mrs. Wagner. She showed a love and academic care toward her students I'll always remember. She also realized Joey and I were struggling through school. She was so patient with us that I sometimes thought she was a part of my own family.

But after school I would neglect the homework Mrs. Wagner gave me to ride in Bubba's new red Ranchero, which he'd customized with white metal teeth on the front end. Everyone knew who owned that car and stayed far away from it because it was Bubba's "pride and joy."

There wasn't a day that Cynthia and I didn't hold hands or kiss in the school hallways. Our relationship was now at a comfortable point to where I felt Cynthia could come to my house.

I was still afraid if she saw my house, she might think differently of me. I didn't want to experience what Joey once did when we lived in the Pink house:

Joey told his girlfriend Vicki that he had chandeliers and that our house was immaculate. He should have never said that because one day she decided to pay him a surprise visit. When Joey looked through the peephole to see who it was, he saw his girlfriend, Vicki. Joey went into a total panic. He didn't even open the door. Instead, he ran into the kitchen, took out the aluminum foil and desperately tried to drape the light bulbs with it to make it look something like chandeliers.

My dad laughed so hard he said, "Hey, Joey, why don't you paint the house, too. Don't forget to clean my room."

It was an amusing moment, but it really wasn't funny for Joey, because he wanted to impress her. Eventually Joey came to his senses and stopped.

He looked at me with a sad, discouraged face and asked, "Why do we have to be poor?"

I sighed and replied, "If she likes you, Joe, she won't care."

I knew how he felt because I wanted to impress Cynthia and make her like me more. That was why I decided the next time Cynthia asked to come over, I would let her.

That day came sooner than I expected when we drove from a downtown restaurant called Trader Vic's to my house on Albina Street. When we got inside the house, my dog, Yoko, was excited to see us, jumping on Cynthia.

"Yoko, stop!" I said. "Dad, this is Cynthia."

"Hi, Cynthia. Nice to meet you."

"You, too, Mr. Regory."

"Oh, just call me Al. Everybody calls me Al."

"Okay."

"We're gonna be in my room if you need anything, okay, Dad?"

"Okay."

We went to my room, but Dad immediately called me back out to the living room.

"I'll be back," I said to Cynthia.

"Okay."

I knew what Dad was going to say when he called me out there.

"Yeah, Dad."

"Come here," Dad whispered. "I don't want anything goin' on in there."

"I know, Dad. I know."

"And keep your door open."

"Dad, I know. I gotta go back," I said, rushing back to my

room, "Yoko, out!"

Yoko left with her ears back and tail between her legs.

I turned on my small Sony radio and listened to the soft sounds of KINK radio. Cynthia heard a noise outside my window and asked, "What was that?"

"The dogs," I replied.

"Dogs?"

"Yeah, wanna see them?"

"Sure."

I lifted my window shade up and showed her the pit bulls that were chained in the neighbor's backyard.

"Why are there so many?"

"I think the guy does drugs or something."

I caught a surprised look on her face, but that soon passed.

I drew the shade back down and said, "Well, this is the way my room looks."

"I like the way you set it up," Cynthia said.

"You do?"

"Yeah, I do."

"Bed's kind of hard, though."

"So," Cynthia said. "Just the right firmness for us."

"We really can't do anything here," I said. "My dad would know."

"We can't? Oh, I think we could if we really wanted."

"My dad would know."

"How? Why don't you close the door."

"If I did that, he would definitely think something's up."

I tried to be discreet about kissing her.

"Hey, Eddie!" Dad called out, acting like there was something he needed. "Could you come here for a second?"

"Oh, man," I said to Cynthia, "I told you he's paranoid about something goin' on."

I went out there and hurried back to the room.

Amused at my dad's constant calling, Cynthia asked, "Well? What is it now?"

"What do you think? Hey, I have an idea. Why don't we go to our secret place?"

130

"And do it in the car again. Isn't there someplace else we can go? Besides, I get a weird feeling knowing there's a boarding house for pregnant teenagers up the road."

"Well, it's better than me leaving the room every two minutes because of my dad calling."

"Okay. I'm convinced."

Sometimes we searched for anyplace we could relieve some tension, even in the movie room in her house while her mom was in her bedroom sleeping.

Chapter Twenty-One

In June of 1985, Ed was back on another visit and had a few goals: to finish up his time in the military, go to college, and learn to build houses.

A few of us were sitting under the shelter at Wallace Park when we saw this motorcycle enter the park with its headlight on. At first it was hard to see, then it pulled up on the basketball court, and the horn honked.

"Ed, that's so cool, man! This is badass! When did you get it?"

Ed replied, "You wanna go for a ride?"

"Hell, yeah! What kind of motorcycle is this?"

"An Interceptor 500."

I jumped on his motorcycle and we rode off. As the wind brushed past us I shouted in Ed's ear, "Ed, you know, I saw Missy today."

He turned his head over his left shoulder for a second and replied, "Oh yeah, how's she doin'?"

"She's doin' fine," I said. "She told me to say hello to you."

"Did you say hi for me?"

"Did you want me to?" I asked.

"Nah."

"Liar."

"Wanna see what kind of power this thing's got?" Ed asked.

"Go 'head. Let's see. I bet it's gutless."

Ed kicked it into low gear and gave it just a little throttle, and I nearly fell off the back seat.

"Whoo!" I yelled, nearly peeing my pants.

"Told ya this thing had power!"

Weeks later, I purchased a 1985 Kawasaki Ninja 600R so that we could ride together.

Timmy, Bubba, Joey, and some of the other guys had a party for Ed at Tim's house. The weather was warm, and we were drinking beers and eating barbecued ribs. Bubba, at no surprise to any of us, was slamming down a lot of beer.

A pretty Spanish girl named Julie walked up from the park.

"Hi, Tim," Julie said. "You're having a party, and you didn't even invite me."

"Hey! Julie, what's up?"

"You tell me, Timmy. You didn't even tell me about your party."

"Nah ... nah, it's not like I didn't want you to come."

"Sure."

"Well, come on in, have a good time. There's beer in the 'fridge."

I didn't know Julie very well, but I did see her come to the park often. She was about fifteen years old, and when Ed saw her, he liked her right on the spot. Ed was about twenty-one at the time.

"Eddie, who's that?"

"That's Julie. Why?"

"She looks good. Is she taken?

"I don't know, why?"

"She's cute!"

Ed must've drunk a six-pack of beer by now, but he could always fake like he was sober. He approached Julie and started talking.

He later came back to me and said, "Eddie, she wants to go somewhere alone with me. Where am I gonna take her?"

"Ed, c'mon, man. I thought we were hangin' out with the boys today."

"Eddie, c'mon, man, we're just gonna talk," Ed said. "Don't worry."

"Where am I supposed to take you guys?"

"Anywhere ... doesn't matter."

"Tim," I said, "I'll be back in a few."

"Where you goin'?"

"To the store," I replied.

Ed and Julie got into a Ford Granada I'd borrowed from my brother Gerard, and I drove them to Trenton's. Trenton was a heavyset man who had black, curly, frizzy hair and scars on his face and who made a living by selling drugs. He lived by the industrial area in the Northwest. When we got there, Trenton answered the door, looking doped up.

"What's up?" I said.

Trenton replied, "Hey, nothin', man. What the fuck you guys doin' here?"

"Uh … nothin'. Can we come in?" I asked, as Ed stood behind me talking to Julie.

"Yeah, yeah, yeah, c'mon in," Trenton kicked at his pit bull. "San Quentin, move!"

We sat on the torn-up sofa and Trenton asked, "Hey, who's the pretty lady?"

"This is Julie," I introduced. "Julie, this is Trenton."

"Hi."

Ed looked over to Trenton and asked, "Hey, Trenton, can I use one of your rooms?"

Trenton replied, "Uh, yeah, man, go 'head. Just don't get the sheets dirty."

Ed went into a room as I waited for them to finish. After about an hour, Ed came out, tucking his shirt in. We stayed a few minutes longer and went back to Tim's party. Julie was now Ed's new girlfriend.

My friend Stewart bought a Volkswagen bus we named, "The Battlewagon." It had a small tabletop, a seat that folded into a bed, and a small freezer we used for storing alcohol whenever we planned a trip.

At that time, Cynthia and I separated for a while. During our separation, the guys planned a trip to Sauvie Island in Stewart's new Battlewagon. Ed and I followed on our motorcycles.

When we got there, Annette, Stewart's girlfriend, and Dixie, a girl Tim knew, went looking for wood for a campfire.

There were California Coolers for the girls and Budweiser beers for the guys. We joked, laughed, and partied for hours. Dixie was an average girl and on the pudgy side, but we eyed each other most of the night. A few beers later, she was looking fine.

I walked around the fire and asked, "What's up, Dixie? How do you like the party?"

She replied in a high-pitched voice, "The party's great! Why?"

"Well, wanna go for a walk?"

"Okay, where?"

"That way," I replied, pointing north toward a secluded area.

"Okay, bye, guys! We're gonna go for a walk," Dixie said, to everyone as we walked away.

We got about two hundred yards down the river as I continued to drink my Budweiser.

I stopped and got close to Dixie.

She chuckled and said, "What are you doing, Eddie?"

I casually slipped my hand up under her shirt and replied, "Nothin', just let my hands do the walkin' and my body do the talkin'."

Next thing you know, we were on the sand, with most of our clothes off. My underwear was halfway to my knees.

Dixie had the biggest breasts I've ever seen. I caressed them and slowly made my way down her panties. I took them off and slipped a condom on. I spread her legs and penetrated her. She kept saying, "Oh, Eddie, oh, Eddie! Fuck me! Fuck me!"

We suddenly heard some noises around us. I glanced at Dixie and asked, "Did you hear that?"

"What?" she replied, breathing hard.

"Nothin' ... doesn't matter."

We continued, then a light shined directly on us. I heard laughter behind the light. It sounded like Bubba's voice saying, "Look at that small weenie he's got."

We got up and threw our clothes back on.

I heard Stewart yell, "Damn! Dixie, you got some big ol' tits."

I shouted, "What are you guys doin', man? Can't a nigga have some privacy!"

Dixie ran deep into the dark, trying to put her clothes back on.

136

Bubba handed me a beer and said, "Here, let's celebrate your little weenie!"

"Fuck you, guys!" I said. "Why you gotta mess up my score?"

Stewart laughed and said, "What are you gonna to tell Cynthia now?"

"Fuck you, Charlie Brown!" I shouted, walking back to the campfire. "You guys are punks."

Dixie showed up at the fire, crying, and said, "You guys are assholes!"

"Why am I an asshole?" I asked.

"'Cause Eddie, they're your idiot friends."

"Ooh, we're idiots," Bubba teased. "At least I'm not a slut!"

"Fuck you, Bubba!"

Dixie went with Annette for a walk, and we stayed by the fire drinking our beers.

Chapter Twenty-Two

I flunked my senior year and decided I needed to go back and get my diploma. I was now in the class of 1986 instead of 1985. This time, all I needed were a few credits to graduate. Students at Lincoln couldn't believe I had flunked my senior year. Some thought it took a lot of courage to come back.

It was Thanksgiving, and Edith prepared muffins, biscuits, a huge turkey, cranberry sauce and pies, which melted in your mouth. After dinner, Ed and I went to his room.

"Hey, Ed?"

"Yeah?"

"Can I have this Ranger beret?"

"Yeah. You can keep it. Do you know what the wings on the pin are for?"

"What?"

"They're my Ranger wings. I earned them."

"It's a cool hat," I said, "I wonder what it would be like if I were in the Rangers?"

"You can still join."

"Nah, it's not my style."

Ed said, "It's not all bad for you. You can learn discipline, responsibility."

I said, adjusting the beret, "It's a little small."

"Let's see," Ed said, taking the hat then stretching it out with his hands, putting it back on my head. "How's it feel now?"

"Fits better, but not great."

"It looks good."

"Think so?"

"Yeah. You look like a soldier."

"That's right, boy. So don't give me any lip."

Ed chuckled and went to the bathroom. I went back into the

living room and sat on the soft beige recliner, which faced a radio that was built into a turntable. I heard a song, which reminded me of our friendship. The lyrics were beautiful. The song was called "He Ain't Heavy" by the Hollies. I was listening to it when Ed suddenly came out and sang, "He ain't heavy - he's my brother…."

I said, "Yeah, man, that's our song."

Edith laughed because she knew we were like brothers and said, "Is Eddie your brother?"

"Yeah, he's my brother, Mom, and he ain't heavy," Ed replied humorously.

Edith laughed and said, "This is a joyous occasion.

Our rich friend Woody from Lincoln had another party at his mom's house, and a bunch of us showed up. Ed and I drove his mom's black AMC Gremlin there. We walked past a fountain with a statue of a naked man in it. I knocked on the door and Woody opened it.

"What's up, guys?" Woody said, gesturing a greeting with his can of Budweiser. "Welcome!"

We replied, "What's up?"

"Enter the house of beer!" Woody said.

We walked in and couldn't believe our eyes. There was alcohol everywhere. Bubba was mixing drinks in the kitchen.

"Woody," I asked, "where'd you get the beer?"

Woody was showing Tim his new big-screen television. He looked over and replied, "From Trenton. I gave him a hundred bucks, and he bought all the stuff and kept the change."

There were two half-gallons of Bacardi, and some Mai Tai and Pina Colada mix on the kitchen counter. I strolled toward the refrigerator and opened it. Most of the food had been taken out, and it had been re-packed with cans of Budweiser beer. I knew there were going to be a lot of sick people by the end of the night. I grabbed a cold one and watched Bubba mix the drinks.

"You know what you're doin'?" I asked.

"It's real simple, Eddie," Bubba said. "You see, this here's a man's job. That's why Woody gave it to me. First you take the Bacardi, then you take a sixteen-ounce cup—fill it with Bacardi—"

"Damn! That's too much," I blurted out. "It's gonna taste like shit!"

"No, no, it's the right amount," Bubba said with confidence. "You put it in the blender, grab some ice—put it in the blender— grab the mix—put some in the blender and top it off with a little bit of this beer. Grab me the Tabasco."

"What? Tabasco? Another one of your weird concoctions. You already messed it up with the beer," I said, handing him the Tabasco.

Bubba ignored me and continued, "Put a few drops of this Tabasco in—mix it and, voila! I'm done."

"There's no way I'm gonna drink that shit," I said, "no way."

"No, here, try it. Try it!" Bubba insisted.

"Okay, just a little," I said, sipping some and almost spitting it out on Woody's cream-colored linoleum floor. "That's the nastiest shit I've ever tasted in my life."

Bubba poured sixteen ounces of his concoction into a cup and said, "Watch this," and he began to drink it. "Shit! That's strong. I think I'm feelin' a little sick now."

I said, "I told you, man. Ain't nobody gonna drink that crap. I'll just stick with my beer."

Ed came up from the living room, opened the refrigerator, and grabbed a beer. He saw Bubba sweating profusely and asked, "What's wrong, Bubba?"

I interjected, "Oh, well, Bubba thought he could be a big man by drinking a cup of that atrocious mix of his."

Ed walked over to the blender and smelled what was in it. He quickly lifted his head back and blurted, "Damn! That's nothin' but Bacardi. What's that brown stuff in there?"

Bubba rubbed his stomach and said, "I gotta sit down, bro."

He went into the living room and sat on the sofa. Meanwhile, Ed and I grabbed several beers and sat on the steps outside of Woody's house. It was a quiet night, except for the loud noises of laughter and slurred dialogue inside the house.

I sipped my beer and asked, "Hey, Ed?"

"Yeah."

"Have you ever killed anyone in the military?"

He looked at me strangely, drank a big gulp of his beer and replied, "Nope. But I've seen things I wish I hadn't."

"Like what?"

Ed shook his head from side-to-side, glanced at the ground and replied, "Hungry kids, oppression, you name it. You know, I really didn't know how lucky I was 'til I joined the military and saw how much hurt there was out there."

"Do you regret joining?"

"Nah. I regret not making something out of my life," Ed said. "Here I am drinkin' beer, and I don't feel like I'm goin' anywhere."

"You are somewhere," I said, "You're with family. You're with me."

Ed said, "Ya know, one day I'm gonna get married, spit out a few kids, watch 'em grow up, and just be happy."

"Married?" I said. "Man, I can't imagine either of us gettin' married."

"We have to. It all just can't be drinkin' beer and aimlessly goin' nowhere. There has to be more to life."

"Ya know, my dad always says that if you follow God, you'll never need to look for anything else," I said. "You think if we did that, we wouldn't want anything else?"

"I don't know, maybe. I do know that I'm fittin' on downing this beer," Ed said theatrically, as he lifted his can of Budweiser and gulped it to the last drop.

I nudged him and said, "Damn! I could down a beer faster than that."

"Well, c'mon, missing link," Ed said, making a funny face.

We rushed inside and got six beers out of the refrigerator and laid them across the kitchen counter. I looked over into the living room and yelled, "Bubba! … Woody! … you guys, come 'ere! Ed and me are gonna have a slammin' contest."

Bubba got up off the sofa, ran up the stairs, and said, "I gotta see this."

Everyone else followed. Ed grabbed two beers off the counter, lifted both tabs up and handed me one.

Stewart barged between us and said, "Okay, wait. I'll give you guys the go-ahead. No sipping … no cheating—that means you, Eddie."

"Man, shut up, fool! I ain't gonna cheat."

Ed and me each held a can, of beer close to our lips and waited for Stewart's signal.

Bubba said, "Y'all just a bunch of wimps. I could slam one faster than both of you put together."

I started to sip the foam off the can and Tim shouted, "You're cheatin'! No cheatin', Eddie."

"I'm not! Chill out, Tim."

Cynthia said, "Eddie, don't do it. You're gonna get sick."

"Don't worry, baby. This is for you," I said, acting as if I knew what I was doing.

Stewart proceeded to say, "Okay, drinkers get ready, get set. Go!"

I lifted the can up and felt the beer drizzle down my lower lip as I tried desperately to gulp as much as I could.

Bubba was shouting, "Go! Go! Go! Go!"

I beat Ed by a couple of seconds. Bubba handed us two more beers, and this time, I could see in Ed's face he was determined to win the next round.

Bubba said, "Okay, drunks ready? Cans to your lips, get set, go!"

I gulped as fast as I could, but Ed was taking bigger gulps than I was. Beer began to trickle down the sides of his mouth.

"Go! Go! Go! Go! Go! Go! Go!" everyone cheered Ed on, since I won the first round.

Cynthia was all I needed for encouragement. I wanted to win for her.

She said, "C'mon, Eddie! C'mon. You can do it! You can do it."

Our cans tilted further and further back. After four to five seconds of no breathing and fast drinking, Ed drank a last gulp, then crushed the can with his right hand and yelled out an Airborne Ranger shout, "Yeah! Ar-uah!" then threw the can on the floor.

I felt my head rush from drinking so fast.

Yet that didn't stop Ed from proclaiming his victory over me.

He said, "You see, boy. You're just a squirrel tryin' to get a nut."

I said, "Okay, punk ass. Another one."

Bubba said, "Wait! I got an idea. Woody, do you have two empty two-liter bottles?"

"Yeah, they're under the kitchen sink."

Bubba walked briskly to the sink and opened the cupboard beneath it. There were several of them lined up in a row. Bubba grabbed two, then pulled a knife from the kitchen drawer, cutting them in half.

"Okay, you guys think you know how to slam? Well y'all mother fuckas gonna have to drink outta this!" Bubba said, holding the two, two-liter plastic bottles up high.

There was no way I was going to back out. Bubba gave them to us and we put the spout close to our lips.

Bubba continued, "Okay, now I'm gonna get two beers and pour these fuckers right into the bottles. First one to drink it empty wins. And no cheatin', niggas."

Bubba grabbed the beers, lifted the tabs and held the two beers over the cut two-liters. Ed and I tilted our heads back and waited for the beer to be poured in.

"Alcoholics ready, get set, drink!"

He quickly poured both cans into the liters.

You could see the strain in Ed's neck trying to gulp every ounce.

Woody shouted, "Go! Go! Go! Man, I can't believe they're doin' this."

Bubba shouted, "Woody! Open two more of those Budweisers!"

Bubba took the other two beers before we could finish the first and poured them into the two liters. I was consuming more than I could swallow. So I stopped, brought my head down and quickly spit whatever I had left in my mouth into the kitchen sink.

Ed still kept drinking the beer out of his liter, and so everyone started to cheer simultaneously, "Do it! Do it! Do it!"

He quickly brought the bottle down, looked at me and exclaimed, "You don't know how to drink it, that's what it is. Rangers lead the way!"

"Ed, man, I'm feelin' fucked up, dude." I said, arched over the kitchen sink, throwing up dry heaves.

Ed patted me on the shoulder and said, "Maybe next time, young 'un."

It was about eleven-thirty p.m., and Ed lost count on the beers he drank, slurring most of his words. Everyone else in the living room was drunk except for Cynthia.

She said, "Eddie, I have to go home now."

"Why? The, the party's just startin'," I slurred.

"Eddie, you're too drunk to even talk."

"Nah … I'm … I'm not drunk. I'm just feelin' a little uncoordinated," I said, swaying, trying to stay in one place.

"I gotta go, Eddie. Call me tomorrow."

"Don't go, Cynthia. Are you upset with me?"

"I just don't like seeing you this way."

I followed her outside, and she got in her car.

"Bye, Eddie."

"Cynthia!" I voiced loudly as she drove off.

I went back inside the house and into the living room.

Ed asked, "Where've you been, bro?"

"I've been outside takin' care of business."

"Oh, yeah, I know what kinda business you've been takin' care of," Bubba said, moving his right hand up and down pretending he was masturbating.

"Man, y'all wish you had some business you could take of," I retorted.

Ed threw me an extra can of beer he had beside him. "Here, have another one."

After drinking a while longer, Ed walked up to me and said, "Eddie, I gotta go, man."

"Why?"

"'Cause, I gotta … gotta get my uni ... uniform," Ed slurred.

"You gotta get your uniform? What the hell for?"

"I hafta."

"Ed, man, I don't know, dude. We're all fucked up?"

"I'm fine," Ed replied.

"Ed, we're too fucked up. But if you know what you're doin'."

Ed wrapped his arm over my shoulder and said, "C'mon. Hey, Woody, I'm goin' to my house for a minute." Woody just nodded.

"What?" Timmy exclaimed. "You're not goin' nowhere!"

Timmy began to search Ed's pockets, looking for the keys to the Gremlin. "Where are they? Where'd you put your keys?"

"There in uh … safe place," Ed replied, grabbing a can of Copenhagen chew out from his back pocket. He dipped his right fingers into the can and put some under his bottom lip.

"C'mon, Ed. Quit messin' around," Tim said. "You're in no condition to drive."

Ed pushed us away and said, "All right, all right. I won't go. Just chill out."

"You promise?" Tim asked, pointing his finger at Ed as if he were a child.

"Yeah, I promise!"

"I'll watch 'im, Tim," I said. "If he tries to go anywhere, it'll be with me."

Ed turned and dashed toward the door. Everyone else came running. He beat us to the Gremlin and locked himself in the driver's side.

"Ed, c'mon, man, open the door!" I pleaded.

Stewart marched to the back of the car and leaned on it, jumping up and down on the bumper.

Bubba stood in front of the car and said, "Nigga's gonna hafta go through me first."

"C'mon, Ed. Get out!" Tim said, beating on the driver's

146

window.

Ed was teasing us with the keys in his hand as if he was going to start the car and drive.

Tim said, "Okay, Ed, follow me down the hill and if I think you're driving okay, I'll let you drive the rest of the way."

"What? Dude, are you nuts?" I blurted. "He's too fucked up! Even I know that and I'm messed up too."

"I'm using psychology on him," Tim whispered.

Ed cracked the window open and said, "You promise?"

"I promise," Tim replied.

"Don't fuck me, Tim ... don't you ever fuck me, Ed said, acting out and mimicking the words from the movie, *Scarface*."

I began to laugh because it was so funny.

I walked briskly up to the driver's side and said, "Ed, Tim will let you drive, but you gotta let me ride with you."

He opened the passenger's side and said, "C'mon, homeboy."

Tim got into his Maverick and started it.

Ed said," Put it on KGON. Find KGON on this piece of junk."

"I can't. This radio's just AM," I replied, pushing all the buttons on the panel.

Ed started the Gremlin, rolled down the window, and pinched a glob of chew from his lower lip, throwing it on the pavement. Bubba jumped into Tim's car and they slowly drove off.

Tim waved his arm outside his Maverick window and yelled, "C'mon! Follow me."

Ed's foot depressed on the gas pedal too fast. I got slightly whiplashed as the car took off down the hill away from Woody's house. We rode down Chehalem Street past Council Crest Park. I could feel my head swaying with the car movement. That's how I knew Ed was not driving in a straight line.

"Whoo!" Ed yelled out. "Whoo!"

Ed followed Tim's car onto Greenway Avenue, which all downhill. We began to accelerate, and I could feel the car weave from side-to-side. Suddenly, I heard the tires screech, and the car did a 360 degree spin down Vista Street.

Ed shouted, "Oh shit! Oh shit!" trying to take back control of the car. The car spun again and came to a halt. I vomited, and when I looked over the dashboard I saw a stone wall.

"Wha' … what … what happened?"

Ed replied, excited, "I was handling it! Handling it! Did you see that? Did you see that?"

"What the ... the fuck happened? Where are we?"

"Did you see that Eddie? You missed it. We almost hit a wall and went over the cliff!"

Ed tried to start the car, but it wouldn't turn over. Cars drove around us and Tim made a U-turn and drove back up Vista toward us. We found ourselves on the right side of the narrow road. Tim turned his car around and parked in front of us. Tim and Bubba opened their doors and ran toward us.

"Ed! What happened?" Tim asked.

"Are you guys okay?" Bubba asked.

"Yeah, man. Did you see that? The car spinned several times down the hill," Ed said.

Tim replied, "Yeah, we saw it. At first we thought it was a cop car with his lights on."

"Ed, we gotta get this car outta here before the cops come," Bubba said.

Tim said, "Bubba, I'm gonna drive the car, and you drive my Maverick back up to Woody's."

"Okay, give me the keys."

Tim was intoxicated himself, but capable of driving. When we got back to Woody's, we partied a little longer and stayed the night. Bubba slept on the sofa while the rest of us slept on the living room floor.

The next morning I woke up when the doorbell rang. I had a severe hangover, and my shirt was off. But I managed to get up and move unsteadily toward the front door. I didn't bother looking through the peephole. I unlocked the door, and Edith was standing there with a shocked look on her face.

"Oh, my God," she said in a surprised tone.

I looked befuddled and said, "Hi, Edith. I'll get Ed."

"Are you okay?" she asked.

"Yeah, Mom ... hold on."

I went into the living room, but Ed wasn't there.

"Ed, Ed!" I shouted.

"What?" Ed replied, in the bathroom next to the liquor cabinet.

"Dude, your mom's here; she's at the front door, man."

"I know. I called her to come pick me up."

"You called her? Why? She's gonna know we've been drinkin'."

"I need to go home. I'm tired of being here."

Edith walked in and saw the empty beer cans and blue 16-ounce cups scattered all over the kitchen floor. She didn't say much and patiently waited for Ed to finish.

As Ed was leaving I said, "Hey, I'll see ya tomorrow."

"Okay."

Shortly after, I struggled into the bathroom to throw some water on my face and saw the most inconceivable sight. When I fell asleep, the guys must have decided to play a joke on me by using my body as a human billboard. I had the word "fuck you" on my forehead, and smiley faces drawn on my body with mascara and lipstick. That's when I knew the reason for Edith's reaction.

Chapter Twenty-Three

In March, Ed was coming home for good. I thought it would be a nice surprise to have a party for him at my dad's. Julie, Tim, Bubba, Joey, Jaeger, Stewart, and Cynthia stayed at the house to surprise Ed when he walked in. Edith and I waited for him at the airport. When his airplane arrived, it was one of the best feelings I ever felt. I thought, *Now my best friend is here to stay.*

He walked down the corridor in his Airborne Ranger uniform, a wool, black beret that tilted off the right side of his short hair, and medals pinned to his uniform symbolizing the rank of an established soldier.

His rosy, red cheeks, clear hazel eyes, and slender body were signs of a true athlete. He held a green duffel bag, which had everything he owned in it. Edith and I greeted him with open arms as he walked toward us.

"Hey, Mom, Eddie!" Ed said, kissing his mom on her cheek.

Edith was crying and said, "Hi, baby, my beautiful son is home for good."

The kissing and hugging lasted for several minutes.

"So you think you're a tough Ranger now, huh?" I said, grabbing his duffel bag and walking toward the car parked outside. "How's it feel to be back home?"

Edith got in the car, and I loaded Ed's stuff in the trunk.

"It feels good, Eddie. I'm glad I'm outta there and knowing I'm gonna be a civilian again."

"Why, was it too tough for ya?" I said. "You're just a little girl."

"Boy, I'm an accomplished Airborne Ranger!" Ed declared, with a closed-fisted right hand to his chest.

We got in the car and headed toward my dad's.

"Where we goin'?" Ed asked.

"We're goin' to the base where the rest of the soldiers are at,

151

grunt!" I answered, pretending I was an authoritative figure from the military.

Ed said, "You'd be a good sergeant, Eddie. You should join the Rangers. It's not just a job, it's an adventure!"

"No way, man. I don't think I'd like it if someone sprayed spit in my face all day."

We arrived at my house.

"C'mon, Ranger. Time to see my dad."

I had Ed lead the way toward the front door. He was excited to see my dad because he loved and admired him. There were many times Ed would call him from the barracks and ask him questions about the Bible.

We walked several feet into the dark hallway, turned left, and headed toward the living room, and Ed asked, "Why is everything so dark?"

That's when the lights came on, and everyone said, "Surprise!"

Dad sat in his old, beat-up recliner. He wore his blue cotton hat, his 62-inch size pants, and suspenders with streaks of cornstarch on them. He used cornstarch to bathe himself with because showers were hard for him to take.

There was a crayon-colored banner pinned on the wall above the entrance, to the kitchen that read: "Welcome Home Ed!" I showed him into the kitchen.

"Hey, Ed," I said, "see what we made? There's lasagna, garlic bread, white rice, potatoes, chips, and plenty of soda pop and beer. "It's an all-you-can-eat buffet, man."

"Looks good," Ed replied. He walked over to my dad, hugged him, and said, "How ya doin', Al? It's good to see ya!"

"Hey, Ed, thank God you got home safely!" Dad said, holding the Holy Scriptures in his hand. "I prayed for you every day."

Everyone mingled around and took turns talking to Ed and blasted the music to the pop-rock station, Z100.

Edith said to Ed, "I have to go now, honey. What time will you be home?"

"Later, Mom. I just want to spend some time with my

friends."

"Okay, call me if you need a ride."

"I'll be okay, Mom. Bye, I love ya."

"I love you, too."

Gerard came by later to eat some food and also left. Cynthia stood there quietly in the small, crowded living room while I spent most of my time with Ed.

I saw Jaeger standing in the kitchen, digging his fork into more than a half-plate of lasagna and said, "Hey, Jaeger, you should try comin' up for air."

Jaeger laughed and replied, "Man, this is grubbin'!"

"Yeah, it is."

Almost everyone left. Ed went into my room with Julie to talk with her, but he did more than talk. Every time I interrupted them, they were kissing on my bed. Cynthia and I tried to keep my dad talking so he wouldn't get up and get into his wheelchair to go to his room. If he did, he'd catch them kissing.

Dad was about four hundred and eighty pounds then, and was usually bedridden. Every day he moved from his room to the television in the living room in his custom-made wheelchair. That was why Dad didn't take showers, because he was too big and afraid of slipping in the bathtub. Instead, he stocked up on corn starch. He put it under his breasts, around his scrotum, and any place that chaffed easily. Even when I offered to help him take a shower, he never accepted. He felt ashamed, and thought it was biblically wrong for me to look upon his body.

Dad conversed with Cynthia a little about his life, and I went into the kitchen to clean up. After a while, Ed came out of my room, and Julie's hair was slightly messed up.

Ed said, "Hey, Al," as he walked over to him and wrapped his left arm around his obese shoulders. "I missed home."

"Hey, Ed, how'd you like your party?"

"It was awesome! All the great food, my beautiful mother, my buddy, Eddie ... it was awesome! Awesome!"

"Good, good. Ya know, we all worried for you and prayed for your safety," Dad said, patting Ed on his lower back.

"Especially when they sent you guys to Libya. That worried all of us."

"I worried for you guys, too," Ed said, looking at Julie standing in the hallway. "Yo, baby, why don't you bring your fine self over here."

Julie chuckled and walked toward Ed, saying, "It's Julie to you."

Ed looked over to me and asked, "Where's your Ninja?"

"In the garage."

"Oh, you mean the shack. Let's go check it out."

"Okay, let's go."

Julie and Cynthia were reluctant to stay behind and said, "Oh, okay, the girls will just sit right here like little dogs."

"Nah, baby that's not how it is," I responded in a cool manner.

We walked into the kitchen toward the back door and into the small, run-down garage.

Ed glanced at my motorcycle and asked, "Did you just clean it?"

"Yeah, I did the other day. Looks pretty good, huh?"

"Looks real good!" Ed said, lightly touching the seat and handlebars.

"We gotta go ridin' tomorrow ... if it's nice," I said, "unless you're afraid of the Ninja."

Ed smiled and said, "The Interceptor rules!"

We both chuckled.

Suddenly Ed had a serious look.

"What's up? Something up?"

He sat on my motorcycle, and stared at the controls.

"Nothing's wrong, just that, well, I just missed home real bad."

"I know, man. We missed you as much as you missed home."

"Cynthia seems like a nice girl. Is that her car out front?"

"Yeah. She'll probably never have to work another day in her life. Her mom and dad are rich. Nice car, huh? They let her drive any car she wants. You know it would take us a million

154

years to have one of those Audis."

"Rich girl goin' out with a poor boy," Ed said smiling. "Yeah, that's what I'll call you, poor boy just like those poor boy sandwiches."

We laughed, and I replied, "Ah, man, that's cold, cold."

The serious look on Ed's face was there again.

"Eddie, I think Missy's pregnant."

"What?"

"I think Missy's pregnant," Ed repeated in a low tone.

"How? When? What do you mean she's pregnant?"

"She wrote me a letter and said she was pregnant."

"You're kiddin'. What are you gonna do?"

"I don't know."

"Well, are you sure she's pregnant?"

"That's what she said. It's probably some other guys and now she wants to blame it on me."

"You gotta talk to her, man," I said. "Did you tell Julie?"

"No way."

"If she's pregnant, what are you goin' to name the baby?" I asked jokingly.

Ed replied, "Twinkle Toes."

"Well, that's a good name."

"I'll deal with it."

"You will? How?"

"I'll hafta take care of the baby."

"When did all this happen?" I asked.

"Last time I came up to visit."

I sighed and said, "Come on. Let's go back inside. We'll get into this later."

"Yeah," Ed agreed, stepping off my bike.

Chapter Twenty-Four

Now that Ed was home for good, he would make time to see his real dad, Buzz. Edith was separated from him because he was an alcoholic.

His dad lived in the Columbia Villa, which was a low-income housing neighborhood in North Portland. One day it was raining, so I borrowed my dad's white 1965 Ford station wagon. We drove to Columbia Villa searching for Buzz.

We came across an apartment complex, which was run-down like all the other apartments around us. It was the only place that reminded me of where I used to live in the ghetto. Ed knocked on one door and a lady opened it.

The place smelled of marijuana, and the lady had four kids who surrounded her, wearing no clothes. Her breath smelled of alcohol and she asked, "Yeah, what?"

"Do you know someone they call Buzz?" Ed asked.

"Who?"

"My dad, Buzz. He lives in one of these apartments, but I'm not sure which one."

"A man ain't lived here for months. Try that apartment over there," She said, slurring her words as she pointed over some brown grass to another door.

"Thanks," we said.

We walked across the brown grass and knocked on that door. A fat, tall man with messy hair, no front teeth, and a bottle of Night Train answered the door, "Yeah?"

"Does Buzz live here?" Ed asked.

"Buzz?" the man replied in his coarse voice.

"Who is it?" someone in the background asked.

Ed said, "Yeah, my dad, Buzz."

The man opened the door wider, looked behind him and said, "Someone's looking for you."

A short, stocky man wearing boxer shorts with holes in them

and welts on his face got up from the cut-up, urine-stained sofa and exclaimed, "Craps!"

For some strange reason, Buzz always called Ed Craps.

Ed replied, "Hey, Dad!" as he walked in to hug him.

There were chairs haphazardly around the apartment, and wine bottles everywhere, and a small black-and-white television on an old kitchen table. His dad was surprised to see the only family who ever came to visit. Buzz proceeded to slur, "This is my ... drinkin' buddy, Judd."

We said, "Hi."

"So, what have ya been doin', Marine punk?" Buzz asked.

Ed chuckled and replied, "I'm an Airborne Ranger, Dad. Just like you were, remember?"

"Fuck the Rangers! Goddamn pussies!"

Buzz raised both his hands into a karate formation and said, "C'mon, Craps. Let's see how tough you are."

Ed laughed and copied his dad's moves, and jokingly said, "Dad, I don't wanna show you my Ranger skills. I might hurt ya."

Buzz said, "Oh, yeah, c'mon, Craps. I'll fuck you up."

I began to laugh.

Ed advanced toward him and helped his drunk dad to the sofa, saying, "Dad, I could kick your ass all over this apartment. Sit down over here and let's just talk."

"Eh, fuck it!" Buzz said. "I'm too tired to kick your ass."

We laughed.

Ed asked, "So what've you been doing with your life?"

"Drinkin' booze and more of it," Buzz replied, with a drunken smirk on his face.

"Drinkin' booze?" Ed said. "You know that stuff's not good for ya."

"Whatta ya talkin' about? It's better than sex!"

"Is it?" I replied.

"Goddamn right it is!"

We all laughed.

Ed said, "So whatta you gonna do today?"

"Get me a woman."

That amused Ed, and he said, "I thought you said booze is better than sex?"

"It is," Buzz replied.

"Then why do want a woman?"

"'Cause I do it better when I'm drunk."

"How do you know you can still even get it up?"

"Whatta ya mean? I could be unconscious and my dick would still be hard!" Buzz said.

Ed laughed and said, "Dad, you're crazy. What's on the tube?"

"Nothin'. There's nothin' ever on," Buzz said. "Hey, why don't you get me a woman?"

"Dad, I'm not gonna get you a woman. Besides, the woman I would get would be a slut. You don't want that."

"How do you know what I want? You don't know shit, punk!"

Ed said, "Dad, you'll just get a disease or something, then you won't be able to have sex at all."

Buzz said, "I'll put a rubber on."

"Let's talk about something else," Ed suggested. "I'm tired of talking about women."

"Ah," Buzz said to his roommate, "hey, Judd, get me a drink."

"Hey, Ed," I said, "we have to go."

Ed asked, "Is there anything you need, Dad?"

Buzz slurred, "Yeah, yeah, why don't you get me some wine down the street?"

"Some wine? You don't need wine. Look at that gallon you have sittin' on the table."

"That's my backup bottle," Buzz replied.

Ed and I laughed.

"Backup? That bottle should last you a few weeks."

Buzz smiled and slurred, "I could drink that bottle in twenty minutes. So why don't ya go to the store and get me a bottle of uh ... Night Train."

Ed got up from the sofa and said, "We gotta go, Dad. I love ya!"

We walked toward the door, and I opened it. Buzz grabbed Ed by his jacket before we left and slurred, "You need some money, food stamps or something?"

"No, Dad, I don't need any money. Why don't you use that money to buy some underwear."

"What's wrong with my underwear?"

"They've got holes all over them!" Ed exclaimed.

"I just wear these around the house."

"We gotta go, Dad. I love ya," Ed said, leaving the apartment as I followed.

"Come see me again, punk!" Buzz yelled out, as we walked toward the car.

We drove off, and there was a silence in the car as if Ed was thinking about something.

I wanted to break the silence, so when I came to the third or fourth stoplight I asked, "Why do they call your dad Buzz? Is it because he's always buzzing?"

Ed grinned and answered, "No, man, his name is Edmond. Though I never thought about it that way."

Weeks later, Ed discovered Missy wasn't pregnant, which took a huge burden off his mind. The following weekend, word got out I was having a keg at Macleay Park. That Saturday we drove to the industrial area in the Northwest where there were several different breweries and rented a keg of Budweiser and a Diamond tap.

We brought it to my house and put it in a tub of cold water. We later took it to Macleay Park in Stewart's Battlewagon. Bubba grabbed the keg from the Battlewagon and lifted it on his back. We walked up the trail and passed the first bridge and found a spot where there were lots of leaves. It was the perfect place to put the keg because if any cops came that night, we could camouflage it and come back later.

Everyone was there, including Wendy, Annette's thirteen-year-old sister. Their parents never really cared about where they were or what they did.

Stewart said, "Hey, Bubba, are you goin' to drink forty-eight cups of beer tonight and get sick all over the trail?"

"I'm gonna fuckin' drink this whole fuckin' keg before anybody gets here."

I laughed and said, "Bubba, if you drink that whole keg, Ed will lick your ass."

Stewart laughed and added, "Yeah, and Timmy will get sloppy seconds."

"That's nasty!" I said, with a disgusted look.

It was getting cold, but when it came to beer, it was easy to let the forces of nature pass us by. At about nine o'clock, people started to show up. Bubba was in charge of the keg and tap. Before anyone could drink beer, we collected three dollars from each person and gave them a sixteen-ounce, red plastic cup.

"Eddie," Bubba asked, "get me a cup so I can pour some of this brew?"

"Here," I replied, handing him the cup.

Bubba poured the beer into the cup and said, "Watch this."

He practically swallowed it.

"Damn! Bubba. You didn't even breathe."

"That's the way a man drinks beer."

I put All the money I made selling beer that night in my socks because I didn't have any pockets. By now Wendy was extremely intoxicated. I also noticed she kept forcing herself onto Ed.

Ed kept saying, "You're just a kid ... you're just a kid."

At the same time, Tim was saying, "Hey, Ed, what do you think about me joining the Marines? You think I could do it?"

"Yeah, Tim. You could do it," Ed said. "Wendy, why don't you go back to the Battlewagon or something."

"Why?"

"Wendy, I told you you're just a kid."

Tim said, "Ed, Ed, what do you think?"

"Why don't you join the Rangers?" Ed asked.

"'Cause I wanna be a Marine."

"Marines are Jar Heads!"

"They're the toughest out there."

"Tim, don't let the commercials fool you."

Cynthia stood beside me and the keg, watching everyone mingle. Suddenly someone from the bottom of the trail shouted, "Cops!"

Everyone panicked. I looked over to Bubba and yelled, "Bubba, help me hide the keg!"

We set the keg down and quickly threw leaves over it.

"Fuck, fuck, fuckin' cops, man!" Bubba said angrily. "I can't even fuckin' slam a beer without some pig showing up!"

"C'mon, Bubba! Hurry up!" I exclaimed. "They're getting closer."

People dropped their filled cups of beers and tried to find a place to hide. Bubba and I ran up the dark trail. I could see two flashlights not far behind us. We ran as far as an old, cement building we called "the Witches' Castle." There was a long-time myth about witches who lived up there at one time.

I couldn't find Ed, so I yelled, "Ed! Ed! Where are you!"

We ran further and further up the dark trail. Ed was on the second bridge just past the Witches' Castle. I couldn't believe my eyes. Wendy and Ed were kissing. With all of the commotion going on, I ignored what they were doing and kept running up the trail. As the lights behind us got closer, I heard laughter, then turned around.

"What the hell?" I said, "I can't believe it! They're Lincoln students."

"What?" Bubba added, "I'm gonna kick some ass."

"Chill, Bubba. Chill," I said, stopping him.

"I'm pissed, Eddie ... makin' me run all the way up this trail and shit."

"Hey, man, at least they're not real cops."

Bubba wiped the beads of sweat off his face with his forearm and said, "I need a beer."

At first we were all upset, but that didn't stop us from going back to the keg and finishing it off. The party ended about twelve-thirty a.m., and we brought the empty keg back down the trail. We all saw Ed walking toward the Battlewagon with Wendy. I pretended nothing was wrong, but was angry with him for kissing her.

162

The following morning we ate breakfast and jogged across the Broadway Bridge. We jogged passed Wallace Park and up at least a hundred stairs, which led us to Hillside Community Center, a place where all the rich kids went to play basketball. Our walk back down gave me the opportunity to talk to Ed.

"Ed, what were you doing kissing Wendy last night?"

"Wendy's a nice girl."

"Ed, she's just a kid."

Ed went silent for a moment and said, "Yeah, I know."

"Well, why'd you do it?"

"I don't know. She's a lot smarter than you think and acts a lot older."

"C'mon, Ed, you can't be serious." I said. If you keep doin' this shit, you're gonna go to jail."

"I kept tellin' her she was just a kid, but she still kept comin' at me."

"Ed, out of all the crazy things you've done, this is the dumbest," I said, with an authoritative voice. "You can't see her Ed. You can't!"

"Yeah, I know. You're right," Ed said, "let's just forget it for now, okay."

"All right, but promise me you're not gonna see her anymore?"

"I promise. I promise."

"Cool."

As often as Ed tried to avoid her, Wendy didn't make it easy. She constantly visited Ed at his house and partied with us on weekends.

Chapter Twenty-Five

In order for me to graduate with the class of 1986, I had to study harder than ever to pass my "competency tests." I showed up every day to class, and Mrs. Wagner stepped me through my math, reading, and comprehension skills. It was hard because many times I just couldn't stay focused, but I knew it was important to my dad and myself for me to get my diploma.

When the day came for me to receive my diploma, I had butterflies in my stomach on the bus toward Civic Auditorium in downtown Portland. Across from the auditorium was Keller Fountain, which consisted of several, man-made waterfalls. Later, Ed and Edith met us there and took pictures of us in a parking lot south of the fountain.

Cynthia and I walked toward the fountain and admired the waterfall.

"This is beautiful," I said. "I'm glad you're here, Cindy."

"I wouldn't miss this for anything," she replied, kissing me on the cheek. "You worked hard for this."

"Hard to believe that, well, I'll be outta high school."

"Now you're going to move on to bigger things," Cynthia said.

"Yeah," I replied. "I don't know what's gonna happen from here."

"I'm sure whatever does happen, it's going to be good."

Edith showed up.

"Hi, Cindy."

"Oh, hi, Edith."

"Would you like to go inside with me?" Edith asked.

"Okay," Cindy replied, then to me she said, "I'll be inside with Edith. I love you and good job."

"Thanks, babe."

Ed swung his arm around my shoulders and said, "I'm proud of you. Your mom would be, too."

"Yeah, I wish she was here right now."

"She is, Eddie. She is. She's watching down from Heaven right now saying, 'There's my little, Puerto Rican wetback son. I'm so proud of him.'"

I laughed.

"You think so?" I asked.

"That's what I would say. C'mon, let's go inside. It's almost time."

"Okay."

We went inside the auditorium and when the ceremony began, Bubba and I couldn't find our seats along with several other students, so we held up the ceremony for several minutes. The announcer came out on stage and began to give a speech about the class of 1986. One student a few seats down threw his graduation cap up in the air and yelled, "Whoo!"

The announcer said, "I'm not embarrassed, they're your kids."

Everyone laughed.

For the second half of the ceremony, all the seniors went backstage and waited to be called on to receive their diploma.

A staff member came up to me and asked, "Eddie, how would you like your name to be announced?"

"Um, how 'bout *Eddie Stallion Regory?*"

"Is that what you want?" he asked in a hurried manner.

"Yeah, that's how I want it."

When it was time for my name to be called out, the announcer said, "Eddie Stallion Regory!"

I felt proud wearing my red robe and cap in front of all those people, but I wished my dad could have made it. I walked out toward the stage, received my diploma, and did a two-step dance.

When the ceremony ended, they had a pizza party for the seniors at the YMCA Club. There were card games, bingo, and other activities that lasted all night. The next morning, we went on the *USS Kansas City* for breakfast. When I left the ship for home that next morning, I felt a sense of accomplishment.

The best thing about summer was that Ed and I rode our bikes everywhere. It was a bond we had. So one day, we rode our bikes all over Portland. We even raced down Burnside. It felt like moving at the speed of light, as people watched us weave in and out of traffic. We rode side-by-side.

"Hey, Eddie?" Ed yelled.

"Yeah."

"Let's go play tag at Couch Park."

"Right now?"

"Yeah," Ed answered, "it'll give us something to do."

We rode there and parked our bikes close to the school. It was about eleven o'clock in the evening. We played tag on the structure, and minutes later, we saw a police car drive through the park. The car slowed down and stopped in front of the structure. A police officer stepped out and proceeded toward us.

"Hey? You need to get down and leave the park, now!" the cop demanded.

I stood there on the structure staring down at him and said, "Why? It's not even twelve o'clock. Doesn't the park close at twelve?"

Ed didn't say anything. Instead, he stepped off the structure and tried to be inconspicuous.

I continued, "That's not right! We shouldn't hafta leave the park if we're not makin' noise or botherin' anyone."

The impatient officer reached his right arm over his club and quickly pulled it out. He clenched his hand tighter around the handle and said, "Get down or get hurt!"

Ed walked further away when the officer demanded, "You stay right there! You don't go anywhere. I want to talk to you."

I proceeded nervously toward the officer, as he'd requested. He held his club close to his body while I stood there wondering what was going to happen next.

The officer asked, "Why didn't you come down when I asked you?"

"Because I … I … I don't think it's right for you to push us around, man."

He shouted, "Get on your stomach, now!"

I didn't think that was wise because, where I came from, getting on your belly for a cop could mean your life.

"Why?" I asked.

That's when my insurrection caused the cop to grab me by the back of my shirt and throw me down toward the cement ground.

"Get down!" he shouted, putting his heavy foot on my back, where the heel of his shoe depressed firmly on my spine. I felt the point of his club solidly pressed against the back of my neck. He did a pat-down search. "Stupid kid."

At this point I didn't know where Ed was.

I then heard Ed yelling, "Leave my friend alone! Leave him alone! We didn't do anything to you."

The officer suddenly released the pressure of his foot. I quickly got up and turned my head, and saw Ed holding a huge, heavy steel, garbage can lid. I saw the officer put his hand on the grip of his gun.

I shouted, "Ed, run!"

Because of Ed's diversion, I ran the opposite way. I glanced over my shoulder and saw Ed running faster than I've ever seen him run. There was no way the officer could catch him.

"Hey! Stop! Stop!" the cop, yelled.

I ran behind the backyards of some old houses. It was dark and I couldn't see. I suddenly came to a complete halt when I ran into a clothesline.

"Ugh!" I gasped one last breath and landed flat on my back.

I grabbed my neck, rubbing it to soothe the pain, and stayed there for a while. The officer didn't know we rode to the park, so I knew Ed would later meet me by our motorcycles. I got up and wandered around the neighborhood. I walked to the Food Mart a couple of blocks west from Couch Park.

I glanced at the clock on the wall and saw it was one o'clock in the morning. I walked back to Couch Park to see if Ed was there. Staring across the basketball court, I saw Ed standing there by our motorcycles, looking around to see where I was.

I cried out, "Ed!"

"Eddie!"

"What happened? Where's the cop?" I asked.

"Man, Eddie, I was scared. He called for backup and they looked for me in the building Hazel and Tamara used to live in."

"You mean that building on Everett?"

"Yeah, that one," Ed said. "That fuckin' cop was an asshole!"

"You tellin' me, man," I said. "Why do ya suppose he was pushin' his shit around like that?"

"I don't know ... maybe it's because we're white. I knocked on Hazel's old apartment, then remembered she didn't live there anymore."

"So what'd you do?"

"I hid," Ed said. "But before I got to the building, I stopped and looked at the cop straight in the eyes and pointed my finger at him and said, 'The laws of justice will put you in your place.'"

"What did he say?"

"Man, I just ran after that. That fat cop couldn't catch me."

We laughed.

"Damn, dude. I can't believe what you did. You were movin' out."

Ed replied, "I never ran so fast in my life."

"I know. One second you were there, the next, about three blocks down."

"Let's get outta here 'fore he comes back," Ed said.

We got back on our motorcycles and rode to the 7-Eleven on 39th and Powell. Ed bought two Big Gulps. We rode back to Ed's house and went into his room. I could see he was a bit distressed. He took off his Nike running shoes and sat on his bed.

"Ed, you okay?"

"Yeah, I'm just ticked off," Ed replied, tilting his head down. "Why did he have to come and do that for? It's just not right."

"Because he was a prick!" I blurted. "Dude didn't have anything else to do."

We didn't say much after that. Ed turned off the lights and

we fell asleep. About five-thirty that morning, Ed was screaming, "Ah! Ah! Ah!"

I woke from the noise and my eyes weren't adjusted to the dark, so I quickly asked, "Ed, Ed, what's wrong?"

I was startled, but not surprised, only because I'd seen him do this before. Ed mumbled some gibberish and went back to sleep. I knew it was a bad dream. Ed thought his violent dreams were because of the spicy food he ate. I felt it was because of the military and how they deprogrammed his mind into being a different person.

Chapter Twenty-Six

About one-thirty, Ed went into the kitchen to make breakfast.

"What's up, Ed?"

"Nothin'. Have a seat. I'm makin' some energy food."

"What is it?"

"It's my power breakfast. It has white bread with eggs, cinnamon, vanilla extract, and butter."

"Sounds healthy," I said sarcastically. "Whatta you call it?"

"Peanut butter French toast."

He put two plates of French toast on the table and grabbed a jar of Adam's peanut butter out from the cupboard.

"This is the best peanut butter in the world," Ed said, "try it on your French toast."

"You want me to put this on my food?" I asked, leery of what it might taste like.

"Yeah, go 'head. It's good. Try it," Ed said, as he picked up a butter knife and spread some on my French toast. He then opened a new bottle of syrup and drenched my French toast with it.

"That's enough, man," I said, "that's way too much."

Ed said, "Mom, did you know Al met his wife at thirteen? Right, Eddie?"

"Yeah," I replied, still eating my breakfast.

"He did?" Edith asked. "Well, he must've loved her very much to see her at thirteen years of age. How is your dad doing?"

"He's okay, Edith. He sends his love to you."

"Well, you tell him I love him, too."

"I will." I looked over to Ed and said, "Say, man, this is awesome! Where'd ya come up with this peanut butter French toast idea?"

"A guy from the barracks showed me how to do it." Ed

suggested enthusiastically, "Hey, why don't we take the bus downtown today"

"The bus? Are you crazy! We've been takin' buses for years, and now that we have wheels you wanna take a bus? No way, man. Not me."

"C'mon, man. It'll be good for us," Ed said. "We'll go see that movie *Heartbreak Ridge*."

"All right. But we'll hafta come back and get our bikes later, because I'm not fittin' on stayin' out all night without my wheels."

After breakfast, we got dressed and caught the number 9 bus downtown.

It was about three p.m., and the movie wasn't starting until five-fifteen at the Fox Theater. We began to walk toward the Old Town area north of Burnside.

We saw homeless people lying against dirty alleyways, and some roaming the streets with cheap bottles of wine.

"I bet my dad's down here," Ed said. "How can a country so rich treat the people who live in it so poorly?"

"I don't know, man. It's just the way it is."

Ed walked over to a homeless person sitting against a storefront and asked, "Hey, buddy, you hungry?"

The man, with his dirty, long beard, wrinkled face, and tired eyes looked up at Ed and nodded.

"C'mon," Ed said, helping the man up to his feet. "We'll take ya to get some food."

We took the man to the Burger King on West Burnside. Between the both of us, we had about twelve dollars. Just enough money to see the movie and buy concessions. But Ed didn't think about any movie. His purpose now was to give this homeless person a warm meal and whatever else he needed.

I wasn't surprised, because Ed was very generous and caring. If anyone needed something, he gave it to him or her with no questions asked. Like the time he took a new pair of army boots off his feet and gave them to his uncle because he liked them.

The old man was a bit incoherent, so Ed ordered for him.

"Hi, uh, how 'bout two whoppers and fries."

"Is there anything else?" the cashier asked.

"No, that's it."

Ed paid, and we sat down and watched the man eat his food. He didn't say much. Although you could see in his eyes he was thankful.

Ed put his arm around the man and said, "Hold on there, buddy. You're gonna choke if you don't slow down."

The old man smiled while eating his two Whoppers and fries. I knew we were going to miss the movie, but I also knew it was for a good reason. The man finished his food and sat quietly.

Ed asked, "Hey, buddy, you want us to take you back?"

The man nodded his head, and so we walked him back.

Before we left him, he looked at Ed with his sad, oppressed eyes and quietly said, "George."

"George? Good to meet ya, George," Ed said. "Eddie, give me a couple of bucks."

"Why?"

"Because I'm gonna give it to him."

"But he'll buy alcohol with it."

"Does it matter? If it'll make him happy before he dies, so what."

I gave Ed my last five-dollar bill, and he gave it to the man. Afterwards, we didn't have enough money to see the movie, so we walked over to Keller Fountain.

Ed said, "Ya know, I gotta quit drinkin'."

"Well then, let's both get in better shape like we used to be and stop drinkin'," I said. "Ya know the one thing I'm afraid of?"

"What?"

"Not gettin' anywhere with my life," I said. "When my mom died, I promised her I'd do something with myself, and here I am, doin' nothin'."

"You ain't no bum, Eddie. You're just a Puerto Rican wetback," Ed said jokingly.

"Don't you ever wonder where you're goin' or what you're

gonna do with your life?" I asked.

"Yeah, I do all the time," Ed replied quietly.

"Maybe I'll write a book or something," I said. "My dad always told me that I was philosophical."

"What would you write?" Ed asked curiously.

"I don't know. Maybe I'll write about you," I said. "Yeah, I'll write about how you wish you were like me and that I have enormous power over your weak, Airborne Ranger ass."

I laughed and pretended I was going to push him into the water. I kept doing it until Ed surprisingly jumped into the cold, running water with his clothes on.

In disbelief I yelled, "Dude! You're nuts!"

"C'mon in. The water's cold."

I hesitated, but couldn't stand knowing my best friend was having all the fun making a complete idiot of himself, so I jumped in too.

"Whoo!"

We splashed the water and played in it like two kids. When we were done playing, we dripped water all the way back to the bus stop. People looked at us like we were crazy, but we didn't care. When we got to Ed's house, we put some dry clothes on and stayed up to watch the Johnny Carson show.

The next evening we rode our motorcycles to Wallace Park and sat in the shelter, the whole time watching Tim try to play basketball against Bubba and Joey. We had two beers left from a six-pack we'd bought at Thurman Mart, a storefront across the street from Friendly House. We saw headlights of a car slowly making its way into the park. We knew it was a cop car so Bubba shouted, "Hide the beers!"

We weren't intoxicated, but some of us were under-age at the time. Ed was the only one who could purchase alcohol. The car made its way toward the basketball court, and two cops stepped out. At first I couldn't see their faces, but when they proceeded closer, I saw them clearly. Ed sat beside me, and I knew we thought the same thing: one of them was the same black cop who saw us at Couch Park.

"Whatta ya guys doin' out here?" the cop asked.

We were nervous and scared that the cop would know who we were.

"Nothin'," we replied.

I tried not to look him in the eyes too much, afraid of him recognizing me as well.

The cop asked, shinning his light around the area, "Have you guys been drinkin'?"

"No, we haven't. We've just been playing hoops," Joey answered.

I noticed he was paying a little more attention to Ed.

"I think I know you," the cop said with uncertainty.

I decided to interrupt and politely said, "Officer, we can leave now if you'd like."

"I know you guys," the cop said. "You're the same guys who were at that other park."

"Other park?" I exclaimed, acting like I had no idea what he was talking about.

"You just cut your hair, didn't you?" the cop said to Ed. "Stand up. Turn your back around—give me your hands!"

The cop handcuffed him, put him in the police car, and questioned him awhile longer. They took Ed downtown from there. We were pissed-off, and the next day, Ed got out on his own recognizance.

Part Four: Year 1987

Chapter Twenty-Seven

Tim decided to join the Marines even though I tried to convince him not to. I managed to get a new job at the Lloyd Cinema Theater in Northeast Portland, working the graveyard shift as a janitor. I loved it because I could hang out on the rooftop and eat my lunch. The bright neon signs, huge theater screens, and THX sound gave me the feeling of being in Hollywood. But I'd always had a sincere passion for the movies and often dreamt of being in one.

I saw all the free movies and often asked Dad if he wanted to go see one, but he felt he was too fat to fit in the seats and thought people would look at him and think he was a freak. I assured him I wasn't embarrassed and didn't care what people thought, but often wished he was healthier so we could do more things together.

When Dad had nothing to do, he enjoyed working with wood. He'd build boats or cut out pictures from animal magazines to use as patterns for his next wood project. When he was done, he'd give them away to the neighbors or anyone who liked them. It was a way for him to keep his sanity, especially after Mom died.

Sometimes we would have long talks about Mom, and he would cry wishing Mom was alive. Many times I felt helpless in trying to comfort him. When he was in anguish about Mom's death, I would sit on his bed powdered, from the cornstarch, and wrap my arm around his obese back, showing him kindness.

But being without a mother was difficult for me. Even though Dad proved he could be a father and a mother.

When Dad was in the mood, he sang opera while doing the dishes. He surprised me with his talented voice. I encouraged him to sing more, but he would always say it took too much air out of him.

I didn't always get along with Dad. Once I came home upset from school and Dad noticed.

"What's wrong, son?" he asked.

"Everything ... everything Dad. I'm tired of just gettin' by, seein' everyone else get ahead. I'm sick of all these minimum wage jobs, never having enough money to get what I want, and I can barely make my motorcycle payments."

"You'll get yours someday. Just give it time. Life's not like the movies. You gotta work for what you want, and you gotta work hard for it!"

"I'm tired of working hard. I am working hard, all the time ... I work and what do I get? Nothing," I shouted. "Why do we have to be poor? Why couldn't you make things better for us?"

"Son, I tried! Don't you think that if I had the money I would give you whatever you needed. Don't you think if I could've given your mother a better life I would have? I would help your sister get well again and help your brothers. I hate livin' this way! I can't even afford a pair of decent underwear because I'm in hock up to my ears. Who knows, maybe I could've had your mom live a little longer. My poor wife, she didn't deserve to die!"

Dad got into his wheelchair then rolled himself back into his room (like he always did after an argument) and cried on his used-up handkerchief.

I felt crappy. Then walked into his room and said, "Dad, I'm sorry. I didn't mean to say those things."

"It's not your fault. You're right. All my life I've worked nothin' but labor jobs, barely gettin' by … prayin'… hopin' for somethin' better to come along. But nothing's gonna knock on your door and give you your dream," Dad said, then blowing his nose with his white handkerchief. "You gotta go out there and earn it. You gotta want it so bad you can taste it. But if you live your life the way I did mine, you'll never want anything but death."

"Dad, don't say that. It's not your fault. Life's not so bad. I just see people like Cynthia who have all these nice things and new cars and wish I had them."

"You'll get them, Eddie. You will. But what does it all matter if you don't have God in your heart. You could die tomorrow, and then where would you take your money and cars. Follow your heart? Do the important things in life, and the rest will follow. I promise! You got your mother's will and ambition ... you've just gotta believe, believe you can do anything."

I moved closer and said, "I'm sorry. I shouldn't have gotten so angry."

"It's okay, son. Come here."

I sat beside him on his bed and he put his hand on mine and said, "Eddie, you have the most precious, wonderful gift in the world. You have your health. Once you've got that, nothing can stop you from making a buck. But remember this, if I die tomorrow you will go on with your life whether you make it or not. You will survive. And one day you'll realize that after everyone you ever loved is gone, making it will not seem as important. If I were a rich man today, I'd give all of it away in a second to be with your mom. I would not think twice about it. But that's not how it works."

Dad blew his nose.

I got up and said, "You really think we'll see mom again?"

"If I didn't, I'd be dead now."

I left the room thinking about what I had said. Dad always said, "Words can cut harder than actions." How true that was.

Dad fought in the Korean War, earned every medal possible including the Bronze Star, and got nothing in return, except for a small place to live and an occasional, disrespectful idiot who came over from housing (Section-H) to check on the apartment.

I'll never forget the day I stayed in my room because some guy from Section-H was coming. I wasn't supposed to be living there because I was eighteen.

The man knocked on the door and Dad answered, "Come in, sir. Come in."

I stayed in bed and listened to the conversation they had.

The man proceeded to say, "So, did you bust any walls in the house?"

"No sir, no sir. House is in good shape," Dad replied humbly.

"Where's your bathroom?" the man asked rudely.

"Over there, sir. Right around the corner."

I wanted so bad to go out there and tell him to fuck off! I knew Dad was hoping the man wouldn't check my room, because if he did, there was a good chance they might take away Dad's Section-H privilege. And Dad was in no condition to work a job and pay his own rent.

The Section-H man checked every room in the house except for mine. He walked right past it and headed for the door with his clipboard and pen.

The man said, "You keep this place in good shape, you hear?"

"Oh, yes, sir. Sometimes my sons come over and mow the lawn."

The man left. I quickly got up and rushed into Dad's room and asked, "How could you let him talk to you like that? How?"

"Because son ... when ya have nothin', ya have to humble yourself."

"But, Dad, don't you have any pride?"

"Eddie, what do you expect me to do? If I told him I didn't like the way he was talking to me, he might've kicked us both out. And you're not even supposed to be here."

"Just because he's from Section-H doesn't mean he can step on you."

Dad got into his wheelchair, pushed himself into the living room, and sat quietly on his recliner.

I followed him out there ashamed of what I said.

"Dad, I'm sorry!"

"It's okay, Eddie. Forget it," Dad said, blowing his nose with his handkerchief. I went back into my room, turned on the radio, lay down and stared at my ceiling.

Chapter Twenty-Eight

A week before Cynthia's graduation, Barry, Cynthia's step dad, lent me a red 1987 Porsche 944 Turbo with spoilers on it. It was like a dream come true for me. I felt like the "king of the road." The same week, Cynthia went looking for a prom dress, and my tuxedo wouldn't be ready until the day before the prom.

I hurried over to Ed's place and knocked on the door.

"Hey, Eddie, what's up?"

"Ed, come check this out!"

"What?"

"Come out here," I said, motioning him to follow me. "This is gonna flip your lid."

Ed walked out with me and said, "Can't you just tell me what it is?"

Suddenly I saw Ed's eyes open wide, focusing on the 944 Porsche parked on the street.

"Whatta you think?" I asked.

"Whatta you mean?"

"What do I mean? I mean this is my ride for Cynthia's prom."

"No way. Are you serious?"

"Dead serious," I said, "come on, I'll take you for a ride, poor boy."

Ed laughed and said, "I gotta tell my mom I'm leaving."

"Okay."

Ed rushed back, and we cruised 82nd Avenue for awhile, then merged onto the I-5 freeway. We hit a high speed of 137 mph. Ed put a tape in the Blaupunkt stereo, and we blasted to the sounds of "Staying Alive" by the Bee Gees and raced the Porsche northbound toward my house. When we got there, we parked the Porsche in the beat-up garage.

We strolled in the back door, and my dad was sitting on his recliner watching HBO on cable television.

"I dig your shades, Al," Ed said sarcastically, referring to the black garbage bags stapled over the living room windows.

I stood there laughing at his comment.

"Hey, man, they work," Dad replied.

"You too poor to buy blinds," Ed said theatrically, and with a funny expression on his face. "I gotta couple of bucks. Let me help you out."

"Yeah, I am poor. You got money? You gonna buy me some?" Dad said, slightly leaning over his recliner with his hand out and eyes wide. "Tch, man, you're not gonna buy me nothing."

"Yeah, Al, I'll buy ya some."

Ed was making me laugh so hard I couldn't breathe.

"Oh, man, I gotta sit down. This is too funny," I said. "Ed, you gotta quit."

Ed wrapped his arm around my dad's shoulders and said, "Youza poor nigga ... need me to buy ya some shades."

"Nah, man. I don't need you to buy me nothin'," Dad said proudly. "I like my poor man's shades."

Ed chuckled, then walked into the kitchen to get something to eat. Seeing a silver pot on the stove, he asked, "Whatcha cookin', Al?"

"Old recipe my mom used to make: hamhocks, chicken bones, chicken feet, beans ... all that good stuff."

"Mmmm ... sounds good ... yeah ... I like body-part soup."

"Ya know, you don't have to eat it, Ed," Dad said. "I'm not proud. I'll eat it. All of it, too. You know, you come into my house and start talkin' crap about my shades and food ... you can leave, Ed. The door swings both ways."

I interjected, "Dad, you'd eat anything that had a food label on it."

Dad pointed his finger at me and said, "Ah ... you see ... you forget where you came from."

"No, Dad, I didn't forget where I came from, I just know I ain't never ate that crap before."

"As far as I care, both you guys can starve!" Dad said. "I don't care."

"Say Ed, let's go out for tacos," I suggested.

"Yeah, maybe we can throw the tacos in with the soup," Ed added, laughing after he said it.

I laughed and said, "That's cold. That's cold-blooded."

"Go 'head, make fun if you want," Dad said. "But when you're hungry and your stomach is tight and bloated with air, you'll eat my body-part soup then."

"Al, I ain't ever gonna eat that soup!" Ed said, laughing so hard he began to tear. "You couldn't pay me."

"You wanna burrito or something, Dad?" I asked.

"Nah, man. I'm gonna eat my body-part soup and be content."

"Okay."

We drove to the Taco Time on Interstate Avenue in Northeast Portland. We ate two crispy burritos and cruised around until two o'clock in the morning, then headed back to my house.

"Hey, Ed."

"Yeah."

"Let's flip a coin to see who gets the floor."

"That's okay, I'll sleep on the floor."

"Thanks Ed. You da man."

We fell fast asleep, and later that morning, I heard noise coming from Ed. Because I was so tired, I stayed in bed and ignored him.

Suddenly I heard Ed screaming, "Ah! Ah! Ah!" raving through the house like a madman.

I then heard the television fall over. My dad was sleeping in his recliner when this happened. Finally Ed woke up, and I turned on the bedroom light. I saw him standing there in an incoherent state of mind.

"Ed, you okay?"

He shook his head and wiped the sweat off his forehead, then went back to sleep. I went out into the living room and saw a hole the size of a fist in the sheet-rock. I picked up the television and put it back on its stand. Dad looked shocked by what had just occurred.

"Dad, you okay?"

"He's not sleeping here no more," Dad said quietly.

I knew Dad didn't mean it, because he loved Ed like a son. I went back into my room, turned the light off, and crawled into my bed.

I quietly said, "Must've been the tacos."

The next day I said, "Ed, remember what happened this morning?"

"What?"

"Dude, you went crazy in my house."

"I did?"

"Yeah. Don't you remember?"

"Sort of."

"I can't believe you don't remember," I said, dropping the subject.

We drove the Porsche back to Ed's house to get our motorcycles. We rode to Terry and Jacob's house, and when we walked in, it was the usual scene: beer, marijuana, and cocaine laced the bar counter as the sounds of Jimmy Hendrix played in the background. Terry and Jacob were a couple of friends who lived up the block from Tim. They always had parties at their house. Partly because their mother was rarely home.

I went upstairs and grabbed two beers.

"Ed!" I called out, "here's a cold one."

"Thanks."

We went downstairs and sat on the sofa, watching Madonna on MTV on their big-screen television. At about three o'clock in the afternoon, I got up from the sofa, and Ed was at the bar talking to Jacob.

"Ed, let's go," I urged him.

"Hold on," Ed replied, cutting up lines of cocaine with a razor blade on the bar.

"Whatta you doin'?" I asked.

"Hold on," Ed said. "I'm trying to finish this."

He borrowed a straw from Jacob and quickly snorted two lines. At first I couldn't believe my eyes.

"What's it feel like?" I asked.

"It numbs your nose," Ed answered. "It's no big deal."

"Why you doin' it, then?"

"Nothing else to do."

"Let me try it?"

"Nope. It's not good for ya."

Jacob chuckled from behind the counter and said, "Just let him try it, Ed."

Ed said, "If I give this to him, he'll start trippin'."

"Man, I'm not gonna trip. You're the one who's trippin'," I said, motioning like I didn't care about trying it anymore. I sat down to watch MTV.

Chapter Twenty-Nine

On June 6th 1987, after Cynthia's graduation, we decided to celebrate at the Alexis Hotel on the waterfront downtown. Ed showed up with Julie and so did Tim and Bubba. It was a casual party with champagne and a lot of joking around. At about nine-thirty in the evening, we were feeling tipsy from the drinking. I heard a knock on the front door and went to answer it. It was two guys in hotel uniforms.

"Hi, we're hotel security and we just wanted to make sure everything was okay in there."

I answered, "Yeah, everything's fine. Why?"

"Well, one of the guest's said there was loud noises coming from this room."

"I'm sorry. We'll try to keep it down."

"Thank you," they said, and left.

I closed the door and blurted, "Man, I paid a hundred and fifty bucks for this room with no windows, and they're bitchin'."

"What happened?" Bubba asked.

"Oh, just a couple of wannabe cops at the door checking up on us rowdy graduates."

I went into the kitchen, and Ed followed behind.

"Hey, Eddie."

"What's up?"

"Can I talk to you for a sec'?"

"Yeah, man, what's up?"

"Let's go in here," Ed said, walking into the master bedroom.

He had a perplexed look on his face as if something was seriously wrong.

"What's up, Ed?"

"Sit down."

I sat on the bed and anxiously waited for whatever he was going to say.

He continued. "Eddie, man, I gotta tell ya something ... you're not gonna like this."

"What, what?"

Ed was making hand motions and rubbing his head in bewilderment, then blurted, "Wendy's pregnant."

"What?"

"She's ... she's pregnant," Ed reluctantly repeated.

"What? How? What do you mean she's pregnant? She's only thirteen years old!" I said. "How could that happen?"

"I know. I know."

"What the fuck! Ed. How did it happen? I mean, I know how it happened but why?"

"It just happened."

"Ed, I want more than just that."

"It just happened. It just happened," Ed said, in a distressed tone.

"Goddamn! Ed, this has to be the most fucked-up thing you've done. Do Wendy's parents know?"

"Not yet. You're the only one I've told. Eddie, I'm scared, man."

I tried to be as sympathetic as possible, but I really didn't know how to handle it.

"Are you still seeing her?" I asked.

"No, not really. I don't want to abort it, Eddie. I'll take care of her and the baby."

"It's not that easy, Ed. You got a big problem. What if they find out? What are you gonna do? How long has it been since you've known?"

"I don't know, a while now," Ed said. "I'm sorry, Eddie! I'm sorry!"

"Are you gonna abort it?"

"No, no way!" Ed said firmly.

"Ed, you gotta think about this. I don't believe in abortion either, but do you really think her parents are gonna let her have the baby? I doubt it."

Ed began to cry.

"It'll be okay, bro. Things will work out." I hugged him and said, "Look, we'll finish this later. Let's go back out there, and I'll meet you tomorrow and we'll talk about this more."

"Okay."

"Here, wipe your eyes," I said, handing Ed a wet towel from the master bathroom.

After five minutes or so, we left the room. Even when I made love to Cynthia that night, she knew something was bothering me.

One hot, sunny day, Cynthia invited me to go swimming at her grandfather's house. I was having a good time doing belly-flops and backward dives. Cynthia's mother was sipping her Margarita in the pool house. Cynthia's grandfather didn't even bother to come out and say hello to me. After a couple of hours of playing in the pool, I was so hungry I would've eaten liver.

I heard Cynthia call from the patio, "Eddie, let's go!"

I got out of the pool and wrapped a white towel around my waist.

"Put your clothes on, too," Cynthia said.

"Okay."

When I walked into the house, the maid was preparing hamburgers. My mouth was salivating, and I could feel the hunger coming on even stronger. I knew if I were at my house, I would've been picking the meat out of the pan.

Cynthia said, "Eddie, follow me."

"Where are we going?"

At first I thought we were going to eat somewhere else.

Cynthia said, "I'm gonna take you to your house, okay."

"Why?"

"Well, my grandfather wants me back up here."

"Why, Cynthia?

She hesitated and answered, "He wants me to eat with them."

"I thought you were gonna eat with me?"

"I'm sorry, Eddie," Cynthia said, "he … he … he told me to take you home."

I vehemently said, "What the fuck! Why? Are you guys

short on burgers or somethin'? Or is it because he's thinks I'm a poor, ghetto piece of trash!"

"No, Eddie. That's not fair. He just wants to make it a family thing."

"Cynthia, I don't know where your family's from, but where I'm from, when you invite someone to your house, you treat them as a guest, not like shit! And that's the way I feel I've just been treated. Didn't you say something to him? Didn't you think it was sort of wrong? Or are you just protecting your future investment?"

"What's that supposed to mean?"

"You know exactly what I'm talking about. Why should you stand up for me? You got everything anybody could ever want, freely! Why should you care about me?"

"Eddie, it's not what it looks like. He doesn't hate you."

"How could he? He doesn't even know me."

"Eddie, stop," Cynthia said. "What am I supposed to do? What do you want of me?"

"Cynthia, don't you have any control of your life? Why are you always trying to please your family? You could have told him he was wrong. Even when my dad does something I don't like, I tell him. But I think it's deeper than what I'm saying ... I think you're afraid because he's got your future in the palm of his hand. Why should you blow it on me? I've got no rich future for you. I've only given you my love and my heart, but I guess that wasn't enough."

Cynthia began to cry.

When we arrived at my house, I hurried out of the car and slammed the door. Cynthia rushed out after me.

"Cynthia, just leave! Leave!" I shouted. "I'll go to McDonald's or something."

"Eddie, wait!" Cynthia said, trying to stop me from opening the front door to my house.

I slammed the front door, and she knocked heavily saying, "Eddie, open the door. Please, Eddie, open the door! It's not what you think."

"Cynthia, go home. Go home to your rich daddy and

mommy," I declared from behind the door. "You think I like knowing I've got nothing to offer you. You think it's easy for me to not be accepted into your world?"

Eventually, she left, and I called Ed.

"Hey, Ed."

"Whazzup, wetback?"

"Hey, Ed, you wanna go to Terry's and Jacob's house?"

"Sure."

"I'll use my dad's station wagon and pick you up."

"Okay."

About an hour later we got to Terry and Jacob's.

Terry answered the door, "Hey guys, come in."

The house smelled of marijuana.

"What's up, Terry?" I asked. "What's goin' on?"

"Not much. Party's downstairs."

We followed him. I saw Bubba, relaxed on the sofa watching television and drinking a Hamm's beer.

"Hey, Bubba," I said sarcastically, "I see you've upgraded your beer."

Bubba replied, "Yeah, just like your woman."

We laughed.

"Why you gotta go there?" I asked.

"You asked for it," Bubba replied.

People were lined up at the bar taking bong hits of marijuana through a plastic round tube. Ed went over there, and I began chatting with Bubba. I looked over my shoulder, and Ed and Jacob were taking bong-hits together.

I got up from the sofa and asked, "Say, man, let me try that?"

"You don't smoke," Ed said. "Besides, it's not good for you."

"You guys don't know how to smoke that shit. That's the problem," I said, acting cocky. "Ed, let me try it, c'mon."

"It's not a good idea," Ed said, inhaling more smoke from the bong.

Ed didn't always smoke pot, but when he did, he inhaled

huge hits beyond belief. Terry passed me the bong.

"Whatta you want me to do with this?" I asked.

"You don't know?"

"No, man. Show me."

Terry brought the bong close to his lips and said, "Make sure you seal your lips around it, then suck the shit out of it like this."

He began sucking the smoke from the bong, held it for a few seconds then let it all out.

"That's it?" I asked.

"That's it," he said, "child's play."

I picked up the bong, and Ed watched. I inhaled more smoke than I wanted. For a few minutes I didn't feel anything, then everything started to spin around me, and my legs began to feel heavy.

"Ed, man, something's happening. I can't breathe!" I said, walking unsteadily toward the sofa. "This is weird."

"Eddie, just relax," Ed said. "Go lay down."

"Okay."

I went to lie on the sofa, and for most of the evening, I was in another state of mind, not able to control any of my actions. I kept laughing at anything and anyone, then got to a point where I felt like I was going to die.

"Let's go home, stoner," Ed said, with a chuckle.

I got up slowly and said, "Damn, this isn't gonna go away."

"Just give it time. You smoked a lot at once."

Ed merged onto the I-5 going north. I looked up at the freeway sign to Seattle and said, "Ed, I keep seeing the Seattle sign, man. There it is again! Ed ... what's goin' on?"

"Just relax," Ed said. "It's the pot trippin' you out."

Everything seemed like slow motion. It took forever to get where we were going.

Finally, we got to Ed's house. He parked the car out front and said, "Why don't you go walk it off."

"Where do I go?"

"Anywhere. If you're not back in twenty minutes, I'll come lookin' for you."

"Okay," I replied and started walking.

After walking awhile, I saw a phone booth and made a collect call to Cynthia.

"Cindy?"

"Eddie?"

I asked, "Whatta you doin'?"

"Nothing. What are you doing? You sound strange."

"I'm high," I said. "Can you come pick me up?"

"What do you mean you're high? Do you mean *pot* high?"

"Yep."

"Where are you?"

"I don't know. I think ... I think ... I see a lot of cars around," I replied.

"Eddie, do you know what time it is?"

"No, uh ... forget it. I'll find my way back."

"Find your way back? To where?"

"It doesn't matter. I gotta go! Bye."

"Eddie," Cynthia said before I hung up the phone, "I love you!"

"Yeah," I replied, then hung up.

I realized I wasn't far from Ed's house because some of the area began to look familiar. Maybe because the marijuana was wearing off. I found my way back to Ed's and saw him sitting on the steps waiting for me.

"Hey Ed," I said, walking toward him, "dude, I'm feelin' better. But I'm never gonna smoke that shit again."

I sat beside Ed, and he looked distressed.

"What's wrong?"

He shook his head from side-to-side, gesturing to me nothing was wrong. But I knew Ed better than that.

I continued, "You gonna talk to me or what?"

"Yeah," Ed replied quietly.

"Well, if you're not gonna talk to me—dude, I'm never smoking dope again. That was potent!"

Ed grinned and glanced at me, and I noticed his eyes were glossy from crying.

"Ed, man, tell me what's up?"

"Wendy's parents are pressing charges," Ed said. "They wanna … they wanna kill my baby, Eddie. They wanna kill my baby!"

All I could do was listen.

I sighed and said, "Look, Ed … I uh … I don't know what to say, man. Does your mom know?"

"No. And they won't let me see or talk to Wendy or tell them that I'm willing to be the father of the baby. I fucked up, Eddie. I fucked up."

"Ed, we all fuck up … some fuck-ups are worse than others, but we have to tackle them the best we can. I take it they're gonna have Wendy abort it."

Ed said, "I talked to Annette, and she said Wendy had no choice in the matter. I wish I could start over."

I had no words of advice to give him. It was difficult for me to take and understand. Shortly after, we went up to his room and neither of us said a word.

The next day we drove back to my house to pick up our motorcycles.

I didn't tell Cynthia about Wendy's pregnancy, partly because I didn't want her to think differently of Ed. He had problems, big problems, and I felt they had only gotten worse when he tried to re-adjust as a civilian.

Chapter Thirty

When Cynthia left on vacation, I kept every note and postcard she sent to me. She would keep every letter and card I gave her in a little shoe box. This time Cynthia had looked into several more colleges and knew that once she left, we would separate.

I thought it was an opportunity for her mother to finally get rid of me. I never believed that Cynthia's mother liked me. I didn't see much of her father, either. He was always playing tennis or working at the Porsche dealership.

It was obvious that the only time Barry wanted to play "Dad" was when he was nosy about Cynthia's private life. I once got a call about nine o'clock in the evening. It was Cynthia, crying over the phone.

"Cynthia? What's wrong? What's wrong?"

"Eddie, this is embarrassing for me to say … but … Barry … Barry found my shoe box."

"And?"

"Eddie, he found out I was on the *pill* and confronted me on it."

"What? Well, what did you say?"

"I didn't know what to say. I was too embarrassed … I … I'm sick to my stomach. He said he was ashamed of me."

"Cynthia, he has no right to be prying into your business like that. Put him on the phone!" I demanded.

"No, Eddie. I don't want any trouble."

"Cynthia, I'm going up there!"

"Eddie, please! Don't come up here. It'll only make things worse."

I sighed, debating on what to do.

"Okay, I won't. But are you gonna be okay? Do you want me to meet you somewhere?"

"No. It's okay. I'm going into my room to stay in there

forever," Cynthia said. "I've got to go."

"Okay."

When she hung up I couldn't stand feeling helpless, so I decided to call a cab and proceeded to head toward Cynthia's house, with the intention of talking to Barry on a mature level.

I began to practice over and over in the cab what to say: "Barry, I don't think it was right for you to take Cynthia's shoe box the way you did. And I don't feel it's any of your business that she's on the pill."

The driver looked at me crazy in his rear-view mirror. When we approached the long driveway to Cynthia's house, I said, "Stop right here, right here."

I reached in my back pocket for my wallet, and realized I'd left it at home.

"Damn," I said angrily. "Look ... um ... can you wait here for me?"

"Yeah," The cab driver said, "but the meter's gonna be running."

"Fine. Fine."

I rushed out of the cab, briskly walked up the driveway, and knocked on Cynthia's front door.

"Eddie? What, what are you doing here?"

"Cynthia, I just wanna talk to your dad, please. I'll be calm."

"Eddie, I don't know. I don't think it's a good—"

Barry shouted from the living room, "Cynthia, who's at the door?"

I tried to walk in, but Cynthia blocked my path so I wouldn't.

"Cindy, I just wanna talk to him."

Barry heard my voice and said, "Cynthia, is that Eddie? Let him in and close the door."

I felt this sudden impulse to say whatever was on my mind.

"Barry, I wanna talk to you, now!" I declared, in an authoritative voice.

"What?" Barry replied, disliking the tone in my voice.

"I wanna talk to you. I don't appreciate you going into

196

Cynthia's personal box. You should mind your fucking business!"

"Don't you use that language in my house!" Barry said angrily. "How dare you!"

"I'll use any Goddamn language I please!"

The yelling got worse as Barry got up from his chair and rushed toward the front door. Shocked by my audacity, I could see his face burning with anger.

Cynthia's mother stood there, baffled, as Cynthia said, "Stop it, Dad! Stop!"

I barged my way closer to Barry and yelled, "Why did you hafta pry into Cynthia's box? Tell me? Why?"

"What?" Barry shouted back. "Who the hell do you think you are? Get out of my house!"

"I'm not goin' nowhere 'til you tell me."

"You little punk kid!" Barry said, then grabbed me by my throat and pushed me up against an expensive, imported Japanese painting behind me.

The glass shattered. I grabbed Barry's hands, pushing them off of me, and demanded, "Get the fuck off!"

We wrestled each other into the living room.

I continued, "You wanna fuck with me, old man … c'mon … fuck with me!"

I knew I could hurt Barry and from the looks of it, he knew it too. I kept thinking, *You don't want to hurt him, Eddie.*

I rushed at Barry and punched him in his jaw, holding back the power of my punch. Blood spurted from his lip, and he stepped back in shock. Cynthia's mother stood in front of Barry and shouted, "That's enough! Barry, that's enough!"

Cynthia grabbed my hand and said, "Eddie, come on! Let's go."

Before we left, Barry looked at me one last time and shouted, "I'm gonna sue your ass off, Eddie!"

I replied, "Sue me for what?"

Cynthia turned around, stared Barry in the eyes, pointed at him, and said with a firm voice, "No you're not! I don't think so."

We hurried outside.

Cynthia said, "I can't believe what you just did."

"Neither can I. I'm ... I'm sorry. I didn't mean for it to happen that way."

We proceeded down the driveway. I saw the distress on her face and continued, "Cynthia, I'm … I'm sorry. I wanted to tell him how I felt and how wrong he was. I didn't mean for it to turn out this way."

"Eddie, I can't believe what you did, but, well, he's had it coming for a long time."

I felt this sense of approved relief. We sort of laughed it off, and she walked me back to the cab.

"You better go home," Cynthia said, as she walked away from the cab.

"Cynthia," I asked with an embarrassed look, "you got some cash 'til tomorrow? I forgot my money."

She reached in her jeans pocket and gave me some.

"Thanks."

Cynthia headed up the driveway. I got in the cab and rolled the window down.

"Cynthia."

She turned around.

"Thanks for standing up for me."

She smiled and walked away.

Chapter Thirty-One

Wendy's abortion destroyed Ed. I stood by his side through the whole mess. Ed wanted so badly to speak with Wendy and tell her how sorry he was, but her parents wouldn't allow it.

So he waited outside Friendly House every day, hoping to see her walk by. Then one day he saw her come out of Friendly House.

"Wendy?" Ed asked, "Wendy, can we talk?"

Wendy would not respond to his questions, ignoring his feelings. I knew she wouldn't listen, but I didn't want to discourage Ed from trying.

Ed began to cry and said, "Why, Wendy? Why? Why did you have to kill my baby?"

"It wasn't my choice, and I'm not supposed to talk to you!" Wendy exclaimed. "So leave me alone."

He became angry and shouted, "Whatta you mean? Our baby is dead, and you can't even talk about it?"

It was the side of him I had hoped he would control.

Wendy began to walk away when Ed grabbed her arm and continued, "Don't you have any feelings? Don't you care that it was a life?"

Wendy answered, "It's not my fault! It's not my fault!"

"C'mon Ed. Let's go," I said, barging between them.

"No, no! I just wanna talk to her," Ed said, swiftly moving his way around me toward Wendy.

"Ed, no! C'mon! This ain't cool. You're gonna get in trouble."

"Leave me alone!" Wendy shouted, "You've already caused enough problems!"

"What? Your parents kill my baby and you can't even talk to me," Ed said angrily.

People inside Friendly House heard the commotion and Brian (the new counselor) ran out and said, "Eddie, it'd be best if you get Ed out of here."

"I know. I know. I'm trying," I said, rushing back toward Ed. "Ed. Ed, c'mon, man. Let's just get back on our bikes and go. We'll go wherever you want. Just let's go before the cops come."

Ed wrapped his hands over his head and said, "This is crazy. What am I doing?"

He got on his Interceptor and sped down Thurman Street toward the freeway, and I followed behind on my Ninja. We weaved in and out of traffic, taking the West Burnside exit. We rode to Couch Park and parked our motorcycles. Ed got off and sat on the rail where we first met.

"Ed, you okay, man?"

"Yeah."

There was a minute or so of silence ...

"Remember this place?" I asked, trying to cheer him up.

He looked around and didn't say a word. I sat beside him on the rail.

Ed then glanced at me, shook his head, and blurted, "Damn, I was goin' fast, wasn't I?"

"Yeah, you were. But not as fast as my Ninja," I said jokingly.

Ed said, "I don't even know why I did what I did."

"Look, man, it's already done. I wouldn't dwell on it."

"Yeah, maybe you're right."

For the rest of the day we hung out and played tag on the structure, and that evening shared a forty-ounce bottle of St. Ides.

Ed said, "I feel like ridin'."

"Let's do it," I said. "Where do you wanna go?"

"Doesn't matter. Anywhere but the Northwest."

"We could cruise down McLaughlin Boulevard," I suggested.

"Sounds good," Ed said.

We got on our bikes and rode. I noticed an old, blue, half-ton truck in front of us. It had three guys in it, one of them wearing a cowboy hat. We rode past them, and before we knew it, the truck passed us. Well, Ed and I were always up for a good race, so I saw Ed pass the truck again and followed. In doing this, the race went out of control.

The truck tailgated Ed's motorcycle, inches away from his back tire, then got behind me and zigzagged. The truck was not nearly as quick as our bikes, but it must've had a powerful engine because it was definitely faster in the long run. I saw Ed motion his hand at a gas station sign about two hundred yards ahead. I understood the signal and kicked my clutch into low gear. We sped into the closed gas station as the truck followed behind us. We stopped our motorcycles and quickly parked our bikes.

Three big guys stepped out of the truck, tensed, and their fists clenched. But that didn't scare Ed. We approached the guys, and I began thinking, *Oh, God, this isn't gonna be a fair fight.*

Ed walked tumultuously toward one of the guys he thought was the leader and yelled, "You could of fuckin' killed us, asshole! What were you thinkin'?"

"Well, why were you trying to race us?" the leader slurred, as if he'd been drinking.

The guy in the cowboy hat seemed like an oversized idiot who went along with whatever his leader friend said. The cowboy mimicked, "Yeah ... yeah ... uh ... why were you racing us?"

It appeared as if we were dealing with some backwoods rednecks, and I was afraid one of them might head back to their truck and pull out a gun or something. I also thought this was a bad time to get Ed angry.

I got between Ed and them and said, "C'mon Ed, forget it. These guys are out of it."

"No, Eddie! No. They could've killed us! Did you know that, asshole?" Ed turned and yelled at the leader. "You could've killed my best friend because you decided to ride on our asses with a two-ton fuckin' truck!"

"Well, we didn't know," the leader replied.

Ed pointed at the leader and said with a brutal tone, "Don't you ever! ... Ever get that close to anybody ridin' a motorcycle! You have a truck, and I'm on two wheels. We could've gotten killed. And you could've ran over us—don't you ever do that again!"

They backed up, and the leader said to his friends, "Let's go ... come on."

I stood beside Ed and watched them take off in their truck. After it was over, I felt proud to be his friend. Especially after the way he stood up for me.

Ed grinned at me and said, "Did you hear the way that guy with the cowboy hat talked? 'Duh ... uh ... duh.'"

"He was a joke. But they were scared," I added.

Ed said, "Let's go."

The next day, Missy called Ed from her parents' house on Thurman Street, just west of Friendly House. Occasionally, they saw each other just out of friendship, but I always felt it was more than that. Ed rode to Missy's and when I got home, Dad was seated in his recliner watching a rerun of the sitcom, *ALF*. Dad really loved watching his shows, especially the Bill Cosby show and *Dinosaurs*.

"Where have you been, Eddie?" Dad asked.

"I've been out with Ed. Why?"

"Why do you think? Because I was worried."

"I'm sorry, Dad! I should've called."

"Jeez, man, yeah, you should've. You could've been dead for all I knew."

"I know. I'm sorry."

"Hey! Why don't you take me to Fred Meyer so I can look at the tools?" Dad asked eagerly.

When Dad felt strong enough, he loved going to Fred Meyer. I had to make double-sure he wanted to go, because he would often change his mind.

"Really? You wanna go to Fred Meyer?"

"Yeah, man. I wanna go! Go get my slippers and beige pants and checkered shirt, the one with the Velcro."

I went to Dad's room and got the same pants and shirt he always wore when he was going somewhere special. Besides, it was the only clothing that really fit him. A Christian lady made the clothes for him after Mom died. I came out with his pants, shirt, and a pair of "bear claw" slippers Anna bought for him.

It was funny seeing Dad wear those slippers. He was a big kid at heart that way. He also especially liked all of the neat, little McDonald toys that sometimes came out.

"You want me to iron your shirt?" I asked.

"No. As long as it's comfortable."

"But it's all wrinkled, Dad."

"So what, man. Just give it to me."

"Dad, you're not really gonna wear those slippers, are you?"

"Yeah, man, why? What's wrong with them?"

"Well, Dad, people are gonna look at us crazy."

"These are all I got."

"Well, what about a pair of my shoes?"

"My feet are too wide. Besides, they help my feet breathe."

"But Dad, they have claws at the end of them."

"Man, are you gonna take me or are you gonna worry about my feet attire?"

"Look, Dad, let's be reasonable. I'm not gonna take you through Fred Meyer with feet that look like bear claws. We're gonna have to get you another pair of shoes."

I heard a heavy, quick knock on the front door. Yoko kept barking as I went to answer it.

"Whatta you doin' here, Ed?" I asked, surprised.

He walked in, and Yoko was excited to see him.

"Quiet, Yoko," I said, following Ed into the living room.

"I'm gonna go to my room to get my Anacins," Dad said, maneuvering his weight on the wheelchair, then pushing himself to his room. "Move outta the way, Ed. I'm a fat, old man, move!"

Ed stepped out of Dad's way.

"What's up, Ed?"

"I found Missy's diary." Ed replied, as he sat down on the

sofa and pulled out a small, black, leather book from his jacket.

My heart pumped fast, and my blood raced through my veins. My first thought was, *Is he gonna find out about Missy and me.* I had to think of something to say or do to stop him from reading it.

"Well, Ed, that's not right. I mean, maybe you shouldn't read it."

I was terrified of what might happen if he found out about my having sex with Missy.

"You don't think so?"

"Well, I mean diaries are private, right?"

"Yeah, but I've been trying to find this thing ever since we went out," Ed said. "Missy told me she had it, and at one time asked if I wanted to read it."

"She did?"

"Yeah, and she had this right out where I could see it."

He skimmed through the pages reading whatever caught his interest. I stood there quietly and didn't say a word. He stopped reading, stood up, and for a second, we made eye contact.

His eyes looked hurt as his head slowly turned away from me. I wasn't sure if he had read about our affair, but I could feel it.

"Ed, are you okay?"

"Yeah," Ed replied sadly, with his head partially down.

He left without saying another word. I heard the roaring sound of his motorcycle take off. My next immediate reaction was to call Missy. I ran to the phone and dialed her number, but no one answered.

"Eddie, are you ready to go?" Dad yelled from his bedroom.

I walked in there and sadly replied, "No, Dad. I'm sorry."

"What's wrong, son?"

"Nothing."

I went outside and felt sick inside knowing I had betrayed my best friend.

Chapter Thirty-Two

It had been days since I'd seen Ed, so I called Missy's house.

"Hello?"

I cleared my throat and said, "Missy, this is Eddie."

"Hi, Eddie."

I sensed she knew exactly why I called.

"Missy, I need to ask you something. It's about Ed."

"What?"

"Missy, I need to know if you put in your diary what had happened between us?"

"I knew it would come to this," Missy said, "I'm sorry, Eddie. Yes, I did."

"Missy, how … how did he get your diary?"

"I left it on the bed and he grabbed it."

"On the bed? Why? Why did you do that if you knew he was there?"

"I forgot it was on my bed when Ed came over to see me. He went upstairs into my room and saw the diary lying on the bed. He grabbed it without me knowing and said he had to go see you about something important. I didn't want him to go, but he was persistent."

"Missy, did you put everything in the diary?"

"Eddie, I'm sorry."

"Well, when he came over, he must've saw what we did in there, because I haven't heard or seen him in a week. I'm worried."

"He hasn't called me either. Maybe he's at Julie or Tim's house," Missy said. "Eddie, I'm sorry he found it, and I hope this doesn't end your friendship."

"Yeah, well I hope it's not too late for that," I said, hanging up the phone.

I felt Missy was lying to me about how she had mistakenly left her diary on the bed. She felt as guilty about our affair as I did, and as a last resort for the truth to be known, purposely left that diary on her bed for Ed to find.

I drove Dad's station wagon to go see Neil, a friend of Tim's and mine who lived in Clackamas. When I got there, I knocked on the door.

"Eddie! What's up, man?" Neil greeted loudly.

I walked into his spacious apartment.

"What's up, Neil?" I said," I heard Tim was in town. Where is that bone-head?"

I glanced around the apartment and noticed a half-empty six-pack of beer laid out on the kitchen table. Neil had his Sony stereo up loud, along with Madonna singing "like a virgin" on MTV.

"Hey, where's Ed?" Tim asked, as he came out from the bathroom, tucking his shirt into his pants.

"Oh, he's probably ridin'," I replied.

"Where's your weak Ninja?" Neil smirked.

I sneered at him and said, "At least I don't have some old, stinkin', junky, gutless American car."

"Hey, I'm thinking about getting one of those Honda Hurricanes," Neil said. "What do you think?"

I said confidently, "So you can be like me. It'll never be faster than the Ninja! You know that, Neil boy."

Neil opened the refrigerator door and asked, "What kind of beer you want? We have Henry's and Labatt's."

"Thanks, but I'm not in a mood to drink," I replied.

I sat on the sofa.

"Why not? You wimping out on us, spic," Neil said jokingly.

"Yeah, you Puerto Rican wetback," Tim added.

"Man, shut up, Tim. At least I didn't come to America on a boat made out of toothpicks."

Neil laughed and joined me in the insults against Tim.

"Yeah, Castro."

We talked and played cards until about three in the morning. Ed's and my favorite video, "Take On Me," came on MTV.

"So, I wonder where Ed's at?"

"You haven't seen 'im at all?" Neil asked.

206

"No."

"Probably out gettin' laid," Tim implied. "Why don't you join the Marines, Eddie?"

"I'll never join the military!" I said, in a resenting tone. "They fuck with your brain, make you think you're gonna be somebody 'til you get out. Then no one respects or cares about you."

Tim said, "It's for your country, man. It's discipline and loyalty."

"It's bullshit!"

"You're a communist," Tim said.

"See, they already got you brainwashed, Tim."

"Can we get back to playing cards," Neil interjected. "I'm tired of hearing you guys whine."

"Well, boys, I gotta get goin' home anyway," I said, "it's late."

"You're just tired of losing your money," Neil exclaimed, shuffling cards pretending to be some big-shot card dealer.

"I gotta go, too," Tim said. "I'll walk you out, Eddie."

I got up from the sofa and headed toward the front door.

"Thanks for coming by," Neil said, "and if you visit again, don't bother bringing that gutless motorcycle of yours, 'cause I'll have the Hurricane by then."

"Yeah, right."

"Where's your car?" I asked.

It's on the other side of the parking lot," Tim said. "Whatta ya doin' tomorrow?"

"Nothin'."

"Give me a call," Tim said. "I won't be going back until Friday."

"Okay."

I got into the station wagon, drove off, and merged onto the I-205 interstate, then the I-5 going north. By now, I was feeling very tired and falling asleep behind the wheel. I rested my right hand on the visor with the window open and the cheap AM radio on to stay awake.

When I saw the Interstate/Killingsworth exit, I steered onto it and took another left at the flashing red light ahead, quietly saying to myself, "Yeah ... few more blocks before I get home. I can make it."

I turned the car left, and suddenly woke up three blocks down, dead-smashed into a parked car, which had crashed into a wooden fence and then into the back end of a house. Everything had happened so fast. I tried to get myself together and looked over the bent, metal steering wheel. I could see the front end of my dad's car underneath the back end of the other car I'd crashed into.

I forced the driver's door open and smelled gasoline. With what little energy I had, I rolled out of the car and crawled into the street. My chest was in pain as I lay on the yellow-painted street lines, groaning.

I felt a hand on the back of my shoulder and someone repeatedly asking, "Are you okay? Hey, buddy, are you okay?"

Soon after, I heard sirens and indistinct chattering around me. Then the paramedics arrived.

"Can you feel this?" the paramedic asked, touching my fingers and neck.

"What?" I replied incoherently.

"Can you feel this?" he repeated.

"Yeah, I can feel ... feel that," I replied, noticing the reflections of the ambulance lights glimmering off a police officer's badge.

"Do you have insurance?" the paramedic asked.

"No, no, I don't."

I couldn't believe the guy asked me that question while I was in pain.

The paramedic continued, "We're gonna have to take you to the hospital."

"No, no. I don't need no hospital," I said. "See, I'm fine ... I don't need none."

I hastily got up and walked around, trying to rub away the pain on the left side of my chest. I then sat on the curb close to my dad's totaled car and swayed forward and backward.

The police officer looked over my shoulder and asked, "Do

you have a driver's license?"

"Yeah ... uh ... it's in the car."

The paramedic came toward me again and proceeded to say with a calm voice, "Look, there may not be any bleeding outside, but there could very well be some bleeding inside of you."

It seemed as if everything around me was happening in slow motion.

Still swaying and rubbing my chest, I asked, "Are you tryin' to say ... say ... that ... that I could be messed up inside?"

"There is a possibility," the paramedic answered, setting his hand on my shoulder.

No matter how much pain I was in, I kept thinking what it would cost to fix me up.

"So, what's it gonna be?" the paramedic asked.

I replied, "Okay."

They put me in a neck brace and lifted me on a stretcher into the ambulance. When we got to the hospital, they rushed me into emergency and hurried me into a room. They put me through several tests and kept me in a CAT scan.

"Nurse?" I said, inside the CAT scan machine.

"Yes."

"I really need to pee."

"Just a minute," the nurse said, handing me a small cup. "Here, use this."

I relieved myself.

"Thanks," I said, giving her back the cup.

After what seemed like hours of torture, they brought me to my room.

That same night, Michael rushed to the hospital.

"Hey, Mike, what's up, bro?"

"How ya feel?" Michael asked in a soft voice.

"I'm ... I'm okay. How'd you know I was here so soon?"

"Dad told me."

"How'd he find out?"

"Cop told him."

"Man, I can't believe I wrecked the car," I said

disappointedly. "I was six blocks away from home, next thing you know, I was out in the middle of the street. How's the car?"

"We sent that thing to its grave," Michael replied in a funny way. "I wouldn't worry too much about it."

"I bet Dad's pissed."

"He ain't pissed over some dumb car. Don't worry about it," Michael said. "What's important is you! Not a car."

"Look at all this crap they hooked up to me. They're sending me to my grave before I'm dead," I said, motioning at the wires and white patches attached to my chest.

"Well, you're lucky you're not dead," Michael said, "from the wreckage I saw on the way to Dad's house, you shouldn't even be breathing."

"You saw the car?"

"Yep. And it didn't look good."

I sighed and said, "Damn."

"Hey, it's okay. It's not the end of the world. We're just glad you're still here."

"Where's the family?" I asked.

"They're at home, still sleeping. I haven't told them about what happened yet."

"Hey, bro? I appreciate you being here."

Michael inched toward my bedside, put his hand on my head and said, "I love you. You're my brother, and I'll always be here for you. You understand?"

"Yeah, thanks."

"I gotta go now, but I'll be by later with the family, okay."

"Okay."

When Michael left, I fell asleep, and when I woke up, Gerard and Joey were there. I was still very weak, but I managed to talk a little.

"How do you feel?" Gerard asked.

"I feel better."

"Hey, bro," Joey said.

"Hey, Joe. What's up?"

"You okay?" Joey asked.

"I think so," I replied.

210

Joey didn't say much. Gerard walked around to the foot of the bed and looked at the clipboard attached to it. He was pretty smart that way. He always double-checked and questioned everything. Whenever he was around, I could be assured of learning something new.

"Am I okay?" I asked.

"Yeah, it doesn't look too bad," Gerard replied, setting the clipboard back in its place.

"Michael told me about Dad's car ... guess it's pretty jacked up," I said.

"Yeah, you did a number on it," Gerard said, "but the car doesn't matter."

"That's what Michael said, but I know Dad."

"Hey, Eddie," Joey asked, "what did it feel like being in an ambulance?"

"It's no fun, man. When I got here, they had me in a CAT scan for a long time that I almost peed myself."

"So how do you feel?" Gerard asked.

"Oh, I feel a little weak, but better."

Joey asked, "Did the doctor say when you can leave?"

"About two or three days."

"Ah, you just want the attention," Joey said with a smile.

Gerard laughed and said, "Shut up, Joey."

"We should go, bro," Joey said. "He looks okay, and I'm tired."

"Okay." Gerard asked, "Do you need anything? "

"Nah. I'm cool."

He said, "You get some sleep, okay."

"Okay."

"Later, bro," Joey said, giving me a hug.

Then Gerard leaned over and hugged and kissed me on the cheek. When they left, I thought about Ed, wondering where he was. Later that morning, I got a few more family visitors, including Cynthia.

Chapter Thirty-Three

The next day after breakfast I turned the television on with a remote attached to the bed and forced myself to watch *Days of Our Lives*. I noticed the front door open slowly. A hand with a toy motorcycle in it inched its way into the room. The person pretended if he was riding that toy motorcycle, making all the necessary sounds to bring out the realism of it. I felt happy because I knew who it was.

"Ed!" I exclaimed happily.

"What's up, car-wrecker?"

"What's up, bro?" I asked. "Where'd you get the toy motorcycle?"

"Fred Meyer," Ed said. "You're lucky you weren't ridin' your Ninja."

"Yeah, I know. So, where've you been?"

"Here and there. What happened? How did you wreck?" Ed asked.

"Oh, I fell asleep," I replied, chuckling to myself.

"Fell asleep? Dumb, dumb," Ed said, making a funny face at me. "Well, this should show ya not to fall asleep again at the wheel."

I asked, "Hey, did you know Tim was in town?"

"Yeah ... thought about droppin' by his house later."

Ed rested his hands on my bed and said, "You know I love ya!"

"I love ya too, man."

"Don't think I'm mad, 'cause I'm not."

"You're not?"

"What's done is done."

"Thanks, Ed," I said.

"Well, I gotta go," he said a while later, "I promised my dad I'd go see him. You get well, okay?"

"Okay. Hey, you're gonna go see the Buzz man?"

"Yeah, he's lonely ... called me begging for me to come

over … said he'd treat me out to Loaves and Fishes. "

Loaves and Fishes was a place for poor people to eat free meals.

"Are you kidding me?"

"Nope. Isn't that funny?" Ed asked.

"Yeah it is."

"Here, take this," Ed said, handing me the toy. "It'll keep your spirits up and ready to ride again."

Ed proceeded toward the door.

"Later Ed. Hey, I'll call you when I get out of this pit, okay."

"Okay."

Ed left the room and closed the door. My heart had this peaceful feeling when he left, like everything was back to normal.

On the third day I was ready to go home. When I got there, Dad greeted me with a strong hug and kissed me on the cheek, "Eddie, Are you okay?"

"Yeah, Dad. I'm fine."

"Are you sure you're okay?"

"Yeah, yeah, I'm okay."

"Good. Now you owe me eight hundred dollars for the car," Dad said jokingly as he brought his hand out waiting for his money.

I ignored the gesture and asked, "Did I get any calls while I was almost dying?"

"Calls? Who do you know that knows how to dial a phone? You bang up my car and you wanna know if you got any calls?" Dad said. "Yeah you got a call ... from my insurance company, saying you owe them six thousand dollars 'cause that's what it cost to fix you up."

"Six what?" I exclaimed. "No way! That's a rip-off."

"That's what you cost them, and I think they're gonna raise my rates now."

"Nah, they won't. You've been with them too long and have a good record."

"Yeah, but you haven't, and you were under my name."

"I'm sorry, Dad," I said. "I'll tell you what ... I'll buy you a new car when I get rich."

Dad replied theatrically, "You'll buy me a new car? You'll buy spit, that's what you'll buy, spit!"

I laughed and said, "C'mon, Dad, my life's more important. So did I get any calls?"

"Yeah ... uh ... Cindy called," Dad replied, giving up on our conversation.

"Cool."

I picked up the phone and called her.

"Hello?"

"Hey, babe!" I said happily.

"Hi, sweetie! I'm glad you're home." Cynthia asked, "How do you feel?"

"Pretty good."

Cynthia said, "I wanted to tell you the good news."

"What?"

"I found the college I want to go to."

When I heard this, I thought, *Great, just what I need to know right out of the hospital.* I played along as if I was happy for her.

"That's great, Cindy," I said. "I'm real happy for you."

"Are you?"

"Of course I'm happy for you."

"Thanks, Eddie. It means a lot to me to know you care."

"Ya know, maybe, uh, I'll go to college, too."

"Really?"

"Yeah, really," I replied, knowing for a fact that's not what I wanted to do in my life, but I didn't know what else to say.

"Wouldn't it be something if we went to the same college?" Cynthia said, excited.

"Yeah. Then we could see each other every day."

"Oh, that's my mom calling. Can I call you later?"

"Sure."

"Okay, bye."

"Bye."

Chapter Thirty-Four

It was a hot, humid day, in 1988, and Stewart was driving his Battlewagon about eighty-five miles per hour toward Seaside beach. Ed and I accelerated our motorcycles past Stewart's car to see whose bike could go the fastest. I could also see Ed speeding near the Battlewagon, then reaching his hand out to daringly touch the side-view mirrors.

When we got to Seaside, we found a secluded area north of the beach, started a campfire, and drank beers until late evening.

"Hey, Eddie?"

"What's up?"

"Let's get outta here," Ed said.

"And go where?" I asked.

"Back to Portland."

"Party's just startin', man."

"I wanna go ridin'."

"Couldn't we ride around here?" I said. "We'll have to ride a hundred miles back. By then you may not wanna to go ridin'."

"There's nowhere to ride. It's boring over here."

"All right. Come on."

We got on our bikes and rode back to Portland, cruising down Union Avenue, enjoying the cool breeze.

Ed sped closer to me and shouted, "Let's get a hooker!"

"What? Are you serious?" I replied, trying to keep my motorcycle straight.

"Yeah, yeah, let's get a hooker."

"Ed, aren't you afraid of gettin' some disease or something?" I asked loudly, so he could hear me.

He sped closer to me.

"We won't get no disease," Ed said. "Let's just try it! I got condoms."

I couldn't believe what I was hearing. Never in my wildest ideas had I thought of paying for the services of a prostitute. I might have wondered what the experience might've been like, but never thought about actually getting one. At first I was scared and wondered how we were going to do this.

As we rode our bikes up and down the strip, carefully eyeing any potential hookers, the first one we saw was a tall, white woman in a Superwoman-type outfit.

We slowed down and almost stopped in front of her when she signaled for us to meet her around the corner. "Hey! Hey! Lookin' for action? Over here."

We stopped our bikes.

"How much do you charge for head?" Ed blurted out.

"For both y'all? I charge fifty dollars," the hooker replied with an attitude.

"What? Fifty dollars? You hafta be kiddin' us," I said, staring her up and down. "C'mon Ed. We don't need her for no fifty dollars."

"Okay, okay, hold on. Twenty-five!" she exclaimed desperately.

"Well, whatta you think?" Ed asked.

I leaned over and whispered, "Ed, I don't want this skanky bitch. She's not my type anyway."

"Yeah, me neither," Ed said. "Well, thanks anyway."

We rode off as the hooker yelled, "Okay, okay, ten dollars … ten dollars!"

We rode around longer. I noticed a girl wearing a fur coat waiting at a bus stop.

Ed stopped in front of her and said, "Hi."

"Hi," she replied.

"Nice night," Ed said, looking up at the dark sky.

"Yeah, nice night. What are you guys lookin' for?" she asked in a proper way.

"Well … I … we're lookin' for something," Ed replied.

We weren't sure if she was a hooker, so we didn't want to offend her.

"You guys lookin' for action?"

Since we were on the main street, we had to act fast.

"Yeah, we are," Ed replied."

"Whatta you charge?" I asked.

"Fifty dollars for a fuck and thirty-five for head," she said, "that's each of you."

"Damn! That's too much, Ed."

"That's what I charge," she declared, with her eyebrows up high and her arms interlocked.

"Don't worry. I'll pay for it." Ed asked, "Where we gonna take her?"

"I don't know."

"Let's take her to your house," he suggested casually.

"No way, man! If Dad found out, he'd kill us both!" I said, shocked he would even ask.

"Well, we could maybe take her to my house."

"What about your mom?"

"She won't know. I'll tell her she's my girlfriend or something."

"You're serious?"

The hooker snickered at us and patiently waited for our solution to this crazed idea of ours.

"Yeah, let's just take her to my house."

"Where we gonna put her?" I asked.

"Get on my bike," Ed said to the hooker, "c'mon, get on the back seat."

"You want me to ride on that?"

"Yeah, is there a problem?"

"Nope, no problem."

"By the way, my name's Ed, and this is my best friend, Eddie."

"Both of you are named Ed?"

"Yeah," Ed said. "Two Ed's are better than one."

The hooker chuckled and proceeded to get on Ed's bike.

"No wonder you guys get along."

Her fur coat and purple, high-heel shoes were more obvious than Ed's red, white, and blue motorcycle. We rode south on Union Avenue and took Powell up to 37th. The whole time, I was paranoid a cop might see us. When we got to Ed's house, I was relieved.

Ed reached in his pants pocket and said, "Eddie, I forgot my house key."

"Whatta we gonna do?"

"I'm gonna have to knock on the door," Ed said. "Damn! I didn't want to wake my mom."

"Wait! What if your mom asks who she is?"

"You're right. What's your name?" Ed asked the hooker.

"Patty."

Ed said, "Patty, when my mom answers the door and if she asks, tell her your name and I'll say the rest."

"Okay, but I can't believe this," Patty said and grinned.

Ed knocked softly on the door. Edith looked through the peephole and opened it. She was happy to see Ed and said, "Hi, sweetie. Who's this?"

Ed replied, motioning toward Patty, "Mom, this is Patty, Eddie's girlfriend."

For a moment I was shocked, but went along with it.

"Hi, nice to meet you."

"Well, hi, Patty. It's very nice to meet you, too," Edith said looking over to me. "Hello, my second son."

"Hi, Mom."

We walked inside and sat in the living room for a while.

"Would you like something to eat or drink, Patty?" Edith asked.

We both looked at Patty and she replied, "Uh, no, no thank you."

"Are you sure?" Edith asked.

Patty confirmed her answer with a head gesture then said, "Yes, I'm, I'm sure."

Edith hugged Ed and me and said, "Good night, and good night to you too, Patty."

"Yes, uh, good night," she replied.

Edith went back into her room, and we waited until she fell asleep.

"Eddie, you go first," Ed insisted.

"Me? Why me?" I said. "You go first. I've never done anything like this before."

"No, go 'head. If my mom comes out, I can say you're in the room with Patty."

"Man, what am I supposed to do with her?"

"Whatever you want. I'm paying."

I guided Patty into Ed's room and before I closed the door I said, "I don't appreciate you saying she's my woman, either."

I quietly shut the door, not knowing where to start. I stood there as Patty sat on the bed.

"Well, what do you wanna do?" she asked.

"How much did you say it cost for ... for—"

"A fuck. Fifty dollars."

I felt uncomfortable, so Patty stood up and grabbed my hand. She brought me to the bed, unzipped my pants and caressed my groin.

"You like that?"

"Yeah."

"So what do you want?" Patty whispered in my ear, kissing my neck.

"Well, how 'bout head."

"I can do that. But I don't do anything without a rubber on."

Patty pulled my pants, and underwear down and slipped the condom on my penis. She sucked and sucked it but nothing was happening. I didn't want to do this, but Ed told her he would pay only if she did something for me, too.

"This isn't gonna work," I said, "let's just forget it."

"You want me to take the rubber off?"

"I guess," I replied, with uncertainty.

She tried that for a while, but I didn't like it, so I said, "Look, I know this isn't gonna work."

She stopped and said, "You know, your friend is paying for this, so you gotta do something."

"How 'bout your tits?"

"What about them?"

"I'll just get on top of them and fuck 'em or something," I said, nervously waiting to get it over with.

"Okay."

She took her shirt off and lay back on the bed. I left the

condom on and started to squeeze my penis between her breasts, forcing myself to enjoy it.

"I'm coming! I'm coming ... oh, oh, oh!"

Shortly after, Patty asked, "Could you get up?"

"Oh, yeah. Sorry."

I got up, threw my pants back on, hurried toward the bedroom door, and said, "Thanks."

Ed had all the lights off except for a few lit candles on the kitchen table.

"Well, how'd you like it?" Ed asked.

"It was okay."

"What'd she say?"

"Nothing," I said. "It's your turn now."

Ed picked up a candle off the kitchen table and proceeded into the bedroom with it.

I asked, "Whatta you doin'?"

"I wanna make this special," Ed replied, opening the door, then covering the candle from the breeze whisking through the bedroom window. "See you in a bit."

At first I thought he was nuts, but if Ed thought any moment was special, he made the most of it.

I sat on the sofa and waited, tense about Edith waking up. Ed finally came out. As Patty was getting dressed, Ed pulled some money out from his green, army wallet and said, "Here."

"Thanks," Patty said, stuffing the money into her bra.

Ed closed the bedroom door from behind Patty and asked, "Where would you like us to leave you off?"

"The same place is fine," Patty replied, combing her hair with a bristle brush, then layering more makeup over her face.

Ed and I took her back to Union Avenue, rode to the nearest 7-Eleven, and ate some greasy, chili and cheese nachos outside the store.

Ed said, "Man, that was the best orgasm I've had in a long time!"

"You mean ... you did her?"

Ed nodded his head.

"Ed, what did you pay her?"

"I gave her a hundred bucks."

"What? Are you kidding me? I didn't fuck her," I said. "All I did was fuck her tits!"

Ed replied in disbelief, "You didn't?"

"No, no, I didn't," I replied shaking my head.

"Well, she was worth it," Ed said, shrugging his shoulders as if the money didn't matter.

I laughed and said, "She was one expensive ho, but at least she was better lookin' than Superwoman.

We laughed.

Ed said, "Let's head over to your house?"

"Okay."

Chapter Thirty-Five

When we got home, Bubba was talking to my dad.

"Hey Bubba! Whatta you doin' here?" I asked, happy to see him.

"What's up, niggas! Where've you guys been?"

"Ridin' around … partying … kickin' it with the homies," Ed said, making a funny face at Bubba.

Bubba said, motioning to the kitchen, "You're retarded! I bought a case of Bu-Bu-Busch beer for you guys."

"Hey, Dad, did I get any calls or mail?" I asked.

"Who do you know that knows how to dial a phone."

I nodded my head toward Ed. "Well, Ed can dial four digits."

"Ed couldn't find his way out of a garbage bag," Dad said.

Bubba interrupted and said, "Eddie, get me a beer."

"What do I look like to you?"

"Like a reject," Bubba replied laughing. "Now get me a beer."

I stepped into the kitchen, grabbed a beer, lifted the tab off, and said, "Ahhh … you hear that? That's the sound of Buschhh."

"Here. Give it here," Bubba demanded, drinking the whole can in seconds.

"Damn, nigga!" I blurted. "You didn't even come up for air."

"Hey, why don't you give me one of those?" Dad asked.

"Nah, Dad. It's not good for you."

"Yeah, give 'im one," Ed said. "It won't hurt him."

"Ed, you know if he drinks that, he'll fall down and have a heart attack."

"I'm not gonna have no heart attack!" Dad insisted. "Just give me one, silly."

"Hey, Al, Al, watch this," Bubba said, grabbing a beer and

225

teasing him by guzzling it to the last drop.

"Bubba, that's cold-blooded!" Dad said, shaking his head.

Meanwhile, Ed made his way into the kitchen and grabbed three beers.

"Here Al," Ed said throwing him one.

"No, Ed, you shouldn't have given him that. Okay, Dad, I'll tell you what, I'll hold the beer and you can take a sip of it."

"Tch, man, you gotta be kiddin' me," Dad replied disappointedly. "I'm not some kid."

"C'mon, Dad, it's for your own good," I said, opening the beer as I held it with both hands and lifted it up toward Dad's mouth. "Okay, you ready?"

"This is ridiculous," Dad said. "I'm sixty-five years old and I'm being treated like a kid."

"C'mon, Dad, are you ready or not?"

"Yeah, yeah, I'm ready."

I inched the can closer to his lips, and Dad helped me along by wrapping his hands around mine. He quickly started to gulp the beer. Then I lost control of the can.

"Dad, Dad! You promised!" I yelled in laughter. "C'mon!"

"Go, Al, go! Do it!" Bubba and Ed were cheering him on.

Beer was trickling down the sides of Dad's mouth, but he wasn't going to let go of that can for anything.

I shouted, "Dang, Dad! You see, next time you ask, I'm not gonna trust you."

"Man, youza sucka! You should know better than to trust your old man," Dad said, wiping the foam off the sides of his mouth.

The whole time, Bubba and Ed couldn't stop laughing.

"You see, Dad, because you drank that whole can of beer, you're gonna have a heart attack now and die a slow, slow death," I said, pointing my finger at him.

Ed pointed at a toy water gun by Dad's window and asked, "What's the water gun for, Al?"

"It's for the dogs out here. I keep it by the window so when they bark a lot, I squirt them."

"Let me see," Ed said, trying to grab the water gun.

226

"Don't touch it," Dad said. "Whatta you wanna see it for?"

"I just wanna check it out."

"No, dummy. Don't do that," Dad said, pushing Ed's hands away from the water gun.

Ed said, "I wanna see the doggies, too."

"Why do you wanna see them for?"

"'Cause."

"Nooo ... nooo," Dad said in a funny way. "What part of *no* do you not understand, the 'n' or the 'o'?"

"C'mon, Al," Bubba said, "let's see what happens."

"No ... no ... no," Dad said.

Ed held my dad's arms and yelled, "Eddie, Eddie! Open the shade!"

"Man, you guys. Don't mess up my shade!" Dad implored. "Please! Okay, okay, I'll let you see the pit bulls, but don't break my shade."

Ed released his grip on Dad. Carefully pulling the staples out, he asked, "Why the hell do you have a garbage bag for a shade anyway?"

"It works," Dad said. "See, they're just minding their own business."

Ed tugged at the window, but it stuck.

"C'mon, Ed, you said you just wanted to see the dogs," Dad said, trying to grab Ed's hands away from the window.

"Let me see!" Bubba demanded. "Let me check it out."

"Let me see," I said giggling. "Move, Ed."

Ed got the window partially open, and the three pit bulls and German shepherd were out there. One pit bull was chained to an iron pole about ten feet away from the window. Ed lifted the window up further, then pointed the water gun at it. The pit bull sat there guarding his turf, with his ears erect and an uneasy, tensed, muscular body.

Suddenly, the dog sprang up and sprinted toward the window with a deep, loud bark. It came to an immediate halt, inches away from the window, because of the thick choke-chain tied around his neck.

Ed squirted the gun at him. The pit bull went silent for a

second, looked confused, and backed off. He then came at the window again, and Ed squirted more water at him. Bubba and I giggled while this was happening. He backed up and sat beside his post, realizing there was nothing he could do.

Dad tried to stop us and said, "C'mon, that's enough you guys!"

"Let me try, let me try!" Bubba said anxiously.

"No, man. No Bubba," Dad said, trying to grab the water gun from Ed.

"Okay, guys, time to grow up," I said, closing the window. "Let's shut this thing."

"Spoiler," Ed exclaimed with a funny expression. "You're just a spoiler!"

"One day that dog's gonna be off his chain, and he's gonna come back and eat your hands off," Dad said to us all.

"I'll just slap him around," Ed replied.

"Yeah, sure. I'm goin' to bed," Dad said, with an exasperated tone.

Dad got into his wheelchair and pushed himself back to his room. Dad never really slept because it was difficult for him to breathe while lying down. So instead he would sit on his bed and close his eyes.

I got a small buzz, and Ed sat on the sofa watching Pink Floyd on MTV. Bubba was in the refrigerator, trying to come up with some edible concoction.

I asked, "What kind of nasty mix you makin' now?"

"Man, you ain't got nothin' in this 'fridge," Bubba whined. "All you got is oatmeal."

"We haven't been shoppin' yet. We should go to the store and get some grub," I suggested. "Whatta you think, Ed?"

Ed was too absorbed into Pink Floyd to hear me ask him the question.

Bubba wasn't going to give up on finding food, so he looked in all the cupboards and discovered several bags of Ramen noodles.

He grabbed four of them. "Now this is the one staple no

poor nigga should be without!"

We grabbed a big, silver pot we used for cooking soups or making our favorite, cheese popcorn in.

I said, "You're not gonna make all this weird shit like you usually do, 'cause I'm hungry, too."

"This'll be good—grab me the cheese?"

"Cheese? Man, Bubba, you said you—."

"Eddie, trust me. You'll like this," Bubba said, throwing the noodles and chicken spice from the packages into the pot.

As the noodles boiled, Bubba shredded about a quarter-block of cheese and threw it in with a touch of Tabasco sauce.

I said with a disgusted look, "Man that looks gross! Who's gonna eat that now?"

"Taste it!" Bubba said, holding a fork dripping of melted cheese and Ramen noodles up to my face.

"No way!" I said, backing away from it.

"Ed," Bubba insisted, "com'ere and try this."

Ed got up from the sofa to see Bubba's creation and said sarcastically, "Mmmm ... looks good, Bubba."

"Just try it!" Bubba demanded, as he proceeded to put the fork of food into Ed's mouth.

Ed reluctantly tried it.

"That's not too bad."

"All right ... I'll try it," I said. "But it better be good."

Bubba dipped the fork into the steaming pot of noodles and said, "Here!"

"You're right. That's not bad. You lucked out, man," I said, grabbing an extra fork for Ed.

Instead of using plates, we began to eat out of the pot.

"Hey, this is missin' somethin'," Bubba said.

"Like what?" I hesitantly asked.

"More ... more ... fuckin' Tabasco!" he blurted with gut-bursting laughter.

"Wait! Wait! Before you do that, I'm grabbin' me some more," I said, and washed a dirty bowl out of the kitchen sink.

"Me too," Ed said, doing the same.

Bubba was happy he had the rest of the pot to himself. Ed

and I sat on the sofa, and I grabbed the remote control.

"C'mon, put it back on MTV," Ed pleaded. "I was here first."

"Nope. It's my turn to put it on my channel," I said, turning it to HBO. "Besides, I have the power, now!"

It was about four-thirty in the morning, and we were making enough noise to wake up the neighborhood.

"You guys keep it down! I'm trying to sleep," Dad yelled from his bedroom.

"Okay, Dad," I said. "Let's keep it down a little, guys."

But we kept laughing and joking around, and even wrestling in the living room.

Ed went to my room and turned on the radio to the pop rock station, Z100. It was playing the song "Take On Me" by A-ha. Bubba and I got up and went to my room, and saw Ed. He pretended he was riding on his motorcycle, moving his body to the beat of the music.

"What the hell are you doin'?" Bubba asked.

"Ridin'," Ed replied."

"Shut up, stupid," Bubba said. "I'm going to bed."

I tucked myself into bed and said, "Well, y'all have a good sleep."

Bubba said, "Hey, Ed, I'll trade you my blanket for yours."

"Why, what's wrong with yours?"

"You're smaller than I am. This one's too small."

"Okay."

Ed gave Bubba his blanket, then turned the music down.

"Good night," Ed said. "Pleasant, pleasant, pleasant dreams."

"Good night," we replied.

I was about to fall into a deep, wonderful sleep when this loud, banging noise on my bedroom door occurred.

Bang! Bang! Bang!

"What the fu'!" Bubba exclaimed.

"Hey!" Ed said, nearly jumping out of his bed.

Dad was getting us back for making so much noise and keeping him up late. So he waited for us to fall asleep to make the same obnoxious noises we made by banging his cane against the closed door.

"C'mon, Dad," I pleaded, from my bed covering my head with a pillow.

"Nah, man ... you ... you guys wouldn't keep quiet when I asked," Dad said laughing. "I begged, pleaded and pleaded, but you wouldn't stop. So now it's my turn."

Ed turned himself over and covered his head with his pillow.

"C'mon, Al, we're tryin' to get some sleep," Bubba whined, irritated, but laughing too.

Dad kept laughing and banging on the door with his wooden cane.

"All right, Dad, we're sorry!" I yelled. "We won't do it again."

Dad was having such a good time torturing us, he decided to make music with the thumps of the cane hitting the door.

"La - la - la - la - la..." he sang over and over.

I finally got out of my comfortable bed, turned on the lights, and opened the door. "Okay, Dad. That's enough!"

"Are you bums gonna do it again?"

"No. We're not gonna do it again!" Bubba said, in an impatient tone.

"You promise?"

"We promise, Dad. We promise," I said.

"I didn't hear Ed say he promised."

I turned my head and said, "Say you promise, Ed."

"I promise," Ed muttered under his pillow.

"Okay," Dad said, turning his wheelchair around and rolling himself back into his room, laughing.

We tried to go back to sleep.

Dad then cried out from his bedroom, "Next time you'll know better than to mess with me. I'm like the Mafioso. I may not get you right away, but I'll get you later."

Bubba said in a theatric tone, "Ooh, the Mafioso ... I'm scared ... I'll fuckin' kill the Mafia."

Ed and I laughed.

It was obvious Dad felt vindicated, and for the next minute

or so, we talked and laughed quietly to each other.

Chapter Thirty-Six

I had just gotten home from visiting Cynthia, and Yoko kept barking and whining behind the door, waiting to see me.

"Hey, Yoko! Hey, doggie," I said, hugging and kissing her.

I walked further into the hallway and saw Joey sitting on the yellow, vinyl, torn-up sofa.

"Hey, Joe."

"Hey," Joey replied, with somewhat of an attitude in his voice.

I sensed something was wrong with Joey.

"Dad, did I get any calls or mail?" I asked.

"Yeah, uh … Cindy called."

"I just saw her. What'd she say?"

"For you to call her back."

"Yeah, she said you're a has-been and she's looking forward to meeting classy guys in college," Joey interjected rudely.

I didn't know why he was being this way, but pretended I didn't care. He knew Cynthia's leaving for college was a sensitive subject for me.

Joey continued, "Yep, when she leaves, she's gonna look through her year book with her new boyfriend, and when she sees you she's gonna say, 'Oh, and I used to know this guy.'"

Joey did say it in a humorous way, making Dad laugh, but I found it far from humorous. I retaliated by yelling, "Shut up, Joe! You idiot."

Joey stood up, took his right index finger, and put it into a hole he made with his left hand. "You see! This is what she's gonna get. She's gonna get this," Joey stated, insinuating that Cynthia was going to get fucked by some other guy.

After he did that, I rushed up to him and said, "Take it back!"

Joey continued to make the same gesture with his hands, so I clenched my fists and prepared my body for a fight.

Dad noticed the tension and said, "Stop it! You guys, stop!"

Our faces were so close, the tips of our noses practically touched.

I lifted my right hand back behind my shoulder and punched him in his face.

"Ah!" Joey yelled, then tackled me to the floor.

Dad pleaded, "Stop it! Now! Stop! For Godsakes, you're brothers! Eddie, Joey, stop! Stop!"

We continued to fight, knocking down the television and whatever else was in our path. Out of nowhere, Ed walked in and tried to break up the fight, but we were too strong, even for him.

Ed yelled, "Eddie … Eddie … Joe … stop! Stop! Come on! Come on!"

Dad did the only thing he could and called the police, "Hello? I need the police. There's a fight in my house, and I can't stop it." He gave them the address. "And hurry!"

When Joey and I heard him on the phone, we began to pull back our punches. We were tired, but our anger overcame the fatigue. When Ed saw us ease off on each other, he shoved his body between Joey and me to make sure we didn't go at each other again.

"You finished?" Ed asked.

I turned away, then rushed out of the house rubbing my head in distress. I was temporarily incoherent and shocked from fighting in such a hateful way toward my own blood, and thought, *How could I have done this? Why did I do it? Why?*

I suddenly saw a police officer on some steps of a church peeking from behind a wall.

He rushed out and demanded, "Hold it right there! Just take it easy."

I didn't want to listen to anyone. I just wanted to be left alone. I pointed my finger at him as tears started to pour down my face and yelled, "You ain't nothin'! There're tougher cops than you in New York!"

I was scared and wanted to run, but my body was frozen and felt like I couldn't move. He quickly pulled his club out from his right side and shouted, "Turn around! Put your hands behind

234

your back, now!"

I did what he told me. I heard more police cars surrounding the block. The policeman grabbed me and forced me to the ground. My face brushed up against the concrete.

"Next time you think New York cops are tough, remember this!" the cop said, landing a heavy knee hit on my lower back, taking the air out of me.

A lady cop asked, "Why did you do that?"

"Because this punk kid wouldn't listen."

He forced me up off the ground and pushed me into the police car, causing me to hit my head on the rim of the door jam. The windows were rolled up and the circulation to my wrists was slightly cut off from the handcuffs. It was hard to breathe because it was so hot in the car.

After about a half-hour of deliberation with his other cop buddies, he got into the police car, and we proceeded downtown. I didn't say a word. He then made some radio calls to the police station. When we got there, we drove into an indoor parking lot.

The cop unlocked my door and said, "Okay, tough guy, let's go."

I got out and tightened my hands as he escorted me into the police station.

"Okay, relax your hands, tough guy," the cop said, holding the chain link between the cuffs. "Let's go."

He brought me into the station and said, "I want you to look at this wall until I say you can turn around."

I nodded my head. The cop walked toward his cop friends and did some paperwork. I turned my head and saw the cop and his friends staring at me, laughing because I was facing the wall.

I quietly said, "The cuffs are too tight."

They ignored me. I stood there and looked at the wall for at least two hours. Another cop finally escorted me into a small, isolated room. They loosened the handcuffs. I rubbed my wrists in relief and waited there. Another door opened from the other side of the room. I followed the cop.

The cop said, "Take your shoe laces off."

I proceeded to do so.

The cop continued, "Over here. Give me your right hand."

He began to finger print me and brought me into a drunk tank with several other guys.

I looked around me and saw one guy with his shirt ripped to pieces, and another guy with long, unwashed hair and no shirt on, pacing the room back and forth.

There were two overhead cameras. The guy with the dirty hair proceeded toward me and said, "Look, look at this shit? They took my fuckin' shoe laces ... fuckin' ... fuckin' cops, why the fuck did they take my shoe laces?"

I couldn't help but chuckle to myself. The guy looked straight at one camera and flipped it the middle finger and shouted, "Fuck you, pig! Fuck you!"

The other guy with the ripped shirt kept muttering to himself, "My own wife did this to me ... my ... my own wife."

I sat on the floor with these smelly, belching drunks and waited. I didn't even know what time it was.

After what felt like hours of waiting, a policewoman came in and said, "Eddie Regory?"

"Yeah?"

"Follow me."

She brought me to the front counter and said, "Okay, I need you to sign here."

I signed the papers, and she escorted me out of the jail. It was night. I was about to call Ed, but instead called Cynthia. Embarrassed of my situation, I wasn't sure how I was going to tell her why I was in jail.

"Hello?" Cynthia answered.

"Cynthia? It's me."

"Eddie? What's wrong? You're voice sounds different."

"You won't believe where I am ... I'm ... I'm downtown."

"Downtown? Why?"

"Well ... I ... I uh ... I got into an argument with my brother."

"Yeah? And?"

I didn't want to tell her the real reason, so I made up

236

something.

"My brother got out of line with my dad, so I straightened him out."

"So why are you downtown?"

"I just got out of jail."

"Jail?"

"Yeah, jail."

"Over your brother getting out of line with your dad?"

"Well, we got into a big fight after, and the police showed up because of the disturbance."

"Well, where are you? I'll come get you."

"I'm in front of the courthouse downtown."

"Okay, I'll be there in fifteen minutes."

"Thanks," I said, hanging up.

Meanwhile, I sat on the steps of the courthouse and waited. When Cynthia showed up, I was happy to see her face. I walked over to her car and quickly got in.

"Hi."

"Hi, " she asked with concern, "are you okay?"

"Yeah, yeah … I'm cool," I said, "I'm sorry, Cindy."

"It's okay."

"Does your mom know what happened?" I asked.

"No. I told her I was going to see you, but I didn't say where you were."

"That was probably a good idea," I mumbled to myself.

"What was that?" Cynthia asked.

"Nothing."

Shortly after, we got to my house.

"Thanks, Cindy," I said.

"No problem. I hope things get better."

"So do I. So do I," I said, walking away toward the house.

When I entered the house, I said, "Hey, Dad,"

Dad was sitting in the living room with the lights dimmed and his small, tape recorder playing "Memories" again. I knew the song reminded him of Mom, so it didn't bother me to hear it all the time.

"Hey, son," Dad responded quietly. "How do you feel?"

With my head down and ashamed of my actions I said, "I'm sorry, Dad."

"It's not me you have to be sorry to, Eddie, it's your brother."

"I know. I know," I sighed, "but he pissed me off."

"Both of you were wrong. You guys are brothers. You shouldn't be fighting like that."

I asked, "Dad, why did you call the cops?"

"Eddie, there was no way I could stop you guys. I didn't know what else to do. You think I wanted to? I didn't want to do it, but you left me no choice."

"Dad?"

"Yeah."

"I'm gonna move out. Is that okay with you?"

"Eddie, I think it would be good for you to do, but if you ever need a home to come to, my door will always be open. I love you, son. Your mom loved you. You just gotta calm that temper of yours."

"Who will take care of you?"

"Eddie, I lived all these years taking care of myself, I could do just fine without you here."

"You sure?"

"Yeah, I'm sure. Come here and give me a hug?"

I hugged him.

Dad continued, "Now, what you need to do is make amends with your brother. That's what you need to do."

"Okay, Dad," I said. "I'll talk with him tomorrow."

"Good," Dad said. "Gimme hug good night?"

I hugged him and said, "Good night, Dad."

Chapter Thirty-Seven

Cynthia and I finally separated, and she left for college. At first it was difficult, but after a while without her, I actually felt free. On september 10, 1988, it was my twenty-first birthday. Ed, Stewart, Donnie (a friend of ours Ed graduated with) treated me out to a good time. They started by taking me to these clubs downtown. We drank straight shots of tequila and vodka. By eleven o'clock in the evening, we were very drunk. We got into Stewart's Battlewagon and headed for Southeast Portland, to a biker strip bar called Harpo's.

The music in the Battlewagon was playing loud to the song "Taking Care of Business" by BTO as Stewart drove faster. The Battlewagon began to shake from side-to-side because of our jumping, dancing, and singing to the lyrics of the song. We spilled beer all over the floor. When we got there, Donnie forced open the door.

"Ed! Ed! Wait up, man," I shouted, as Ed headed toward the front door to Harpo's.

"C'mon you fuckin' pansy-ass pussies!" Stewart said, laughing at us, then slurring the lyrics to "Taking Care of Business."

"Stewart, give me a chew," Ed demanded, feeling Stewart's pockets, trying to find his Copenhagen.

"Ed, Ed … you don't need that nasty-ass shit!" I said. "Man, what if some fine bitch wants you and you got that shit in your mouth?"

Ed quickly pinched some Copenhagen between his fingers and pressed it under his lower lip and casually said, "Well, then, she'll have to kiss me with it in my mouth."

Stewart opened the door to Harpo's. Donnie walked in first, and the rest of us followed. Wooden pillars stood on the right and left sides of us. The dance floor was straight ahead.

Ed pulled out his wallet and said, "Tim, get some brews for

us," handing him some money.

"What kind do you want?"

"Doesn't matter," Ed replied, walking away.

We sat a couple of tables away from the dance floor, and the stripper signaled for Ed to come closer.

I didn't want Ed to go, because I knew if he did, he would waste his money on her. Ed got up from his seat anyway and proceeded toward the front stage.

"Ed, Ed, don't go up there," I said, "she just wants your money, dude. She's nasty anyway!"

"I'm just gonna see what she wants."

I chuckled and said, "I know what she wants. She wants your money! C'mon, let's go play some pool."

"In a minute … in a minute," Ed replied, as he walked toward the stage and sat down in front of her.

Even after a few beers, she was still the ugliest stripper I'd ever seen. I reluctantly stood up and sat by Ed, watching the stripper slowly take off another piece of clothing to a different song. My face was in disgust by the sight of her cellulite legs, tattooed body, and sagging breasts.

When I turned my head to see Ed's reactions toward the stripper, he had this content look on his face. He reached in his pants pocket and pulled out a one-dollar bill, then laid it on the counter in an erect position for the stripper. The stripper showed Ed more attention and proceeded to squat over the one-dollar bill making sexual gestures at him.

The stripper squatted further down onto the dollar bill and lifted it up by enclosing her vagina over it. We couldn't believe our eyes. Ed and I looked at each other, then laughed.

"Holy shit!" I blurted. "I can't believe it."

"Whoa! Damn!" Ed said, as he bellowed an Airborne Ranger shout, "Ar-uah!"

I blurted, "This bitch is nasty!"

The stripper glanced at me with a scowl then danced around the stage for other customers. I felt Ed watched her for the same reason I did: because it was like watching a freak show. She came back our way and danced some more in front of us. This time, Ed reached into his pocket and pulled out a five-dollar bill. I was surprised, but not in disbelief.

"Ed, don't give her that."

Ed said, laying the five-dollar bill on the counter, "It's all right. It's okay. She deserves it."

I grabbed the five back off the counter and said, "She deserves it? Whatta you, nuts! You're wasting your money!"

The stripper eyed me with resentment and shouted, "Why don't you leave him alone and let him put his money where he wants!"

Ed laughed and said, "She told you."

I looked up at the stripper and theatrically said, "Well, if you weren't so fuckin' fat, and if your ass didn't smell, maybe I would. You're not worth the penny I have in my pocket, bitch!"

I looked around to see the reactions to my comment toward the stripper. Everyone was in disbelief. I looked back at the stripper and saw her pick up an ashtray to throw at me.

"You asshole!" she yelled. "You betta get the hell outta here!"

I quickly got up off my seat and ran for cover behind the nearest pillar. Suddenly, some biker guys stood up from their chairs, gazing at me with their rugged faces and cold eyes.

There was a moment of silence, then Stewart blurted, "We betta get the fuck outta here!"

Donnie was laughing as Ed and I hurried toward the exit.

The waitress said firmly, "Both of you are eighty-sixed out of here! Don't come back!"

We thought for sure there was going to be a fight, but the biker guys didn't follow us. Instead, they watched to make sure we left. Ed was laughing so hard he could barely breathe. It began to rain as we got inside the Battlewagon. Stewart sped out of the parking lot and drove recklessly west on Powell toward downtown.

The music got louder and the partying in the back of the Battlewagon intensified.

I looked out the window and saw one girl with blond hair

and yelled, "Yo, baby! Yo! What's up? Wait! Where you goin'? Can we come with you?"

Ed was trying to open the door to talk to her while the VW was moving.

"What the fuck are you doin'?" I asked, grabbing Ed and pulling him away from the door.

"That girl … that girl was awesome! Did you see her?"

"Ed," Donnie said, "we can find some fine bitches somewhere else."

Donnie passed a half-bottle of tequila around.

"Give me that! Give me that bottle!" Ed demanded, grabbing the bottle away from Donnie's hands.

"Here, fuck-head!" Donnie said laughing. "Take the whole fuckin' thing!"

Ed lifted the bottle to his mouth and guzzled it.

"Ed, man, what the fuck?" I said, in disbelief while Donnie, Tim, and Stewart laughed on.

"I'm an Airborne Ranger!" Ed exclaimed proudly.

"Airborne nothin'. You're a damn idiot!" I said, "give me that!"

I gulped a quick straight shot out of the bottle.

"Stewart!" I shouted because it was hard to hear with all the yelling and loud music bouncing off the small, paneled walls of the Battlewagon. "Stewart! Stewart!"

"What?"

"Where we goin'?"

"How the hell do I know," Stewart said. "Tell Ed to give me some chew."

I looked over my shoulder and yelled, "Ed! Ed! Stewart wants your chew."

"Tell him to kiss my Ranger ass!"

Stewart laughed after he said that and said, "Ed, give me a chew!"

"C'mon Ed, give Stewart a dip before he goes nuts and drives this car even crazier," I said.

Ed threw me his can, then looked over to Tim and asked, "Whatta you lookin' at, Castro?"

Tim was quiet for a second and replied, "Nothin', you Marine wannabe."

"Stewart, where we goin', man?" I asked impatiently.

"We're going to the opera."

"Seriously, Stew?"

"Back to Harpo's."

"Quit fuckin' around," I said, irritated with his not giving me a straight answer. "Where the fuck are we goin'?"

Stewart quickly looked over his shoulder and yelled, "Ed, Ed, where we goin'? Tim, you know where we're goin'?"

Ed shouted, "To the moon, Alice ... to drink some tequila!"

I heard this banging sound in the back, and when I looked over my shoulder, I saw Ed wrestling with Tim trying to take his pants off.

"Donnie, Donnie, help me take his pants off," Ed said, laughing uncontrollably.

Don tried to help him, but Tim wouldn't let it happen easily. He fought back like I've never seen a 135-pound Marine fight.

"Ed, Ed, stop!" Tim begged, using all his strength against Ed and Donnie.

Neither of them gave up as they laughed so hard tears came down their drunken faces.

"Eddie, Eddie, help us!" Ed yelled. "We almost got 'em off."

I rushed over there and assisted them. After so much fighting, Tim couldn't fight anymore and let us take his pants off. We sat there and laughed so hard Stewart couldn't even drive and almost hit a parked car.

"Okay, guys," Tim drops his voice to a lower pitch, "give me my pants back."

"Hey, Tim, you Marine guys sure are tough," I said, holding my stomach in pain from all the laughter.

"Stewart, stop the car!" Ed demanded.

"Why?"

"Because!"

Stewart pulled over by a park, and Ed forced the side door open. He then rushed over to Tim, grabbed him by his shirt, then pulled him out the Battlewagon in his underwear.

"Ed, no!" Tim yelled, frantically trying to fight his way back into the car. "C'mon, Ed! No, no, no!"

"Holy shit!" Donnie said. "That's cold."

Ed got Tim out of the Battlewagon and shut the door.

"C'mon Ed. Let me back in!" Tim pleaded, "C'mon!"

Stewart peeked out the passenger window and yelled, "Hey, Tim, what are you doing out there in your underwear, you sicko?"

"C'mon you guys ... c'mon, open the door!"

After minutes in the cold rain, Ed unlatched the door and opened it for Tim.

Tim rushed back into the VW and said, "Man, that was fuckin' cold. You're all fuckin' assholes!"

Stewart pressed on the gas pedal and peeled rubber and drove away. I whispered a few words in Donnies's ear, and when we were ready, we were going to do what I secretly suggested.

It began to rain harder, and it was almost time for my cue to Donnie. Suddenly, I dashed toward Ed and grabbed him from behind.

"Donnie, Donnie! Help me!"

Tim didn't know what was going on, but that didn't matter because if it was something against Ed, he was in. Donnie wrapped his arms around Ed's legs, and I wrestled Ed toward the floor. Ed was considerably stronger than Tim, so it was harder to take his pants off. We managed to get his pants about a quarter of the way down.

Tim and Donnie gave up, but I persisted. We were five or so blocks away from Wallace Park, and I noticed what started out to be for fun, became a fight between us. I couldn't believe it.

It wasn't the kind of fight where we wanted to hurt each other, because if it were, we would've thrown punches instead. We angrily wrestled until we felt the Battlewagon come to a screeching halt. Our bodies quickly rolled forward toward the front.

Tim shouted, "Damn, Stew, you made me spill my beer!"

Donnie tried to break it up between us and yelled, "Stop you guys! Stop! This is dumb!"

But it was like trying to separate an Anaconda wrapped around a tree.

"Fuck! Stop, you guys! Stop!" Donnie pleaded, over the loud blasting music.

Stewart forced open the side door. Donnie pushed us out, and we fell onto the wet, flooded ground and wrestled through the dirty street. I quickly looked around me and noticed we had stopped on the corner of 25th and Pettygrove. Our clothes were soaking wet as I saw the heavy drops of rain bounce off Ed's face. We rolled near a curb where the water was even deeper.

"Ed! Eddie! Ed, you guys stop!" Tim shouted, trying to break us up.

The shining headlights of cars that beeped their horns at us blinded me. I grabbed Ed's hair between my hands and drenched the back of his head in the dirty, deep puddle of water and shouted, "C'mon! You wanna fuck with me! C'mon!"

I could see the hurt in Ed's face and feel it in my heart as we fought, guilty and ashamed. I noticed no resistance from him anymore. So I began to ease my anger, letting his head slip away from my hands, then watching it drop into the dirty water. Donnie and Tim lifted me up off Ed.

Donnie shouted, "I can't believe you guys! You guys are friends. I can't fuckin' believe it!"

Stewart lifted Ed out of the dirty water. Ed pinched the chew out from his mouth and didn't say a word.

He began to walk toward me, and Stewart said, "No, no, no … I'm not gonna let you go over there if you're gonna go off again, Ed."

"I'm cool … I'm cool," Ed said, moving Stewart aside. "Let's walk."

"Cool," I replied.

Ed swung his arm around my shoulders.

Tim was going to follow us, but Stewart said, "No, Tim. Let 'em alone."

We walked against the rain on the muddy grass toward the basketball court. Ed took his wet, slightly cracked Copenhagen can out of his back pocket, lifted the lid, and put a pinch full of chew into his lower lip.

"You know, you fight like a girl," Ed said, in a casual tone.

For a second I was quiet, then I laughed and replied, "I kicked your ass all over that street. Whatta you talkin' about?"

"You didn't kick my ass," Ed said. "If I wanted, I could've snapped your neck!"

"Ah, shit, man ... I had your head in a puddle of dirty water. Your ass was drownin'."

We hugged each other.

"I'm sorry, bro," I said. "I didn't mean to kick your ass."

"Me too," Ed replied.

We walked back to the Battlewagon and Ed said, "That was fun. We should do that again sometime."

"Cool with me."

I knew there was nothing on earth that would separate our friendship, not even a fight. Afterwards, we drove to 7-Eleven and ate some nachos, and from there, Stewart drove me home.

"Thanks, Stew," I said before closing the door. "Ed, I love ya."

"I love ya, too."

"Now, don't get in anymore fights," Stewart said speeding off.

Later I took a hot shower and went to bed.

Chapter Thirty-Eight

The next morning, I woke up because dad was yelling, "Eddie ... Eddie!"

I quickly got up, opened my bedroom door, and dashed toward the bathroom, where I saw Dad on the floor, crying in agony, "Oh, God, God, why did it have to be me? ... God!"

Dad's five hundred-pound body was stuck between the bath tub and toilet, and his walker that he used to help him into the bathroom was on the floor.

"Dad!" I said rushing to his aid. "What happened?"

"The floor was, was wet," Dad replied, breathing heavily. "Why did you leave the floor wet? God, why?"

"Dad, I'm sorry! ... Sorry!"

I held his heavy, flabby arm in my hands and tried to help him up.

"No ... no ... I just ... just need to lay here for, for a while ... catch my breath," Dad said, resting his head on his left arm.

"Dad, are you sure you don't want me to help you up?"

"Just let me be!" Dad exclaimed, closing his eyes as if he wanted to sleep.

I knew the bathroom floor needed to be dry at all times because of his weight. If not, the chances of him slipping were great.

After about ten minutes, Dad was ready for me to help him up.

He lifted his right arm up and motioned for me to come, "Okay, son, come 'ere."

I held his wrist in my hand and asked, "How do you wanna do this?"

"Okay, lift ... here ... let me see if ... if I can lift some of myself up," Dad said, as he proceeded to put his right hand on the rim of the toilet and his left arm beneath his obese body for leverage. "God, why did I have to be so fat? Why did I do this to myself?"

"Dad, let me do something."

"No. I gotta do some of this myself then you can help," Dad replied, struggling to lift at least some of his upper-body weight off the wet floor. His breasts were so big they moved from side-to-side, making it harder for him to breathe. Dad managed to rest his upper body on the edge of the toilet.

"Okay, come 'ere ... come 'ere," Dad said gasping for air.

He put his right arm around my shoulder, and I could see the cornstarch caked below his armpit as it flaked off his old clothes. He continued, "Okay, grab my walker over there."

I picked it up off the floor and handed it to him. He grabbed the walker with his right hand and grabbed the rim of the toilet with his left hand. He then slowly turned his body toward me and motioned me to come closer, so he could rest his left arm on my shoulder. I knelt down and struggled to keep just the upper part of his body into an erect position.

"Okay, on the count of three, I want you, you to help me up on the walker. One, two, three!"

I lifted and lifted. He was too heavy, but I would not let go. Even together, we could not get him on his feet. At this point, Dad knew he had to do it himself.

"Okay, I want you to help me to the sink. Just get me to the sink."

"You're sure, Dad?"

"Yeah, yeah."

Together we inched his body toward the sink, which was only about three feet away. Dad grabbed the counter and put the walker in front of his body. I stood behind him and put my hands under his armpits.

"Okay, on the count of three, just help me get to my feet," Dad counted. "One, two, three!"

I lifted with all my strength as Dad's obese body moved recklessly. He got to his feet and held the walker tightly, keeping his elbows straight.

"You got it, Dad?"

"Yeah, yeah," Dad replied, slowly inching his way out the

bathroom door and into the living room. He stepped over toward his recliner and flopped on it, and exhaled this sudden burst of relief.

"You okay, Dad?" I'm sorry for leaving the floor wet, but I thought—"

"It's not your fault. It's just this fat, obese body I deserve to have," Dad said regrettably. "I should've never gotten this way. Now I'm paying the price."

I sat down on the sofa and looked over to Dad and asked, "You're sure you okay?"

"Yeah. Just let me alone," Dad said, in an annoyed tone.

I couldn't help but to quietly laugh to myself, thinking of what he reminded me of when he lay helpless on the bathroom floor.

To break the silence I said calmly, "Yeah, man, you were like the Titanic."

Dad looked over to me and quietly chuckled.

I wanted a job where I could use some of my artistic abilities. I thought Dad might be able to help with my first resume, so I walked into his room one morning and said, "Hey, Dad."

"Hey, son," Dad replied quietly, as he lay in his bed with his blue, cotton hat over his eyes.

"Dad, Dad, can you help me for a sec'?"

"I'm tired right now. Talk to me later."

"Dad, I need your help now," I said, softly laying my hand on his right shoulder.

Dad lay on his left side most of the time, so I could see his physical reaction to my persistence. He was tired and annoyed.

"C'mon, Eddie. I'm tired."

"Just for a sec', Dad."

Dad brought his heavy body erect up on his bed and said, "Eddie, you're a pain in the ass! You know that?"

"Dad, c'mon. I need help on this resume 'cause I've never done one before."

"What the hell makes you think I know how to do one?

Especially this early in the morning?" Dad said, looking at his tiny clock on his old, wooden desk. "Six o'clock! Are you crazy! I'm goin' back to sleep."

Dad pulled his hat over his eyes, lay back down, and tried to sleep.

I felt it was time for strategy. I hugged him while he lay there on his bed and whispered, "Dad, I will bug you until you get up, so let's make it easy on both of us. Either you get up and help me on this resume, or I will irritate you to death."

"Eddie, leave me alone, pleeease!"

"Dad, do you want me to succeed in this world? Do you want me to become somebody?"

"Eddie, I don't care what you become ... just let me be!"

I became slightly discouraged and went back to my room. I grabbed a sheet of paper and pencil off the floor and began to write.

After hours of rewriting, I folded the hand-written papers and put them into my coat pocket. I caught the bus to the Safeway supermarket and cashed in the empty beer bottles and Coke cans for the deposit, and used the money to get my resume professionally typed.

Chapter Thirty-Nine

The journey for my first real job began downtown. I walked into an office building and saw a large directory, which showed the office locations of people who had professional practices. I knew it wasn't for me, so I used the same bus transfer and rode to Sandy Boulevard. I searched around the area and noticed a white building. I walked in and saw the receptionist to my right.

"Hi, um ... my name's Eddie, and I was wondering if your company was looking for a hard-working, reliable person."

The receptionist was a bit startled by my forwardness and replied, "Just a minute. I'll get someone for you to talk to." She motioned to a wooden bench. "Have a seat over there, please."

"Thanks."

I was dressed in a sweater, brown corduroys, and penny loafers. I heard heels of heavy boots walking my way, but I could not see who it was, yet I stayed calm and confident. An older man with an authoritative voice said, "Hi, I'm Gage ... hear you're looking for a job."

"Yes, sir."

"Well, what do you know? Do you know anything about screen printing?"

I felt if I didn't fabricate just a little about what I knew, I would have probably passed up an opportunity. So I quickly debated on what answer I should give him and said, "Yes, yes sir, I do. I'm familiar with the process."

"You are? Okay, come with me," Gage said.

I followed him into a warehouse, where I saw Asian women sewing golf bags and using cutting machines of all kinds. He brought me to the back of the warehouse and pushed open some doors, which led us into an art department.

"This is where we do all of our printing. Do you think you'd like to do this?"

"Yes, yes I would, sir."

"Jim!" Gage voiced loudly toward the supervisor, "This is Eddie, and he's looking for a job."

Gage turned around and left, his shoes making the same clanking sound.

The supervisor was a small man who had dark hair and an unshaven face. He looked me up and down and asked, "So, how much do you know about screen printing?"

Instead of lying to him about how much I didn't know, I told him of all my accomplishments in the field of art. "Well, I've developed a board game I tried to screen print myself, and started reading up on stuff about how to screen print. I also graduated from Lincoln High School. I'm ambitious and a fast learner, too."

"Oh, wow, so you're into making games, huh?"

"Yes sir."

"Just call me Jim," he said, looking over to a girl working on some sort of stenciling, "although some people call me other names."

Jim proceeded to show me around the semi-clean shop and introduced me to the other ladies, including a deaf lady who did all the embroidering.

"So, when do you think you can start?"

When I heard this, my heart was pumping from excitement. I felt like jumping in the air and banging my feet together like in that Toyota commercial.

"Right away! I can start right away!"

"Well, how 'bout Monday since it's the start of a new week."

"That's fine. Perfect!"

"Okay, so, we'll see you Monday."

"Great. Thank you very much. Monday it is."

He escorted me out the front doors and shook my hand.

"Eddie?"

"Yes?"

"Welcome aboard."

"Thanks."

When I walked out, I was so happy I couldn't wait to get

home and tell Dad. I thought, *Yes! I got me a real job.*

My first day on the job, I came dressed in jeans, a blue, loose-fitting shirt, and a white bandanna wrapped around my head. It was the same bandanna I wore when I went running.

"Hey, Eddie! You look ready to work."

"Yeah, I'm ready."

I noticed another girl in the shop I didn't see the first time. She was thin and had blond hair. She seemed sort of shy. Jim showed me to a Hopkins printing press a few feet away and asked, "So, have you ever worked on one of these before?"

I wanted to impress Jim with my knowledge, but didn't want to sound dumb. I gave the only answer I thought feasible, "Yeah, um … this is a printing press."

"Yes, that's right. It's a printing press. So you have worked with one of these?"

"Well, I'm familiar with the process, and I've seen one of them at work but never really worked on one myself."

I began to sense Jim knew I didn't know as much as I had portrayed. But he liked me, so he was willing to show me the ropes. Jim grabbed a white towel and laid it on the palette. He took a small can of red, soluble ink and layered some below the image on the inside of the screen. I watched on with interest and the desire to learn this new trade.

Jim said, leaning over the screen, "You pull the screen down over the palette and flood the image. Rest the screen over the palette and hold the squeegee with both hands. Tilt the squeegee a little, and pull the ink through the screen onto the towel on the palette."

Jim lifted the screen up, and I was amazed.

"Whoa," I quietly said, "that's cool."

"You try it."

I got behind the press and grabbed the squeegee.

"Like this?"

"There ya go. You got it," Jim said. "With a little practice, you'll be busting out these jobs in no time."

I flooded the image on the screen and pulled the ink through.

"Wow."

Jim said, "Pretty cool, huh?"

"Yeah, it is."

"Eddie? Let me ask you something?"

I stopped what I was doing and listened attentively.

"You really didn't know how to screen-print, did you?"

I brought my head down like a sad puppy and said, "No. Not really."

"Hey," Jim said, "doesn't matter. I didn't know either. Everybody needs a start. Here, practice on these towels."

He walked away from me, and I felt nothing but respect for him. Suddenly all my feelings of failure and no hope for something better were now in the past. And it was all because Jim believed in me.

That weekend, I was anxious to celebrate with Ed about my new job. I called him up and said, "Ed! Ed! Guess what, man?"

"Whazzup, cuz?"

"I got a job!"

"Cool, where at? What kind of job?"

"I'm gonna be a screen printer!"

"Hey, that's great, Eddie. When do you start?"

"I already did."

"Hey, you know where I'm goin'?"

"Where?"

"California with Tim."

"California? Why? When?" I asked.

"In a couple of months."

"Why?"

"I just want to get myself together and quit drinking and do something with my life."

"So how's California gonna help you with that?" I asked.

"Well, I signed myself in this rehabilitation center out there."

At that point, I forgot about my new job and thought how I was going to lose him.

"So, how long are you gonna be there?" I asked sadly.

"Just a little while. Just long enough to clean myself out,

and I'm gonna start running every day. When I come back, I'll be in really good shape again. We can both start running again."

"I'm gonna miss you, man."

"I'm gonna miss you too, bro," Ed said. "But I'll come up and visit."

"So, what do you want to do tonight?" I asked.

"Par-dy!" Ed squealed loudly.

Chapter Forty

We later met and rode in Ed's new Volkswagen bus. We called it, "the Battlewagon 2." It was about nine o' clock in the evening, and we partied at an area east of the Willamette River, below the Hawthorne Bridge.

It always gave me a good feeling to be there. There were times Ed and I would park our motorcycles on the pedestrian walk on the Hawthorne Bridge and stare at the city lights.

Neil, Joey, Bubba, and Tim showed up later. After drinking some Budweiser beers, I noticed Ed wasn't around.

"Tim, where's Ed?"

"I don't know. He was here with Neil a minute ago," Tim said, looking over to Stewart, "Stew, give me a chew."

"I don't have any more, Cuban."

"Bubba, have you seen Ed? Has anybody seen Ed?" I asked.

"No, I haven't. I saw him a while ago."

"Where the hell can he be?" I said. "I have no idea where to look. I haven't seen him since we got here."

"Ask Joey. Maybe he saw him," Bubba suggested.

"Man ... where the hell is he?" I quietly said, pacing around the Battlewagon 2.

I gave up looking and patiently waited for Ed to show up.

Bubba's face looked surprised and said, "What the fu'?"

I turned around and saw Ed.

"Ed? Where the hell have you been? You're wet!"

"I know. I jumped off the bridge," Ed said.

"What?"

"I jumped off the bridge."

"He did. I saw him do it," Neil said. "I couldn't believe it either."

"You saw him do it?"

"Yeah, man, I saw him. I couldn't believe it."

"Ed, did you really?" I asked.

"Yeah," Ed confirmed, taking the chew out from his mouth. "Stewart, give me a another chew. This one's wet."

"I'm not the chew supplier here," Stewart said, grabbing his chew out from his jeans pocket and handing it to Ed. "Here!"

I didn't know how to respond. Maybe because I was in denial that he could do something so stupid.

"Ed tell me you really didn't do that."

"I did. Hey, can I use your shoes?"

"My shoes? What am I gonna wear?"

"Wear those shoes in the van. The ones I gave you."

"Those are boxing shoes."

I looked down at his running shoes and saw they were soaking wet. I slipped my penny loafers off and gave them to him.

"Here, man. These are my only dress shoes, so don't mess 'em up."

"Thanks, brutha."

I tried forgetting what had happened, faced Bubba, and conversed with him. Shortly after, I began to get hungry for nachos. I was going to ask Ed if he could drive me to 7-Eleven, but he was nowhere to be found again. I looked up at the Hawthorne Bridge to see if he was up there. Suddenly, Ed was walking toward me again.

I yelled across the lot, "Ed! Come 'ere, man!"

He appeared a little drained.

I continued, "Where'd you go now?"

Ed replied almost out of breath, "I jumped off the bridge again."

By now I was angry and not in denial. I glanced down at the shoes I lent him and bent over to touch them.

"They're soaked! What the hell are you thinking, man?"

I noticed a penny from the left shoe was gone.

"I did it 'cause I was bored."

"Ed, man, because you're bored?"

Ed didn't take me seriously and blared, "I'm an Airborne Ranger!"

"You're gonna be an Airborne nothing if you do that shit again," I said, in an angry tone.

The other guys sort of laughed in disbelief.

"Ed, please, man, don't do that again?" I asked, resting my hand on his shoulder.

It was late, and the party was dying down. Bubba and the other guys went home.

Ed and I stayed out and decided to go to a tavern called the Belmont Inn on Southeast Belmont.

We sat a few seats away from the empty dance floor. The waitress came up to us and asked, "You guys know what you want?"

"Yeah," we replied.

"What would you like?" she asked.

"How 'bout a pitcher of Henry's ... um, a side order of onion rings—Ed, did you want something to eat?"

Ed replied, "Nah."

Before the waitress left, I said, "Oh, and ... uh ... your phone number, too."

She smiled and replied, "Sorry, but that's not on the menu."

"Well, can we put it on the menu?"

She chuckled and said, "I'll be back with your drinks."

"Dude, she was fine!" I said, staring at her ass as headed back toward the bar.

Ed reached in his pants pocket and pulled his wet can of Copenhagen out, pinched a large amount between his fingers, put it into his lower lip, and replied, "Yep."

We sat there and looked at this empty dance floor, listening to the sound of oldie music. Ed was intoxicated, but hid it well. Which was also why he wasn't talking much. His eyes were slightly red, and I could tell he was in deep contemplation about something.

"Here's your pitcher," the waitress said, setting it down with two coasters and glasses.

"Thank you," Ed said, pouring beer into my glass first, then his.

I took a sip and said, "Ed, give me a dip."

He smiled and replied gesturing like I was crazy, "You don't dip."

Ed kept staring at the dance floor, thinking of something.

Then they played "Jail House Rock" by Elvis Presley over the huge, loud speakers. Suddenly Ed got up and walked toward the dance floor with his back facing everyone. He began shaking his right leg to the beat of the music. He lifted his collar up and started dancing as if he was Elvis himself. I couldn't let my best friend go up there alone and have all the fun, so I joined him.

Chapter Forty-One

The next day Ed and I got up and ate one of his power breakfasts.

"How'd you like your breakfast?" Ed asked.

"It was good." I asked, "Do you remember what you did last night?"

"Kind of, why?"

"'Cause, man, you did some crazy shit."

"Like what?"

"Like what? Man, you were fucked up," I quietly uttered, shaking my head. "Ed, you jumped off the Hawthorne Bridge. Don't you remember?"

"Yeah," Ed replied.

"Ed, if you're gonna do that, we can't go out drinkin' anymore."

"I know … I know. You're right. That's why I'm goin' to rehab'," Ed said, changing the subject. "Hey, you feel like rappelling?"

I used to watch those army movies where guys would rappel from helicopters, and often had a curiosity about what it would be like. That's why he asked.

"I don't think so. I've never rappelled before."

"That's okay. I'll teach you."

"Nah, man. I'd be too scared."

"Well, I'll bring the ropes anyway. Just in case."

Ed went into his room and got his ropes and clips.

I heard him say, "Damn!"

"What's up?" I asked.

"I think Timmy's got a clip of mine."

"Do you need it?"

"Sorta. That's okay. I think these do," Ed said, grabbing whatever clips and rope he had available.

We headed out the door and got into the Battlewagon 2 and

drove to Northwest Portland. We drove past Wallace Park, and Friendly House Community Center, and right then Ed blurted, "I know where we can go."

"Where?"

"The Thurman Bridge."

"Why?" I asked.

"To rappel."

"Are you serious?"

"Yeah, we won't be there long. Let's just try it."

"All right," I agreed hesitantly.

The Thurman Bridge overlooked Macleay Park. We drove there and parked just west of Missy's mother's house. Ed pulled out his ropes and clips, and we proceeded to walk up the hill, halfway up the bridge. I was kind of excited about doing it, but I was also scared.

Ed asked, "You wanna try it first?"

"No way, man! What if some cop comes by?"

"I'll go first, then you can try it."

"I don't know, Ed ... this looks pretty scary."

"It's really easy," Ed explained, "I'll strap this around your waist and use these clips for the rope. The gloves will protect your hands from getting rope burn."

"It's easy 'cause you know how to do it. I don't think I can do it," I said. "Let's just forget it."

"Let me show you," Ed said, tying a few clips to the rope and around his buttocks, making sure everything was tight and secure.

He then tied the rope on the outside part of the rail and proceeded to step over it. I looked over the rail, and my eyes froze at the sight of the cement path about one hundred feet down.

"Ed, I don't know, man," I said, nervously watching him hold tightly to the rope and put his body into an "L" shape position off the edge of the bridge.

Ed explained, "You see ... you hold tightly, then you push off with your legs."

Ed proceeded to count as I watched with anticipation, "One,

262

two, three!" he cried out, gliding down the rope like a bird glides in the air.

When I saw how easy he made it look, I was eager to try it. He landed softly on the ground and shouted up, "See! Told you it's easy."

"I wanna try it," I yelled down.

Ed unclipped himself and walked up some stairs which led him back up to the bridge.

"You wanna try it?"

"I do and I don't. Whatta you think?"

"I think you should try it. You saw how easy it was for me."

"Okay!"

He wrapped the rope around me making sure everything was safe and secure. He held tightly to my shirt as I stepped over the rail. I was too scared to do the same "L" shape position off the bridge, but after some pep talk, I did.

"Eddie, listen … just let your hand loose of the rope from behind you, and you'll glide down," Ed said. "Don't be afraid. Like I said, the gloves will stop the rope from burning your hands."

"Okay."

"Don't be afraid. Just push off," Ed said.

"I don't know, man."

"Just do it."

I slowly eased off the rope from behind me and began to glide toward the ground. I pushed the rope flush up against my back, then suddenly stopped about a quarter of the way down. Ed was saying something, but I couldn't understand him because I was concentrating on what I was doing. I released a little more rope from behind me and the front of my shirt got tangled into my front clip. I was now halfway between the bridge and the ground. Ed had made sure everything was secure, except for my shirt not tucked in tight enough into my pants.

"Ed, Ed! My shirt … my shirt is caught."

"What?"

"My shirt is stuck! It got caught in the clip."

"Can you swing yourself to the left, close to the hill?" Ed

asked.

"I don't know. I'll try," I answered, swinging as hard as I could but getting nowhere. The rope began to cut off the circulation around the upper part of my legs.

"I can't do it."

"Okay, hold on," Ed said, "I'm gonna have to cut your shirt."

Ed ran back to the Battlewagon 2 and grabbed a bowie knife. He rushed back and walked midway down the stairs near the bridge and started to climb it. He managed to get to the middle of the bridge and said, "Eddie, can you swing toward me?"

"I think so."

I began to swing myself.

"C'mon … c'mon … gotcha!" Ed said grabbing the rope.

He cut some of my shirt, but it would have been too dangerous to take it off.

"I'm gonna go back down and swing you over toward the hill by the stairs."

"Hurry up, man. My legs are killin' me!" I urged him, almost crying from the pain.

Ed grabbed the rope from the ground and swung me to the left, so he could run back up the hill to grab me. After several attempts, I swung as hard as I could one last time, and Ed snatched me with both hands.

"Damn, get this rope off me!"

"You okay?" Ed asked.

"Yeah, I think so."

When we got back to the car, I was extremely sore, and the inside of my legs had red indentations from the rope.

"You was a little sissy," Ed teased, making this funny, crying face at me.

I kept rubbing the pain away from the insides of my legs.

"Man, you try havin' a rope wrapped around your fuckin' ass cuttin' your circulation."

"Youza little girl," Ed continued. "Nah, I'm just joking."

"Man, shut up!"

Ed left for California, and after a while on my new job, I got a small raise and decided to buy my first new car. I was going to buy one of those Yugos, then decided to have Stewart help me buy a Volkswagen instead. We went to Volkswagen of America in downtown Portland.

I spoke with a saleslady who seemed fairly nice and worked within my budget. I pretty much knew what I wanted, because a girl at my job let me drive her car to see what it was like. With two hundred dollars down, I bought my first car. I was so excited.

Thrilled about my new car, I called Bubba.

"Bubba! I got a new car. An '89 Volkswagen Fox."

"How much did it cost?"

"About seven thou'. I bought a stereo and bra, too."

"Come get me!" Bubba said eagerly.

"Okay."

I dashed out the door and drove to Northwest 29th and Vaughn Street where Bubba lived, and honked my horn for him to come out.

"Buddy!" Bubba exclaimed. "Look here. Nice!"

"Get in, man. Where do you wanna go?"

"Can I drive?" Bubba asked.

"Yeah, c'mon."

He anxiously got in the driver's side and we drove around the Northwest.

"Hey, let's go to Wallace Park," I suggested.

"Why?"

"Because I wanna see who's over there."

Bubba drove there and parked the car on the north side of the park. We walked up the grassy hill.

I looked over to Bubba and said, "Maybe Hazel's here."

"Maybe."

Right when I said that, I noticed a girl sitting on the ground, watching the other guys playing basketball. At first it was too dark to see who it was, but when I paced closer, I became happy and surprised.

"Yo, Hazel! Whatta you doin' here?"

She had a little smile on her face as if she was also happy to see me.

"Nothing."

"Well, how's your sister? How's your mom?"

"They're fine."

When Hazel stood up from the ground, she was the most beautiful girl I'd ever seen. She didn't even look pudgy anymore.

"Hi, Hazel," Bubba said. "Eddie told me to come to the park 'cause he was lookin' for you."

Hazel smiled.

"Hey, um … I got a new car. You wanna drive it?"

"Sure," she replied, slightly surprised I would even ask.

"Bubba, give me my keys," I said. "I'll be back, bro."

We began walking toward the car.

"Yeah, sure you will. You found Hazel. You're not coming back," Bubba said jokingly.

I walked Hazel to the driver's side and opened the door for her. She got in, then I quickly got in on the passenger side.

I asked, "You know how to drive a clutch?"

"Mm-hmm."

I showed her where the gears were. She started the car and we drove off.

"How do you like it?" I asked.

"It's nice." Hazel asked, "Where did you get it?"

"At a Volkswagen place downtown."

"It's nice."

We drove around a little longer and finally came back to the park.

"It's about time!" Bubba said, gesturing as if we took forever.

"Hey, I was showing Hazel my new ride. Hazel, you gonna be here tomorrow?"

"Um, no."

"Well, can I get your phone number so I can call you guys?"

"You have a pen?"

"Bubba, you have a pen?" I asked.

Bubba said, "Bubba, give me the key … give me a pen … what do you think I am."

"Thanks, man."

Chapter Forty-Two

The following weekend Hazel and I met at Lloyd Center Mall. I saw her waiting for me by the railing on the bridge overlooking the ice skating rink. She was wearing a red leather skirt, black nylon stockings and a rayon blouse. I sneaked up behind her and softly touched her hips with both my hands.

"Yo!"

She turned around and said, "Hi."

"What's up?"

"Nothing."

"Where do you wanna go eat?" I asked.

"Doesn't matter," she said, "wherever you want."

I wanted to take her someplace nice, but only had about twenty bucks on me.

"Well, why don't we drive around and see if we can find a place."

"Okay."

We got into my car and drove toward the Sandy Boulevard area. I saw Sylvia's (an Italian restaurant) and said, "Hey! Why don't we try that place?"

Hazel nodded her head and said, "Okay."

I parked the car and opened the door for her. We stepped into the restaurant. I tried to be gentleman-like in everything I did.

The host approached us and asked, "Two for lunch?"

"Yeah," I replied.

"Here are your menus. Your waitress will be with you in a minute."

"Thanks," I said. I turned to Hazel, "So, um, you look great."

"Thank you."

The waitress came.

"Hi, my name is Sonia and I'll be your waitress this

afternoon. Is there anything I can get for you to drink?"

"Um … Hazel, would you like something to drink?"

"I'll have a Coke."

"She'll have a Coke, and I'll just have some water for now."

"Okay, that's a Coke and a water."

I opened the menu, and I was shocked at the prices. Your average meal was about twelve dollars.

I didn't want her to think I didn't have the money and said, "Order what you want."

I figured I could have the soup if she ordered something too expensive.

A few minutes later …

The waitress asked, "So, have we decided what we want?"

I looked over to Hazel and she said, "Um … I'll, I'll have the calzone."

As soon as she said that, I casually looked for what she ordered on the menu to see the price. I couldn't find it quick enough and said, "I'll just have the soup of the day."

I looked over to Hazel and thought she probably felt like a pig ordering the calzone while I only ordered the soup.

"Is that all you want?" Hazel asked.

"Yeah. I had a huge meal before I met you 'cause I didn't think we were going out to eat."

"Oh."

"So, uh … what've you been up to?" I asked.

"Nothing much."

"Where do you live now?"

"Aloha."

"Where's that?"

"It's past Beaverton but before Hillsboro."

I was happy she said more than two words to me.

"Why did you guys leave Portland?"

"My mom married an engineer."

"An engineer?" I asked. "That would have something to do with computers, right?"

"I'm not sure. I think so."

"Hmm," I said. "It's been a long time, Hazel."

She just stared at me with her puppy-like eyes.

I continued, "You know, uh ... I wanna say I'm sorry for not coming to your graduation when you invited me. I really wanted to, but uh, I uh, well, I got caught up in a lot of things. I hope you're not upset."

She listened carefully.

I continued, "Anyway, I'm glad you're here. We gotta lotta catching up to do."

Hazel said, "It's okay."

"What?" I asked, not sure of what she meant.

"It's okay you didn't show up for my graduation."

"It is?"

She nodded her head. Her calzone came with my soup and bread.

"Is there anything else I can get you?" the waitress asked.

"Nothing for me. How 'bout you, Hazel?" I asked hoping she would say no.

"No, I'm fine. Thank you."

I was relieved, because when the check came, I could barely cover it with the tip.

After that date, Hazel and I met almost every day. Sometimes she came to my job and brought me lunch. During the weekdays, I would go home to take a nap so I could meet Hazel later in the evening at our favorite meeting place, The Blue Moon on 21st and Glisan. It was also across the street from my new favorite pizza place, Silver Dollar. We sometimes stayed and talked until closing, even if we had to go to work the next morning.

I left my first printing job, and desperately began the search for another printing job. Hazel continued to encourage me about how I could find one if I didn't give up. During this time, Ed came up from California to stay for a while.

Stewart now lived on his own in the Belvoir apartment building a few blocks north of the Vista Bridge. Ed began going there more to drink beers with him.

I paid Ed a surprise visit at Stewart's. When I got there, he was drinking a 40-ounce bottle of St. Ides watching Run-D.M.C. on MTV.

"What's up, Ed?"

"Hey, Puerto Rican! Come in."

I worked my way through Stewart's first-floor apartment window.

"Where've you been?"

"I'm living with Cheryl now."

Cheryl was a girl he had known since high school.

"I know. Your mom told me." I asked, "Where's that at?"

"About three blocks from Lloyd Center."

I grabbed a glass from Stewart's kitchen cupboard and poured some of Ed's beer in it.

"I thought you went to rehab'?"

"I did. How's Hazel?" Ed asked, casually avoiding the subject.

"She's fine."

"Eddie's gonna marry Hazel someday," Ed blurted out to Stewart.

"I heard you got a new motorcycle," I said.

"Yeah, it's the Hondamatic!" Ed said with a funny face. "You wanna see it?"

(We called it the Hondamatic because Joey used to have a Honda motorcycle that didn't have a clutch and changed gears on its own).

"Yeah, dude! Let's go check it out."

We left the apartment back out the window. The motorcycle was parked out back.

"Whatta you think?" Ed asked.

"Check it out, man," I said, with this look of disdain on my face. "This things a piece of junk!"

"It's the Hondamatic!" Ed exclaimed. "This is a fine ride. I get all the women on this."

"Probably all the nasty ones."

Ed said, changing the subject, "I'm going back to school."

"Oh, yeah, whatta you wanna do?"

"I wanna get into architecture."

"Ed, why are you drinking?"

He looked at his bottle and submissively replied, "I don't know. I know I shouldn't."

"I thought that was why you split to rehab', so you could clean yourself out."

I noticed he was getting irritated.

I continued, "Ed, man, you know you can tell me anything."

Ed straddled over his motorcycle and didn't say a word.

"Ed, what's up?"

Ed looked at me, got off his motorcycle and shook his head, then walked away.

"Ed, what's up? Where you goin', man?"

Ed said, walking back to his motorcycle and starting it, "I just wanna be alone."

"Ed, Ed! Wait man," I yelled desperately, as he took off and waved bye.

I hurried to my car and drove around looking for him, but he was nowhere to be found.

A few days later, I decided to pay another visit to Stewart's. I knocked on the first floor window and Stewart opened it.

"Eddie," Stewart greeted loudly, "What's going on?"

"What's up, Stew. Has Ed been here?"

"Yeah, he's in the bathroom."

Ed came out and saw me at the window. His eyes were a little red, like he hadn't had much sleep.

"Hey, brutha … whazzup?"

"Hey, Ed, can we talk?"

"Yep."

He crawled out the window.

"Hey, Ed, I'm sorry, bro. I shouldn't have been talkin' about your drinkin', especially when I was drinking. I know I'm not a good example, and I just want to say I'm sorry."

Ed nodded his head, assuring me everything was okay.

"I'm sorry, too. I love ya!" he said hugging me

"I love you, too."

"How's it living with Cheryl?" I asked.

"Okay. It's like having my own place."

"How's Hazel?" Ed asked.

"She's cool," I said. "Remember how we used to jog to her house over at the Upshur apartments?"

"Yeah, man. I remember that. That's when Tamara also had a crush on me," Ed said.

"Yeah, she did. Maybe you should try dating her. I could marry Hazel, and you can marry Tamara."

Ed said, "You're lucky you've got someone who loves you. Who'll want to marry you."

"I don't really know if I'll get married."

"You'll marry her. She's perfect. Out of all the girls you've had, I know she's the one. She's liked you ever since you were little."

"Isn't it a trip knowing I didn't even think of her then?"

"Yeah, it is."

"You gonna be around tomorrow?" Ed asked.

"Yeah. Call me."

He got on his motorcycle, started it, and said, "I'll see ya later!"

We gave ourselves the buddy handshake, and I asked, "Where ya going?"

"To see Damon."

"Okay, man," I asked, "How 'bout we go to Sauvie Island?"

"Sounds good," Ed replied, accelerating up the Vista hill, giving me a thumbs-up.

Chapter Forty-Three

On March 31, 1990, it was a cold morning, and I was about to get up and go work out when the phone beside my bed rang.

"Hello?"

"Eddie?"

"Who's this?"

"This is Devin, Ed's brother-in-law. Did you hear?"

"Hear what?" I asked groggily.

"Ed died!" Devin blurted.

"What? What? What is this? A joke, Devin?"

"Ed died," Devin repeated in a serious tone.

"Devin, what are you talkin' about? Quit dinkin' around!"

"I'm not. He died this morning."

I went silent. I didn't know what to say or think. I thought it was a nightmare, and I hadn't awakened yet. Devin rarely called me, so the reality of what he was saying began to sink in. I could hear him on the other side repeating, "Eddie, Eddie, you there?"

I sat on my bed in silence. My heart, oh, God, my heart ... a feeling worse than I have ever felt in all the years of my life came over me. Time was still, and my bones were suddenly weak. My body was in incomprehensible pain.

Still, Devin repeated, "Eddie, Eddie, are you still there?"

I could not speak. *Why*, I thought. My mind had become bewildered and hazy. I needed something. Something to take control of my body, because I couldn't.

I began to pray: "God, help me? God if you're real, wake me up, please?"

I had just enough energy to gasp one, last word from my mouth, "Okay," then hung up the phone.

I got up slowly and forced myself to move faster so I could head over to Edith's place. I threw on whatever clothing was in sight. I opened my bedroom door and briskly walked toward the front door. Dad was sitting in his recliner with his blue, cotton hat over his eyes, snoring.

"Where ya goin? Why you makin' so much noise?" Dad asked.

"Ed died! Ed died!" I blurted, almost choking on my own words.

"What?"

"He died this morning."

"How? God, how?" Dad asked, shocked.

"I don't know ... I ... I ... I don't know," I replied wiping my forehead. "I gotta go!"

I hurried to my car and practically threw myself inside. I started it and sped off burning rubber. Time seemed so slow. It took forever just to get to the freeway. When I merged onto I-5 going south, I was in a daze, but most of all, in denial. I got halfway there, then went out of control in my car.

Hitting the dashboard with a closed fist and slammed my steering wheel with both hands I shouted in anger, "Why, God? Why God? You're supposed to watch him ... take care of him ... watch him!"

The car swerved into the middle lane as people were watching me in their cars, but I did not care. For some reason, I felt compelled to drive to Bubba's work at Fred Meyer first, to tell him what had happened. When I got there, one of the doors was unlocked, and I rushed in. Bubba was sorting the fruit out for that day.

"Bubba?"

"Eddie? Whatta you doin' here so early?"

"Ed's dead!"

"What?"

"Ed's dead."

"How? What happened? Wha' ... whatta you talkin' about?" Bubba asked with this confused look on his face.

"I can't talk right now. Call me later!"

I ran through the doors, back to my car, and drove fast toward Edith's house.

"Oh, God, no! No! No!" I repeatedly yelled in anguish, wiping the tears with my sweaty, red, hurt hands.

When I got there, I screeched into the parking lot, swung my car door open, and ran out, not closing my door. I ran up a flight of stairs and knocked on the front door.

Edith's daughter, Amber, answered with tears in her eyes, "Eddie!"

I walked into the small, two-bedroom apartment, filled with pain, tears, and suffering all around me. I looked for Edith, but she had found me instead. Her eyes were blood-shot and her face was saturated with tears. She hugged me tightly and wouldn't let me go, as I would not let her go. We finally parted, and Edith sat on the sofa.

I looked over to Connie, Devin, and then Amber and asked, "How? Why? What happened?"

"He was hit by a drunk driver between four and five-thirty this morning," Amber answered.

"Where? Who was he with?"

Amber grabbed some tissue and wiped the tears from her eyes, "He was with Damon, in West Linn." Damon was an army acquaintance.

"Who told you?" I asked, sitting beside Edith, holding her shaking hand.

"A sheriff came by this morning and told Mom."

"Where's Damon?"

"Nobody knows," Amber said. "He hasn't called or anything."

"So he's the only one who knows what happened."

"Yes," Amber said. "We're waiting for a phone call from the coroner to identify the body."

"So we really don't know if the body is Ed's?"

"Not for sure."

I sighed a hint of relief.

We waited patiently. The phone finally rang, and it was the coroner.

"Hello?" Amber answered, "yes ... okay ... okay ... thank you. They want us to come down and identify the body."

"I'll come down with you," I said.

"Okay," Amber replied.

"I want to also," Connie said.

277

Right as we were heading out the door, the coroner called again. Amber answered it and this time, the coroner said that it wasn't necessary to come down and that it was Ed.

Right after, Amber started thinking of funeral arrangements. The rest of us were still in disbelief. I stayed there waiting for more answers, but time dragged on, and I impatiently paced the apartment.

We all felt helpless. I stayed there all day and most of the evening. When I left, I had to go somewhere to cope with my shock and my pain. I drove to Macleay Park and walked over to a bench under a wooden shelter and sat there crying.

The next morning, the birds chirped, and I could hear the wind brushing against the leaves of the trees. *Where am I to go*, I thought. *What am I to do*. Nothing on this earth could have comforted my grief. Then the love and hope of seeing Hazel would touch my heart and give me a reason to live.

I calmly walked to my car, still in denial and emotional pain. I started the car and headed home. I rolled the window down and felt the breeze brush against my hair. Everything I drove past didn't seem real. It seemed like a dream. Like yesterday never existed.

When I got home, I parked my car and slowly opened the door. I walked toward my screen door, opened it and unlocked the front door. I softly pushed it open, and Dad was sitting in his recliner with a Bible in his hand.

"Eddie, how do you feel, son?"

"Not good, Dad, not good."

"Eddie, sit down, son. Ed's not dead. You'll see him again. God promises that."

"I know, Dad. I know. But ... but it's not fair. I'm not even sure what happened, except that a drunk driver killed him. I feel like someone ripped my heart out of my chest. Why Dad, why?" I asked, wiping the tears from my eyes.

"Now you know how I felt when your mother died. Like someone had ripped my heart out of my chest. And not just for that day, son, but it felt like that every day. Life can be taken in the blink of an eye. That's why we've got to believe in God, otherwise there's nothing else to live for. Call Hazel. She called eight or ten times."

"Does she know what happened?"

"I told her."

I grabbed the phone off Dad's desk and called.

"Hello?" Gladys answered.

"Hi, Gladys, is ... is Hazel there?"

"Yes. Just a minute."

"Hello?"

"Hazel?"

"Eddie, are you okay?" Hazel asked in a nurturing way.

"I think so. Can you come over?"

"Yes. Do you want me to bring something?"

"No."

"I'll be there soon, okay."

"Okay."

People began calling me to verify if Ed's death was true. The day seemed so rushed and confusing.

For days I blamed God for cheating me out of a fifteen-year friendship. *What gave him the right,* I thought. *How could God want us to serve him when he doesn't even protect us?* I felt it was insincere and even selfish of him. Hell, I didn't even think he existed anymore. But deep in my heart I knew the truth.

Chapter Forty-Four

Trying to get answers about exactly what had happened to Ed was slow. I had to see my best friend. So that night, I drove to the funeral home where they kept Ed's body and parked my car across the street. I walked aimlessly around, trying to get up enough courage to knock on the front door. My heart was pumping fast and my body felt sick. I managed to get closer to the funeral home, and I was faced with a dilemma and thought, *Do I want to see Ed, or do I want to remember him the way he was?*

I knew if it were me lying dead in that funeral home, Ed would be banging on the door demanding to see my soulless body. I knocked once and no one answered the door, but I didn't give up. I knocked harder and harder until I did see a man walk down some stairs toward the door.

"Yes? Can I help you?"

I was choked up inside, as if my tongue would not allow me to speak.

"Um ... um ... I ... is my best friend, Ed here?"

"Ed? Is there someone here you know?" the man asked.

"Yeah."

"His name is Ed?"

"Yeah, his name is Ed ... Ed Jerome," I replied, wiping the tears away from my face.

"Just a minute, please."

I wanted to sneak in, then realized I would have seen Ed at his worst. A dreadful thought I couldn't omit from my mind.

The man came back and asked, "Are you a relative of the deceased?"

"No, not really."

"Well, you have to be a family member or get permission from the family to see him," the man said sympathetically.

The only words I could say were, "He is my family. He's my brother."

The man said, "I'm sorry ... really, I am. But, your friend is pretty mangled up, and we need to get some authorization from the family saying it's okay for you to see him."

I looked at him and felt a sudden rage, like I wanted to force myself through him and look for Ed myself. Instead I looked down toward the ground and quietly walked away. The man shut the door. Then I heard the locking sound of a dead bolt. I turned my head, and he watched me walk further away before he went back upstairs. I glanced at the front doors to the funeral home, not sure of where I was going next.

I needed to talk to someone. It was about two o' clock in the morning, so I called Hazel.

"Hazel?"

"Eddie? Where have you been?"

"I'm over here, by the funeral home," I replied, still wiping the tears from my eyes.

"Are you okay?"

"Why did it have to be Ed? Why?" I asked, as my emotions became uncontrollable. "We've been friends forever. He's was my life ... my life."

"Eddie," Hazel said, "Ed's not gone forever. He'll always be in your heart, always."

I rested my head on the metal phone box and cried, "Why? Why? Why?"

I could hear Hazel saying, "Eddie? Eddie?"

I put the phone to my ear and quietly said, "I gotta go."

Before I hung up, Hazel said, "Eddie, I love you!"

The day came to see Ed in his casket. It would be the worst day of my life.

I got into my car with Hazel and began to drive. Then Bubba, Jaeger, and Joey followed in Bubba's new Blazer 4x4. The closer we got to the funeral home, the more distressed I felt. I kept thinking about what I was going to see when I got there. How I was going to react and, if I was ready for this since I had experienced the death of a loved one before.

Hazel put her hand on my right leg to comfort me, and I

knew she was the only person who could help me keep my sanity. When we got to the parking lot of the funeral home, my body felt weak. Every breath was hard to breathe, every muscle hard to move. Hazel helped me up the stairs and into the funeral home. I looked over to Bubba and saw Jaeger put his sunglasses on.

An older man dressed in a black suit guided us to where Ed lay dead in his casket. Hazel and I entered this small, slightly lit room. Bubba and Jaeger stood behind. Edith, Amber, Connie, and Devin were sitting to my right on some chairs against the wall. Edith hadn't stopped crying since Ed's death. Her body looked as mine felt.

I approached Ed's casket. I walked a couple of steps further and looked in. My eyes froze and my hands rested still upon the edge of the casket. I could not move my head. *What is happening?* I thought.

I got closer to Ed's barely smiling face and felt my body weaken even more. I stared and stared and stared without saying a word.

"Oh, God! Help me!" I cried silently inside my crushed heart. "Help me!"

Suddenly my knees buckled to the ground, and I cried so loud that people outside the small room heard me. My arms draped over and into the casket. The casket swayed from the weight of my body as I lost control of myself.

I yelled in anguish, "Nooo! Arrrgh! ... Arrrgh! ... Arrrgh!" letting out all the pain I had inside of me.

I could feel Hazel's hand on my shoulder, trying to comfort me. Edith stood up from her chair and stepped toward me, putting her hand on my other shoulder. I slowly stood up as the tears drenched my face to where I could not see clear. I looked in the casket again, and my tears had dropped onto Ed's pressed suit and clasped hands, which rested upon his still stomach.

I lightly touched his forehead feeling the makeup on the tips of my fingers and quietly said, "I love you, Ed ... I love you...." Only then did I conceive what being dead felt like.

I left the room, and Edith came up to me and said, "He's not dead, my son ... he's with God now."

Hazel stood beside me, as I proceeded to walk out of the funeral home toward my car. Jaeger hugged me and said, "Hang in there, man!"

I got into my car, and Hazel drove back home to Northeast 32nd Place.

We tried to comfort each other and bring some laughter back into Dad's small one-bedroom house. We made our beds on the floor in the available bedroom. Dad slept in the living room on his hospital bed. Hazel didn't want to stay because of the limited room we had, so she decided to go home. I knew she was tired because this whole mess had drained the energy out of her as it did me.

Chapter Forty-Five

April 4, 1990, it was about six o' clock in the morning, and the darkest day of my life. The rest of the guys were still sleeping. I got up and put some shorts on and went into the living room, where Dad was sitting in his recliner reading his Bible. He looked as if he was crying. On his yellow, dusty desk, Mom's picture reside beside Dad's tape recorder as the song "Memories" played on.

"Hey, Dad," I said quietly, rubbing the sleep from my eyes.

"Hey, son. How do you feel?"

"Tired."

"Eddie, come 'ere," Dad said. "Sit down beside me."

I grabbed a metal milk crate from the corner of the living room and sat on it close to Dad. He laid his hands over mine and said, "Eddie, Ed's not dead, he's sleeping. You see, son, God promises to bring back all those we love. If it weren't for that promise, I would've committed suicide a long time ago in fear of never seeing your mother again. When she died, a part of me also died. I felt I had nothing to live for, not even for the rest of my family. And when Ed died, also another part of me died. We all loved Ed very much, and we'll all miss him. But we have to go on in hope of the resurrection, because if this is all we have to live for, then there's no sense in living."

I began to cry.

"It just hurts, Dad."

"I know, Eddie. I know. When someone you love so much passes away, we feel as if we can't go on or as if we've been cheated out of life. We wake up every morning and face the ridicule and hurt the world puts on us, so coming home to see our loved ones is what we look forward to. But Satan doesn't want us to be happy. He wants us to hurt. And the only thing we've got between the cruelty of the world and Satan, is God.

"Put him in your heart, Eddie! He will see your pain and give you the hope of seeing Ed again. Parents don't expect their kids to die before their time. I thought I was going to die way before your mom. I was the one with all the problems. But that's not how it always happens. I know it's hard ... very hard. But remember, always remember that all these things will come to pass."

I hugged and kissed him on his cheek and said, "Thanks, Dad."

I walked into the kitchen and made coffee.

It was time to get ready, and I wore a black, two-piece suit, a white shirt, and black penny loafers. Gerard helped Dad get into his wheelchair as they left out the back door, down the wheelchair ramp. The rest of the guys got into Bubba's Blazer, and I got into my car with Hazel. We could hear Yoko whining and barking as we began to drive away. I felt this eating feeling inside of me, like vultures were tearing away at my organs.

Hazel sensed my pain and gently put her hand on my leg to calm me down. As we got closer to the funeral home, I feared that not enough people might have known about Ed's death and not enough would show up. When we got there, Gerard opened the trunk of his car, grabbed Dad's wheelchair, and pushed it around the passenger side. The rest of us proceeded toward the funeral home. Dad would not go inside another church, so he waited outside with Gerard while I was inside with Hazel, meeting with some of Ed's relatives.

The eating feeling inside of me would not go away. On occasion, I would silently pray to myself. Hazel stood close to me and more people walked into the funeral home. I did not know where Edith was, but I knew she would be there and worried for her deeply.

More people were coming in and seating themselves inside the chapel. Before the funeral started, I asked the reverend, "Sir, could you play this song for me?"

"What is it?" the reverend asked solemnly.

"It's our song, 'He Ain't Heavy'."

The reverend knew the song, but said, "Son, I really don't think it's a good idea. This is a difficult time for all of us, and we would like to make it as smooth as possible."

I looked at the reverend somewhat disturbed and confused that he would deny my request, but I was in no condition to argue. In fact, I wanted to punch him in the face.

A few minutes before the funeral, I sat up front with the other pallbearers. The reverend stood in front of us all and made a speech about Ed. I felt strange sitting there listening to this man make his speech about someone he knew nothing about. It was probably the same speech he used for everyone else who died. I looked to my right, and a few seats down was Damon. It was the first time I had seen him since Ed's death. I wanted to ask him why or how it happened. He didn't even look remorseful.

After the reverend's eulogy he had called upon me to read a passage Gerard helped me write for Ed. I got up, looked around, and couldn't believe my eyes. There were more people in the chapel than I thought there would be; there weren't even enough chairs for people standing in the back and spilling outside the church. I proceeded toward the front of the chapel, where Ed's open casket rested behind me.

I looked up at everyone and mentally thanked God for filling the church with all of Ed's friends and family. I noticed my dad in the back of the chapel, seated in his wheelchair, wiping his nose with his white handkerchief, weeping. I was glad he decided to come in. I opened a scroll in my hand and to my left saw Edith behind a black, see-through curtain. My hand shook as I proceeded to read from the scroll:

"In John chapter two Jesus said, *'Lazarus our friend has gone to rest.'* I say, Jerome our friend has gone to rest. But, as Jesus disciples did not know at the time, Jesus was going to resurrect him. So, when the time comes, Jesus will bring Jerome back to life. Because in Revelation it says, *'And he will wipe out every tear from their eyes, and death will be no more, neither will mourning nor outcry nor pain anymore. The former things have passed away. And, the one seated on the throne said, Look, I am making all things new.'* So there will be a healthier and happier Jerome. I believe this, for Jesus does not lie! We will miss Ed until that day we see him again. I love you, Ed.

"AMEN"

I looked behind me at Ed's casket and stood there with this small glimpse of hope that he might rise above his casket, just like Lazarus was resurrected from the tomb. I then sat down and silently cried.

Afterwards, they had Nick, one of Ed's friends speak about the sailing trip they went on. Then Nick sang a song dedicated to Ed. After a couple of more eulogies, everyone lined up to see Ed for one last time. The song "Sailing" by Christopher Cross played over the loud speakers as tears, sadness, and disbelief showed on the faces of those who walked by his casket. Gerard had moved Dad closer toward the casket, but Dad would not look in.

Dad called me over and said, "Eddie, Eddie, put this in the coffin."

He handed me all these medals he got from fighting in the Korean War, including his Bronze Star. I brought them to the casket and laid them across Ed's motionless chest and rested my hand on his still stomach. Stewart put his hand on my shoulder, and I moved up a few feet and saw him put a can of Copenhagen under Ed's jacket. After everyone was done seeing Ed, they closed the casket, and the pallbearers, Stewart, Tim, Arlin, Ed's cousin Robert, and myself grabbed both sides of the casket. We picked it up, and a patrolman at the exit stood erect, tapped his heels, and saluted Ed's body as we proceeded outside. We put the casket gently in the hearse.

Someone handed out copies of the scroll I read about Lazarus. Hazel held my hand and comforted me, leading me to my car. Everyone else got in their cars, and we followed the hearse to the veterans' cemetery. As we drove there, I looked into my rear-view mirror and saw this huge line of cars behind and in front of me. I could see the people who were waiting to pass through getting irritated because of the long line of cars. When we got to the cemetery, we drove up a small hill and parked our cars along the nicely cut lawn. There were so many cars, some had to park further down the hill.

I got out and saw Gerard helping Dad into his wheelchair.

There were uniformed men holding rifles not far from where they laid Ed's casket inside a small shelter. Hazel and I, along with the other pallbearers, walked toward the casket. Edith, Amber, Connie, Ed's dad, Buzz, and some of Edith's other relatives sat near the casket. It was the first time I saw Buzz sober. Not far from the casket, I saw an older man with a cowboy hat and a parrot on his shoulder. I looked around me again and thought, *God, Ed made friends with all kinds of people.*

I then flinched as the uniformed men fired several shots. Afterwards, an officer of the military presented Edith with the United States flag and a last salute. A trumpet played "Taps" as we rested white carnations on the closed casket.

Edith walked toward the casket and lightly touched it as her weak, anguished body shed more tears over her son.

After the funeral, a bunch of us united at Tim's house. It was strange not having Ed there. I thought, *Wallace Park will never be the same again.* I have a picture of that day at Tim's house and look at it from time to time. I didn't know how I would live on without Ed, but I think God gave me Hazel just in time.

I got a new job at the Nike screen print shop in Beaverton. Edith obtained a lawyer and tried to bring the man who killed Ed to justice, but the lawyer was a crook, profiting off her emotions and ripping her off for every last cent. Ed's death drained Edith mentally, physically, and financially. It got to the point where she couldn't fight anymore, just pray and hope that God would someday bring justice to the man who murdered her son.

One day as I visited Stewart to see if he had any old pictures of Ed, he decided to go visit Ed's gravesite. We drove up there in the Battlewagon on the south side of the fence because the front gate was closed. We climbed over the fence, and walked up the wet, grassy hill, passing all the plaques of people who'd died. When we saw Ed's gravesite, it was hard for me to believe his body was six feet under the ground.

Stewart took out a brown paper sack from his bag and pulled

out a forty-ounce bottle of St. Ides. He turned it upside down with the spout above the edge of Ed's plaque and shoved it hard into the wet soil. At first I was upset, then thought maybe that was his way of grieving. We stayed there a few minutes, then walked back to the Battlewagon. For the rest of the ride, we didn't say a word to each other.

Edith often wrote beautiful poems for Ed. One of them I find most dear to my heart:

He consumed drugs & Alcohol got in his vehicle & drove away, not far off, you were jogging as you did at the start of every day. A sad & stressed officer stood at my door, my heart stopped, I knew you wouldn't be coming home anymore. The despair was so profound, only the help of God got us through, denial came, a charade of not believing this could be true. You were so young, so many plans ahead, so much left undone. He robbed you of your life, he robbed me of my only son, this man, who thought he was having fun. You left a lot of beautiful memories, that are in my heart to stay, I love you my son, and I always will, and miss you more than words can say. Merry Christmas my angel, I'll see you again someday.

"Mom"

Chapter Forty-Six

While Hazel was away visiting Peru with her family, I one day decided to go to Lloyd Center Mall. I walked into a Wiesfield jewelry store and began to bargain with the salesman for an engagement ring, which I put on layaway.

After a month of waiting, I showed up at the Portland airport to meet Hazel, Doyle, and Gladys. I wore Levi jeans, a long-sleeve, baby-blue shirt, penny loafers, and had a perfect haircut. Hazel was surprised to see this physical change in me.

"Hazel," I said, as we happily walked towards each other.

She had a look of awe on her face.

"Wow! You look great and I look awful," she said, trying to brush her hair with her hands.

"You don't look awful. You look beautiful!"

"No I don't. I didn't even comb my hair and haven't taken a shower."

"You look fine to me."

"Hey, Doyle, what's up? How was Peru?"

"Oh, Eddie, it was nice," Gladys answered in an euphoric tone.

"You and Hazel are gonna have to go to Peru someday," Doyle said. "It's a beautiful country."

"Yeah, I'd like to one of these days."

Doyle began to speak about how beautiful Peru was, and even though I heard him speak, my thoughts were only about Hazel. It was like a wonderful dream to see her walk beside me. We got into our cars, and I followed them to their house in Aloha.

A couple of days later I took Hazel to Washington Park. It was night, and we walked along the beautifully landscaped paths, which had roses and different varieties of flowers around them. We sat on a nearby bench.

I said, "Hazel."

"Yeah."

"Um ... I love you very much and, well, you've been with me through thick and thin, and, well, I can't see myself going through the rest of my life without you."

Hazel's eyes were focused deep into mine.

I held her hand in mine and continued, "I was wondering if, uh, um, if you'd like to marry me?"

"Yes," Hazel replied very quietly.

"I mean, I'll, I will understand if you don't ... did you say, 'yes'?"

"Yes," Hazel answered, holding me in her arms. I love you, Eddie. I love you."

We rushed down with Doyle and Gladys to a justice of the peace in Vancouver, Washington, and decided to later have a real wedding in March. We took turns helping Dad with whatever he needed, and lived there with him until we had saved enough money to move out.

Once I stayed up late and began to talk with Dad.

"Dad, what kind of jobs did Mom have?"

"Mom worked in factories that paid little money ... sweat shops. She worked hard. I tried to work so she didn't have to, but sometimes it wasn't easy. Once she worked in this factory at a garment center on Broadway in New York. She was making thirty-four dollars a week, and this guy was robbing her 'til I figured out her pay check wasn't right. I went back there and told the boss, 'Hey man, you're robbing her. We gotta go to the National Labor Relations Board, now.' The boss said, 'Relax. Relax. I'll give her the money we owe.' I said, 'Yeah, don't do it again, man.' You see, Mom thought she was ignorant.

"But do you know how smart you have to be to speak and write Spanish? And then be able to speak some English? Mom was smarter than I was. She was articulate. Like Hazel. That means she had brains! That's not a stupid person. Mommy loved you guys. She would've liked Hazel, too. God, she was always cleaning the house. By the time I got her into bed, I was so tired of watching her clean, I felt like I couldn't perform for

292

her. There was nights, man, I was really horny, but Mommy said, 'Nope, first the house.'"

"What about Mom's father? How was he?"

"He used to beat her!" Dad said angrily, "that was the kind of man he was. I don't know why. And he used to bring all kinds of women to live in his house."

"I thought he was married?"

"Mommy's real mother was Maria (my grandmother). He left Maria and brought in other women. I stood between them one day, and I was gonna beat his brains in. But your mother said, 'Please Albert, don't do it.' But after I told him, 'Man, you hit her again, I hear her scream, if there's any mark on her, I will beat you to death!'"

"You really told him that?"

"Oh yeah. I was ready to kill him! That was the woman I loved."

"And what'd he say?"

"He never touched her again. He hated me. He tried getting Mommy not to marry me. But do you know twenty years later, before he died, he said, 'I'm glad you married my daughter. You've been a good husband to her.' It was crazy! It took him twenty years to realize I really loved his daughter. He thought I just wanted to sleep with her and leave her."

"Who is he to judge ... bringing all those women in?" I said.

"But still," Dad continued, "that was his way."

"What about her uncles?"

"I didn't know this about her uncle, but before your mom and me got married, she sat me down and said, 'Albert, would it make a difference if I wasn't a virgin?' I said, 'No, I'm in love with you! I would not have any life without you. My goodness! I'm not a virgin, Santa. I slept with every pig from here to Korea.'"

"Did you?"

"No, but I figured the lie was better than the truth," Dad said in a joking manner. "Anyway, I told her how much I loved her and it didn't matter. Then Santa told me how her uncle raped her when she was seven years old, then we cried. I remember we went to a dance by the East River Drive. This was long before you guys were even born. Your mother loved to dance and waltz in Spanish. Boy, she could dance. She made them hips move real beautifully. She was a work of art. That woman knew how to move. Them other guys in the neighborhood used to ask me, 'Hey, Al, let's go look for some pussy,' I'd say, 'Hey, look, are you crazy! I got a wife at home that gets me more aroused than anything out in the street.

"I remember there were times your mom looked at me and I would say, 'No honey, I'm too tired right now,' but she had me goin' boy—twenty minutes working me over and she had me in the saddle. God I loved that woman! That's why you'll never find another woman like the one you have. You'll never find another Hazel."

"What, what about your career, I mean—"

"My career was work! That was my career, work!"

I began to laugh so hard when Dad said that, I couldn't breathe.

"I worked twenty hours a day," Dad continued, "I did everything, shoveled shit to coal … driving a cab or truck—I did everything. Your old man worked! What career? I had no education. That's why I tell you to learn as much as you can now. The one thing people will never be able to take away from you is your mind, Eddie."

"Yeah, you're right."

"Don't you want to give Hazel a better life?"

"Yeah."

"Then do it," Dad said. "And when you're done with finding your career, you can give me a grandchild."

"No way. We ain't havin' no kids."

"Oh, you think so? Wait 'til that clock of hers starts ticking, then come back to me and tell me you're not gonna have any kids."

Dad was partly right, but realizing how difficult it was growing up myself, I really felt having a child was the wrong thing to do.

294

Part Five: Year 1991

Chapter Forty-Seven

It was our wedding day at Metzger Hall in Tigard, Oregon. I left to pick up Joey at the Greyhound station downtown. His bus came in late from San Jose, California, so when we got back to the house, I took a quick shower and practically threw my tuxedo on.

"Joey, help me with this tie."

"Okay, hold on."

"No, now! I'm gonna be late."

Joey began to help and said, "Just think, five minutes of *I do's* for a lifetime of *yes ma'am*."

"I can't believe I'm gettin' married."

"How do ya feel?" Joey asked.

"Feels pretty weird, especially knowing it's Hazel. I would've never thought."

Joey said jokingly, "Yeah, man, she's gonna be telling you to do the dishes, clean the laundry—your bachelor days are over ... it's gonna be like being in jail!"

"No it won't. This is a good thing, Joe. Don't you ever think about settling down? You can't just keep havin' sex with all these women. Besides, there are all kinds of diseases out there, man. I knew Hazel was the one. Why else would we have seen each other at Wallace Park that day?"

"But I like my freedom!"

"How do you know there's no freedom in marriage?" I asked.

"I just know."

"You don't know nothin'. You'll see, you'll get married someday."

"No I won't."

I chuckled and said, "Yeah, you will!"

I began to have thoughts about what Joey said, wondering if marriage was really like being in jail. We got into to my car and sped off, weaving in and out of traffic, trying to get to the wedding on time.

"You better slow down if you wanna get there."

"Man, I'm gonna be late—shoot!"

Joey said, "Slow down, Eddie."

I slowed down and took a few deep breaths.

We got lost, so I quickly pulled into a gas station and asked an attendant, "Excuse me?"

"Whatcha need?"

"Do you know where Metzger Hall is?"

The attendant told us, and when we found it, I accelerated into the parking lot. I rushed out of my car toward the building, noticing the guests scattered inside the hall.

"Hey, Eddie! Where've you been?" Michael asked. "We're all waiting for you."

"Joey's bus came in late."

"Well, you're lucky, 'cause Hazel's not ready."

"Where's Dad?"

"He's in the auditorium."

I walked into the auditorium, and the first thing I looked for was Ed's picture. I asked Hazel's parents to dedicate a table to it. I saw it with a short passage in a frame I wrote up: *Proverbs 18:24 " ... But, there is a friend who sticks closer than a brother."*

Flowers were around it, and so were some picture albums of Hazel and me when we were kids. Edith was sitting in the crowd, and I made my way over there.

"Hi, Mom, I'm glad you came!"

"My sweet son, I wouldn't miss this for the world!"

"Did you see Ed's picture on the table?"

"Yes, that's the sweetest thing you could ever do. I'm so proud of you!"

"I love you very much, Mom!"

"I love you too, sweetie!"

I worked my way over to Dad.

"Dad, how you doing?"

"Give me a hug, Eddie?"

"So whatta you think of everything?"

"Hey, man, it looks great! Doyle and Gladys did a great job decorating this place."

"Yeah, I think so."

"Now, if only your brother, Joey, could get married," Dad said. "Hey, look over there."

"Where?"

"Over there on the table by the cake," Dad said, pointing at a large bottle of Martini & Rossi champagne. "That's what I wanna taste. The good stuff."

"Sure, Dad, when we open it, I'll make sure you get some," I said, giving him another hug.

"Okay, don't forget."

"I won't, Dad." I said sarcastically, "I like your haircut."

Dad sometimes cut his own hair, but this time it looked like he cut it with a blender.

The wedding was about to begin, and everyone sat down. I stood by the judge and nervously looked over the heads of the people, anxiously waiting for my soon-to-be wife to walk down the aisle.

The wedding song started, and I suddenly saw her beauty move toward me. She looked as pure as the dress she gracefully wore. I couldn't take my eyes off of her. Her white dress and Peruvian skin shone as if she had been sent down from heaven, floating on a cloud. It was my sign of how close true love had been all this time. I began to think how fortunate I was, and understood what Dad meant when he said, "You'll never find another like her."

I didn't have a best man because it would have been Ed. So we gave the rings to Doyle's sister's son, who carried them on a small, white pillow. Hazel and I faced each other, and the judge went through the traditional wedding speech.

"Do you, Hazel, take Eddie to be your husband, in sickness or health, for richer or poorer 'til death do you part?"

"I do."

He looked over to me.

"And you, Eddie. Do you take Hazel to be your wife, in sickness or health, for richer or poorer 'til death do you part?"

"Absolutely."

"You may kiss the bride."

I lifted her veil up over her head and kissed her gently. The judge had us face the crowd and said, "Everyone, meet Edward and Hazel Regory."

Everyone clapped as we walked back up the aisle. The reception started, and the photographer took pictures of us almost everywhere we went. There was so much craziness going on, I don't even remember eating anything.

It was now midnight, and I held Hazel's hand in mine and proceeded to walk with her out the front entrance.

Michael voiced, "What are you doin', bozo, you're supposed to carry the bride out the door!"

I was so excited about getting married I forgot to carry her.

"Oh, shoot! I'm sorry, babe."

I immediately took her hand in mine and briskly walked her back in. I kissed her once and said, "I'll do it right this time!"

I picked her up and carried her out the doors.

"Aren't I heavy?" Hazel asked.

"No way. Besides, it's good for the arms," I said, acting out and mimicking a line from the movie *Rocky*.

I carried Hazel to my car as some of the guests and family followed behind.

The first thing I noticed was a large, yellow cardboard sign on the inside of the back window and big letters that read: "JUST MARRIED!" There were balloons and strings tied to several cans dangling off the license plate that also read "just married." I was relieved nothing unusual was hanging off the car, like condoms or something.

I softly set her down on her feet and opened the passenger door. She got in, and Doyle rushed out and said, "Eddie?"

"Yeah, Doyle."

"Here, take this Visa card and go to a nice hotel."

"Are you sure?"

"Yeah, you guys have a good time."

"Thanks, Doyle. I really appreciate it!"

I was glad for the card, otherwise we would've gone back home. We drove to the Embassy Suites Hotel in Tigard. I parked the car and opened her door. We held hands to the front desk and got a nice room with champagne. As we walked down the hallway toward our room, I opened the door and someone yelled from two floors up, "You gotta carry her in!"

Hazel smiled.

It was all so new to me, and I felt like a heel for screwing it up. I carried her in and yelled up to the guy, "Thanks!"

"No problem. I forgot on my wedding night, too," he replied, as his friends laughed on.

The next morning we had a continental breakfast and left for Seaside beach. We rented a cabin for our honeymoon. I wanted to take her somewhere more romantic, but we didn't have the money.

Chapter Forty-Eight

A few years later, in 1994, Hazel and I moved out of Dad's and into a one-bedroom apartment off of Murray Road in Beaverton. Dad relied on us to take care of him, so it was a big change for him too. He also had heart problems and took Vicodin.

Dad brought in a lady named Susan and her two children to live with him. Susan's father and also his friend, Bob, were in a disagreement, and Dad was not about to let a woman and her children stay out in the streets with no place to go.

One night I got a call from Susan.

"Eddie?"

"Hey, Susan."

"Eddie, something's wrong with your dad."

"Whatta you mean ... is ... is he okay?"

"That's what I'm trying to tell you ... he had a heart attack."

"Did you call the ambulance?" I asked, scared and very worried about what was going on.

"Yeah, I did," Susan said. "The paramedics are here, but they don't have anything big enough or strong enough to carry him out into the ambulance."

"Okay ... uh ... I'll be there right away!" I said, hanging up the phone. I cried out from the kitchen, "Hazel!" "My dad had a heart attack. We gotta go."

"What?"

"He had a heart attack. Let's go!"

Hazel put her coat on and rushed with me in the car toward my dad's house. When we got two blocks away from the house, I noticed a bunch of flashing lights. We parked the car, and I saw a van bigger than an ambulance with my dad in it. He was slightly incoherent and looking at me from his window.

I wanted to go with my dad and asked the paramedic, "Hey? Hey? Can I go with him?"

"Are you a family member?"

"I'm his son."

"Well, we don't quite have enough room, but you can follow us."

"Okay. Is, is he okay?"

"At this point were not sure. You'll be informed when we get him to the hospital."

The paramedic closed the door and the van began to move away from us. I thought I should do something so if Dad should die on the way to the hospital, he would remember me in his last breath.

So I stuck my tongue out at him and made a funny face. He smiled, which gave me some hidden assurance everything was going to be okay. We followed them to the emergency center at Emanuel Hospital in Northeast Portland. Gerard, Joey, Michael—everyone except for Anna showed up. They put Dad in a room, and after hours of waiting, the doctor finally came out.

"Hi, are you the Regorys?"

"Yes, we're his sons," Gerard answered, quickly rising up from the sofa.

"Your father is fine for now, but we'd like to keep him here for a few nights."

"Well, what was the problem?" Gerard asked.

"He had a mild heart attack, and that's why we'd like to keep a watch on him."

"Okay, uh ... can we see him?"

"Yes," the doctor replied, escorting us to Dad, not far from the waiting room.

"Hey, Dad," I said, happy to see him. "How you feel?"

"Oh, I feel okay."

"Man, you put a big scare in me."

The family hugged him.

A nurse came in and said, "Hello, Mr. Regory. We're going to take you to your room now."

Dad looked up at the nurse and asked, "Have you seen that movie, *The Doctor?* Have you seen it?"

She chuckled and said, "No, I can't say that I have."

"Man, that was a good movie," Dad said. "I think every doctor should see it."

The rest of us grinned. When Dad entered his room, I then went downstairs to get a small bag of Doritos from the vending machine. That's when I overheard a receptionist say to another lady, "Did you see that guy in the wheelchair? He was huge!"

I turned around to see the receptionist who said it and saw that she was also very fat. I really wanted to reach over and insult her, but remembered when Dad was made fun of at the Sentry market and promised I would never do the same.

Dad was not getting better, so they transferred him to the Intensive Care Unit. It was eleven o'clock in the morning when Hazel and I drove to the hospital to see him. We walked into the Intensive Care Unit and saw him sitting up on the bed with IVs attached to his arm.

I kissed him on the cheek and asked, "How you feelin', Dad?"

"I feel better," Dad replied with a wheezing sound.

"Well, you look better," I said, sitting down in a chair close to his bed and adjacent to a window that overlooked the parking lot. "Nice view."

"Yeah, it's okay."

I glanced over to the IV, which was putting iron into his body, and asked, "Is the iron helping any?"

"Oh, yeah, man, it's a lot better."

"Dad, you need to eat better when you get out of here."

"I know son," Dad sighed, "I'm my own worst enemy."

I reached my hand over to his.

"Dad, you've made your mistakes, but I love you very much!"

Dad brought his head down and in a soft-spoken voice said, "I'm so embarrassed."

"Why?"

"'Cause I peed myself."

"Don't be embarrassed. You have nothing to be embarrassed about, okay."

303

Dad paused for a second and said, "You've grown to be a fine, young man. Mom would be proud of you."

"I miss her."

"We all do. We all do, Eddie ... funny how we work all our lives to have things, but when someone close to us dies, everything we've worked for is meaningless."

"Yeah."

"Risa's a great girl, isn't she?" Dad said, referring to Susan's friend whom Joey started dating.

"Yeah, Dad. She'll be real good for Joey."

"I'm so proud of all my sons. Mom would be real proud of all you guys."

"Yeah, I know Dad. But she'd be proud of you taking care of us the way you did."

"I didn't do anything."

"Dad, you did a lot."

"I love your sister Anna so much."

"I know Dad, I know you do. She loves you, too, very much."

"Whatever happens Eddie, help your sister out. And if you ever make it in life, help Michael's family, too."

"I will Dad. But right now we have to be concerned about you."

I stood up and walked over to the chalkboard and started drawing my favorite cartoon, a mouse with a sombrero hat.

"My son's a fortunate man to have you, Hazel. You were the best thing to come into his life, and I thank God for that." Dad turned his attention toward me and said, "My son the artist."

"I'm no artist, Dad."

"Oh, yes, you are!" Hazel said confidently. "You're my talented husband."

The doctor came in and said, "How is everyone today?"

"Hi," I said.

"Good, doctor," Dad replied.

"Well, I don't mean to rush you off, but your father could use some rest."

"Okay, doc'," I said. "Dad, do you need me to wash your clothes?"

"Could you?"

"Yeah, where are they?"

"Over there on the floor."

I hugged and kissed him, and tried to smell and feel as much of his facial features as possible.

"I love you, Dad!"

"I love you, too!" Dad said. "Hazel, you've been great to Eddie. I love you."

"I love you, Albert!" Hazel said hugging him. "We'll come back soon."

Hazel used to tell me how much she loved Dad because he respected her. He treated her smart, "like a queen," she would say. That he was very much like a father to her.

The doctor brought us a bag to put my dad's soiled clothes in.

"Thank you, doctor."

"You're welcome."

In my heart I was really thanking the doctor for treating Dad like a human being. Joey stayed in the waiting room with Bob and his son, Jepson. Hazel and I drove to my dad's house and noticed the floor and blankets were caked with cornstarch.

Hazel was angry and said, "I can't believe it. Susan lived here rent-free and she didn't even clean this house. God, that pisses me off!"

"I know, babe. I know. Let's just get this cleaned up, and I'll take his clothes to the Laundromat."

I washed all of his blankets, underwear, and soiled pants. When I got back, Hazel was outside mowing the lawn. She knew I didn't like her mowing the lawn because of how hard it was on her back, but Dad loved a cut lawn.

Late that night, we drove back to the hospital.

We walked into the Intensive Care Unit, and I said, "Dad, we washed your clothes and cleaned the house. Oh, yeah, and I mowed the lawn."

"You mowed the lawn?" Hazel said in a surprised tone.

"Yeah, right."

Dad said, "He's jiving me, ain't he?"

"Yeah, he's jiving," Hazel replied.

Dad felt tired, so I hugged him and said, "I love you, Dad. I'll let you get some sleep."

"I love both of you very much."

We went into the waiting room and stayed there until nine o'clock. Later we headed to my place, and Joey, Risa, and Tyler, Risa's five-year-old son, came along. I put in a movie to try and get our minds off Dad, but just by looking at everyone there, it was obvious that's all we could think about.

Chapter Forty-Nine

April 10, 1994, it was about at eleven o'clock in the morning, Hazel and I went into the waiting room and saw Gerard. He had just relieved Michael from being there all night.

"Good, you guys are here."

"How's dad?" I asked.

"Dad's resting now. He always needs to know someone is here for him; I need to go back to work."

We walked into the Intensive Care Unit. It seemed like Dad was doing better, or maybe I was in denial that these were his last days. Dad saw me and began to get into his joking mood, the mood I've learned to love all my life.

"Hey, guys. Did ya have me a grandson, yet?"

"No, Dad, not today. How do you feel?"

"I feel okay. I'm sick of all the blood they keep squeezin' outta me. You'd think they were selling it or something."

"Now you know how I felt when I was in the hospital," I said, "it sucked!"

"Whatta you guys doin' today?" Dad asked. "Why don't you go out and have a good time."

"Whatta you mean?" I replied. "We're gonna be here all day."

"You don't need to be here," Dad said, "go out and have fun. I'll be okay."

"I don't think so, Dad."

Hazel said, "We like being here with you, Albert."

"I'm just a boring, fat, old man," Dad said. "You're young, you don't need to be here and watch me. Go have fun!"

"We don't want to, Dad. Besides, what make you think we don't like being here?" I asked.

Dad sighed and said, "I don't know. You kids are great, you know that?"

"No, Albert, you're great," Hazel said.

We talked for a while longer then left.

At about three-thirty in the afternoon, I walked into the Intensive Care Unit with Hazel again, and this time Dad was breathing hard in his sleep. For hours, I aimlessly paced the hospital hallways, waiting and praying for a miracle.

I saw Joey walking my way.

"Joey, Hazel and me are gonna go home. You're gonna stay here all night, right?"

"Yeah, I am bro. You go home."

"I love you."

"I love you, too," Joey said hugging me. "It'll be okay."

We left.

When we got home, I couldn't eat or sleep. I thought about my dad's scent, the blue, cotton hat he rarely took off, and all the funny times we had together. How his melodramatic personality was always so humorous to everyone who knew him. And how anxious he was to someday be with Mom once again.

With about four hours sleep, it was time to go to work. I didn't want to go. All I wanted to do was go to the hospital and be with Dad.

I thought, *If this is reality, I hate it! You can't even be with your loved ones because you're afraid of losing your stinking job.*

When I got there, I couldn't work. I kept thinking, *Dad's coming home.*

Nine o'clock in the morning and still no phone call from the hospital. I got sick of waiting, so I called the hospital's waiting room.

"Joe, is Dad okay?"

"Yeah, he still breathing hard though."

"You must be tired, bro."

"Yeah, I am, but Gerard should be here."

"Well, I'm gonna be there after work."

"Okay," Joey replied.

I was happy everything was still okay.

At eleven-thirty in the morning, I called again.

308

"Hello?" Michael answered with a deep, firm voice.

"Hey, Mike. How's Dad doing?"

"Eddie, get down here!"

"Why?"

"Dad died!" Mike said firmly.

My heart was at a total stop. It was the same stop I felt when Ed died.

"What? When? What happened?"

"Just get down here."

"I'm leaving now!" I said, and hung up the phone.

I couldn't think straight, and I felt angry enough to kill.

I quickly walked toward the exit, saw my manager, and said, "I'm leaving."

"Okay," he replied.

I got in my car and peeled my tires out of the parking lot. I raced through a stop sign and began to feel the same daze I felt when Ed died. Unaware of my surroundings, I began to think, *Eddie, calm down. Just be calm. If you wreck this car, you'll never see Dad. Relax Eddie relax...."*

I finally crossed the Fremont Bridge and stopped at an intersection a few blocks away from the hospital. My body was feeling weak and couldn't understand what was happening to me. I rushed out of the car and started to feel dizzy. I ran so hard toward the entrance of the hospital, my legs began to feel heavy, and couldn't run or even walk anymore.

Unable to breathe properly, my stomach began to turn. I wanted to cry, but tears wouldn't come out. I then realized it wasn't me moving my body, but God helping me move.

Getting closer to the elevator, I could feel my blood rush through my veins, pumping the fear in through my heart even faster. I wanted to just fly to the fifth floor and get it over with.

Three, four, five—the elevator door opened, and I nervously stepped out. I looked to my left, and Susan was there crying so hard that for me, it didn't make things any easier. For a moment I felt Susan might have been more concerned about not having a place to stay. Joey was trying to comfort her when he looked up at me and motioned his head toward the Intensive Care Unit.

When I opened the curtain to Dad's room, every bone in my body was weak from the pain in my heart. I froze and was unable to take my eyes away from his partially opened mouth and still, obese body.

That's when I silently cried so the nurses outside the curtain wouldn't hear me. I wanted to be strong inside because, even at the end, that's the way Dad would have wanted it. I cleared my throat and lifted my hand onto his forehead and quietly said, "Now you're in peace, Dad. Now you're with Mom."

There was a sense of serenity in the room that Dad had been praying for since Mom died. He looked just like he was sleeping.

I wiped the tears from my face and walked out of the room. I tried not to feel angry, but it was all I knew how to feel. And once again I would experience the feeling of being dead inside.

I called Maryville Nursing Home in Beaverton.

"Hazel?"

"Eddie? You sound ... is everything okay?"

"Dad died. He died this morning."

"I'm sorry, very sorry, Eddie."

"Can you come here?"

"I'll be there soon."

I hung up the phone.

I walked slowly into the lobby, where other people waited to see their loved ones, and began to stare at the people and cars from the window. I tried to think of all the good things Dad said to me, but it was funny how I couldn't remember a one.

Chapter Fifty

On April 14th they transported Dad to the funeral home, and with two hundred fifty dollars from a burial insurance policy, we were still short another two hundred fifty dollars for the pine casket. A couple of days later, Michael got a call from the funeral home. He later told me what happened.

Michael then called Gerard and said, "Gerard, the funeral home wants to see us about a matter. Could you meet me there in a half hour?"

"Okay, yeah, what's the problem?"

"I don't know. Mr. Jamerson (the one who took care of the funeral matters) and Mr. Wayland (the owner) asked if we could be there as soon as possible."

When Gerard and Michael got there, Mr. Wayland had a regretful look on his face and said, "Gentlemen, we made a mistake and cremated your father."

"What?" Michael blurted. "How can you make that mistake? He was five hundred pounds! I don't understand how you could make that mistake!"

"Well, we had another large man sent to us who was supposed to be cremated and … and so we had two large men. One to be cremated, the other one just buried. By the time we realized our mistake, the process was already two hours underway. The whole process takes about three hours. Isn't that right?" Mr. Wayland looked over and asked Jed, an employee in charge of the cremation department.

"Yes. About three hours, sir."

Michael had a serious, upset look on his face. He walked closer to Mr. Wayland and said, "You guys made a really big mistake!"

"I know sir. We realize that. We're prepared to make full funeral arrangements at our expense." Mr. Wayland said, explaining the type of casket and arrangements they would provide.

Gerard looked over to Michael and said, "Okay. Let's go! We've gotta talk!"

They angrily proceeded toward the exit door of the funeral home.

Michael stopped and looked at Mr. Wayland and reiterated, "You guys really made a big mistake!"

"We know that, sir," Mr. Wayland nervously said, following them downstairs toward the door. "I hope you will consider that we didn't have to say anything about your dad being cremated."

Gerard faced Mr. Wayland and angrily said, "That's not an option!"

"I know that. I know it's not," Mr. Wayland answered meekly.

When Michael and Gerard got to the door at the bottom of the stairs, Michael turned to Mr. Wayland and asked, "Are you sure you cremated my father? You're sure you're not mistaken?"

Gerard also asked, "Yes. Are you sure?"

"Yes. I'm sure it was your father. We have the other body."

"Well, let's see it!" Michael demanded. "Let's go see it."

"Okay."

Mr. Wayland brought them to a room where there was a huge table with a large body covered with a white sheet.

Mr. Wayland motioned toward the body and said, "As you can see, this is also a fairly large man."

He then pulls the sheet off the man's face.

Michael looked over to Gerard and said, "That's not Pop!"

"No, it's not."

Michael and Gerard walked out of the room as Mr. Wayland and Jed followed.

They left the funeral home and drove to Michael's house. Gerard then decided it would be a good idea to call Mr. Wayland to reiterate that the burial would proceed the next day as scheduled.

"Hello?"

"Mr. Wayland? This is Gerard Regory. I just wanted to

confirm that we are still going to go ahead with the burial tomorrow—as planned?"

"Yes sir," Mr. Wayland replied.

"Needless to say, you will pay for all expenses!"

"Of course! That goes without saying. Look, I know I'm in deep trouble here, but I want to make it up to you by at least giving you a nice casket and the best urn we have.

"Well, my concern is that … well … will the ashes spill out of the urn inside the casket?" Gerard asked.

"No sir. The urn will be sealed," Mr. Wayland described the seal and proceeded to say, "And I can give you a sealed casket, too."

"Well, just the plain, wooden casket we originally had planned on will be fine."

"Well, allow me to put a seal around it. I would feel better if I did," Mr. Wayland insisted.

"Okay, fine. Bye."

Gerard hung up the phone.

That evening I was at home with Hazel, having some dinner, when I got a phone call.

Michael's voice sounded very serious and said, "Eddie, I want you to meet me at Gerard's house."

"Why?"

"Just get down here to Gerard's now! And don't bring Hazel."

"Okay, okay. I'll be there in fifteen, twenty minutes."

Michael hung up.

"Hazel, I gotta go to Gerard's house. I'll be back."

"Why? Is there something wrong?"

"I don't know. Michael just said for me to be there."

"Can I come?"

"No babe. He just wants me there."

I got in my car and drove toward Gerard's house.

I buzzed Gerard's apartment on 57th and Fremont, and he came downstairs to answer the front door.

"Hey, Eddie."

"Hey, Gerard," I replied, as we walked back upstairs into his apartment.

Anna, Michael, and Gerard were there. I sat on Gerard's desk as we waited for Joey to show up.

When Joey showed up, there was a minute or two of silence.

Gerard then stood up off his bed and broke the silence, "Now, what I'm about to say is going to be very hurtful, but I want all of you to keep an open mind. Today, Michael and I got a phone call from the guy at the funeral home. Well, when we got there, we talked to Mr. Wayland who was in charge of the burial arrangements and ... well ... what had happened was ... they cremated Dad by mistake."

"What?!" Joey exclaimed. "How could they do that?"

"What do you mean they cremated Dad? I don't understand?" I asked, bewildered and unsure of what Gerard meant.

We all didn't know how to take it. Anna didn't say much at all. Instead, she looked unsettled and slightly disordered.

"What are you talking about, Gerard? How did they cremate Dad?" Joey asked.

"Listen. I don't want anyone going bezerk on me. I want you all to listen. We spoke to the people in charge, and what had happened was, they had mistaken Dad for another man who was supposed to be cremated and—"

"How do ya make a mistake like that?" Joey interrupted. "No way man. I'm gonna sue!"

"Wait! Joey, please ... listen okay." Gerard proceeded, "When we got there, they had mistaken Dad for another man of the same size."

"Are you sure it was Dad?" Joey asked.

"Yes. It was, because Mr. Wayland let us look at the body that was supposed to be cremated. The body was definitely as big as Dad, but it wasn't him."

Michael said, "You see, you guys have to realize something ... there's probably some half-minded guy putting bodies in a burner all day. When he saw Dad's body, he probably thought there was no way another person of the same size was down

314

there and didn't check to see if it was Dad, and so he cremated him."

"That's no excuse for being irresponsible, Michael," I stated angrily, "no excuse."

"I'm not saying it's an excuse. What I'm saying is, is maybe we shouldn't sue or get back at these people because biblically, God wouldn't want it that way."

Joey became furious at this point and aimlessly paced Gerard's small studio apartment. "I don't care! I'm gonna sue!"

I said, "Joey, wait a minute. Is money gonna bring Dad back? And what if we do decide to sue? The guy who cremated Dad will probably lose his job. Is that what you want? Do you think Dad taught us to hurt people that way? No, he didn't. That's why maybe Michael and Gerard are right. Maybe we shouldn't sue, and go forward with the funeral as planned. Anna, what do you think?"

"I don't know, Eddie. Everything is just sad. It's not the money I care about."

Gerard said, "I know how you all must feel, but we have to think this out rationally. Now, Michael and I have talked about this and there are a couple of things we came up with. One is, would it be right for us to sue the funeral home? Two is, we're not out for the money, even though if we wanted, we could hang this guy out to dry. Now, he was sincerely sorry for what he did, but whatever we decide to do, it has to be agreed by all of us.

"Now, Mr. Wayland was the person we talked to. He has agreed to pay for all funeral expenses. Which is without a doubt the least he could do, right? Is everyone here with me?"

"Yeah," we answered.

Gerard's speech continued.

"Now, I had told him to bury Dad in the pine box like Dad had wanted or, we can let the funeral home give us the whole nine yards."

"That's it?!" Joey shouted. "And not make them pay for what they did?!"

I said, "Joey, this isn't a matter of making someone pay for something. It's morals, Joey."

"Eddie, I know about morals. I had the same father, but since Dad moved to Portland, he never got anything from anybody. Yeah, it was a fresh start and we got out of the ghetto, but does that give someone the right to burn him and hope we forget it happened? I'm sorry Gerard, Michael—you guys. I can't let it go that easy. I can't. What if Dad was still alive and he felt himself burn? You know, I've heard of people still being alive while some think they're dead."

"Joey, come on. You can't mean that," Gerard said, "you know you can't mean that."

"C'mon, bro. You're not thinking right," I said. "Joey, at least Dad will get a decent burial. You know Dad always said, 'Funerals are for the living, not the dead.'"

Gerard asked, "Michael, is there anything in your religion that says cremation is wrong?"

"Nope."

Gerard continued, "So why sue the funeral home and possibly have the guy who did the burning lose his job?"

Joey said, "He probably already did."

I said, "You know, Gerard, maybe they're hoping we don't do anything, and then later they can say how they got away with it or something. I kind of see Joey's point. Maybe they saw Dad and said, 'Oh, just another body' and made fun of him, too. I mean, you did mention that this Mr. Wayland said he didn't have to tell you what happened, right?"

"Yes. I did," Gerard replied.

"Well, maybe that's the kind of mentality we're dealing with. You understand where I'm comin' from?"

"Yes, I understand what you're saying, Eddie, but aren't you seeing just the bad side to this?"

"Gerard, what side of it are we supposed to see? We're all confused. Isn't this the reason why funeral homes have insurance? Just for these stupid, uncaring acts they commit. Look, Gerard, I'm not looking for money either, but if we think a little about where Joey's coming from, to the funeral home, it's just a business, not a person. Why should they care if they burned Dad to ashes? This Mr. Wayland may come out and pretend like he cares and say he's sorry, but we all know that to them it's just another body. You know, I want to do the right thing, but something inside tells me maybe we should sue also."

Joey said, "I don't want this funeral home to get a bad rap or get put in the papers for what they did, but I think we should vote on it. Everyone in favor to suing, raise your hand?"

Joey was the only one who raised his hand.

I said, "Well, I kind of agree, Gerard. In a way I don't think we should let them go, but in a way I think we should."

Michael said, "Okay, listen. We have to agree as a family. No one! And I mean no one! Should leave this apartment feeling they didn't do the right thing. We've all been raised what I think is the right way. It didn't bother Dad to be cremated. He only wanted a cheap burial. Frankly, it doesn't matter to me. I mean, I loved the old man as much as you guys did, but dust we came from, and so dust we leave. Funerals are only for the living. Now, before Dad died, he said he wanted to be buried and got out enough insurance to put half down for the casket.

"Now, before this all happened, we were going to have to put up two hundred fifty dollars of our own money. I feel if God had anything to do with it, it was to help us not pay for any funeral expenses. And now we can get Dad a decent funeral for free! I think that's good enough for me. And I think we as a Christian family should take that under consideration."

"You're right, bro," Joey said.

Anna kept quiet during most of our discussion. I thought, *My poor sister was probably more victimized by this than any of us*. Anna wasn't close to Dad like she was to Mom, but she began to love him more toward the end. She gave him more hugs, and before he died, visited him in the hospital. I knew if Dad could have had a last wish, it would be for Anna to love him as much as he loved her.

"So do we all agree to sue or not to sue?" Gerard asked.

"Not sue," we replied.

I saw a disturbing look on Michael's face and he said, "Wait a minute. There's one problem."

"What?" I replied.

"What if we let them pay for the funeral expenses, and they come back at us to pay for, let's say the casket, the urn or any special thing they decide to do for us?"

"Well, we'll have a lawyer put a clause in a contract stating we don't have to pay for anything," Gerard answered.

I said, "Gerard, a lawyer's not gonna do anything for free."

Gerard sighed and said, "Well, this poses a whole new problem."

"So what are we gonna do?" Joey asked.

Michael said, "We gotta see a lawyer and find out what our options are."

"So, does this mean we're gonna have to sue?" Joey asked.

Michael said, "This probably means we're gonna have to talk to a lawyer and find out if the funeral home can come back and slap us with a bill after the burial."

I asked, "So we really can't make a decision right now, is what you're saying?"

"It doesn't look like it, but in the meantime, we can discuss whatever else is on our minds," Gerard responded with a sigh.

Chapter Fifty-One

Dad was being buried at nine o'clock in the morning at the veterans' cemetery, which made it much more difficult for me because of Ed being buried at the same place. We parked along the grassy hill and walked a few feet and saw a forklift lift the casket off the back bed of a truck.

The casket was lowered into a huge cement box, then slowly lowered into the ground. Naomi, Michael's daughter, looked up and asked, "How's Papa gonna breathe?"

I wanted to pick her up and hold her tight in my arms. It was unbearable for me and I couldn't imagine what she was going through.

Michael hugged Naomi and said, "Papa's just sleeping right now."

I began to cry and saw the uniformed policeman who'd escorted us to the cemetery fold the American flag to give to me. I turned away from the officer and wrapped my arms around my head on the roof of a car.

I brought my head back up and shouted, "No! I don't want it!"

The man tried to offer the flag to Anna and again I exclaimed, "No! Don't take it Anna. You know Dad didn't believe in it."

Gerard came up to me and asked, "Eddie? Can Doyle have the flag?"

The tears would not stop, and again I shouted, "No! Gerard. You know how Dad felt."

In a way I felt bad for being so mean to Doyle, but knew he would understand. I felt I should respect Dad's belief as a Jehovah's Witness.

A few days later, Gerard found the name of a good lawyer. The family met again, and this time we faced a new dilemma.

"So what's the deal?" I asked.

"Well, I talked to the lawyer, and he said he feels we should sue and would be willing to take the case on contingency."

"So what happens to the Christian values we talked about?"

"Well, Eddie, I know—we know what the right thing is … but … well I'm just a little leery now on them coming back on us for money to pay for the funeral."

Joey asked, "So we're gonna sue?"

"This is the deal," Gerard continued, "if we get a lawyer, he's not going to draw up a contract for us for protection against the funeral home for free. He knows this is a for-sure case, so he's probably gonna take it for all he can get. So if we sue, we have to go all the way."

I asked, "So we're doing this because of the lawyer?"

"As sad as it is, that's pretty much where it stands."

Michael asked, "Did the lawyer give an amount we're supposed to sue for?"

"Right now we have to agree if we're gonna do this, then we'll hire him and go through the process," Gerard answered.

We agreed.

The next day, Joey and I removed all of Dad's belongings from the house. I perused through his stuff and found a tape by the empty milk jug he used to urinate in because it was difficult for him to go to the bathroom. I played the tape in my recorder, and heard Dad's last words to his family:

"When you hear this tape, I will be gone. But I wanna leave something behind for you guys. I never could give you the wealthy things Mom wanted to give ya's—the nicer things in life. I failed you all—Mom never failed you. But I do love you guys!

"Michael, you've grown to be a fine man. You're doing a good job. Continue serving and loving God. And continue being honest to your wife. To bend … when it hurts, bend some more. Love your children. Do what you can for them. Promise them nothing, 'cause promises can be broken. Take care of them … lead them to God so they have a safe life.

"Gerard, we always called you the peacemaker. You were the one Mom called on to make peace between the family. She

loved you like she loved all of you. I'm sorry I couldn't bury her right, Gerard. I know that hurt you. I don't know what happened to me then. I didn't want it to come out that way. I was so confused; I didn't know. Please forgive me.

"*Anna, my daughter, my only daughter. I've always loved you. How I always wanted to hold you and hug you and listen to what was hurting you inside. I don't know, I guess I'll never find out. But I hope you can settle it between God and yourself.*

"*Eddie, you're married now and you've got a wife to take care of. You've gotta bend too, Eddie ... you've gotta love. It's love you gotta give, not gifts—that's nice, but you've gotta love—you've gotta bend. Talk to her gently. She's precious! She's a gift from God to you. You'll never get another one in your lifetime. You're good in the heart, Eddie. You have a lot of kindness and a lot of dreams, and I know someday you'll make it, because I've always believed in you.*

"*Joey, you make me proud! And I know it's none of my doing. You were serving God, trying as hard as you can to do what is right. I'm proud of you Joey. I'm proud of all my children. You've grown to be men and women. You've grown to love God. And God looks into the heart ... there's where it counts.*

"*Racheal and Naomie, I want to leave this ... maybe you won't remember your grandfather when you grow older, but I love you two guys, and I know you'll grow up to be fine women, because your mother and father are fine. I know you'll grow up to serve and love God, too. You may not be foolish in your ways, for there'll be much wisdom given to you two, from your family and from God.*

"*As for me, I've tried to be the best I could, to be the kind of father my family wanted. But I've failed you all, and I'm sorry. I never fought real hard. I never even tried. I wanted to die so much because I missed your mother. I loved her very much. I've made my mistakes 'cause I was young and foolish and stupid. I was meant to be alone so I couldn't hurt people. It seemed like all the ones I love that I touch, I seem to have hurt. I'm sorry fellas! I'm sorry for not being the way you guys wanted me to be.*

"But never forget this ... I do love you all and pray for you constantly. If we're fortunate through God to see each other again in the resurrection, that'll be a joyous time. Because like God said, 'There will be no more pain, no more crying, no more mourning, and no more suffering.' Jesus never spoke a lie. That was the truth. So I don't know when or how long it will take, but I believe in all my heart that we will see each other again. If it be God's will. I don't know what else to tell you guys. You guys help one another and love one another to the very end of time.

"So where I am, well, maybe we'll see each other as long as we serve God. Good-bye ... all of you, and may God bless all of you."

I've learned many lessons growing up ... some hurtful, some good. But I guess if I had to tell anyone the one most important lesson I've learned, it's the value of human life. I love it and I cherish it. And even though sometimes I forget, I'm then reminded by the memories of the three most important people. When I was a kid, I thought I was poor ... now I realize how rich I was.

I'm not going to say that if I could go back in time, there are things I would change and make better. Instead, I'm going to learn from them. I'll miss Ed, my mom, and my dad, but no matter where I am, their spirits will always be alive in my heart.

I just want to say Mom and Dad if you're reading this, thank you. Thank you for being the angels God sent to guide me through my own life. Until that day when we all rejoice together, I love you.

"When I die, I'll just be asleep, but when I wake up, I'll be rejoicing and thanking God that I made it into the resurrection, seeing everyone whom I ever loved. God, what a day that will be."

–Albert Regory

You know, maybe we will have a grandchild.

322

The End

About the Author

I will always remember the voice of my mother's prayers for a better place to live. We found that place when we moved to Portland, Oregon.

There were times when I felt I couldn't finish this book, that I wouldn't be able to bring out the genuineness of the people who played a significant role in my life. But through the support of my wife I learned that the word "can't" does not exist.

I try to live life to the fullest. To appreciate it, and be thankful that every day I wake is another day I get to enjoy with my family.

When I'm at work, I sometimes think about my beagle dog, Penny and her wagging tail, happy to see me when I get home. And how she sits beside me with her head rested on my lap while I watch a movie. I especially love to eat a meal with my wife and make conversation about anything, or sometimes I'll just sit with her and watch her favorite show, *Party of Five*. I love working on my yard. Especially when I begin a new big project.

I work in the design support department at a shoe company and continue to follow my dad's advice to stay off drugs. I am thirty-two years old and am married to my longtime friend, Hazel Regory.

I've written for a college publication (*Bright Ideas*) and am an associate of the Willamette Writers Group.

I hope you enjoy this book. But most of all, I thank you for helping me achieve my dream by reading it.